Walking with the Saint

Mary Anne Ayer

Copyright © 2005 by Mary Anne Ayer

Tenth Gate Publishing Corporation
1220 North Market Street, Suite 601
Wilmington, DE 19801
www.tenthgatepublishing.com

Ordering Information

Please call 781-820-3900
**Library of Congress
Cataloging-in-Publlication Data**

Ayer, Mary Anne.
Walking with the saint : spiritual practices & insights to enhance
your journey through life/ Mary Anne Ayer
p. cm.
ISBN 0-9755947-0-2

1. Mysticism — Comparitive studies. 2. Spiritual life —
Comparative studies. 3. Religions — Comparitive studies.
4. Ajaib Singh, Sant. 5. Vedanta. I. Title.

BL625.A94 2004   204'.32
                    QBI04-700304

Cover art by Robert Viana.

Salutations and Prostrations
Unto my Beloved *Sat Guru*
and
Master Sant Ajaib Singh
Holy Father and Initiator
to
The *Sat Purush* whose Compassion
Has sent our Master Ajaib Singh
And others to bring the suffering Souls out of
The regions of entrapment and back to
Their real home, *Sat Lok.*

Introduction

In a quest for spiritual answers, I have traveled thousands of miles and spent countless hours in study and meditation. At last, I feel it is time to give what the universe has given to me so generously to those who have similar intentions, but who may not have had the time for the spiritual search. Life is much more sacred and meaningful then we are led to believe. We only need to look in the right direction and the truth will be shown to us.

This book is about my search over a thirty-year period, both in the external world and within meditation. My first laboratory was my life's experiences, including journeys to India and around the world. My experiments encompassed reading textbooks in the original language of Sanskrit, dated more than 2,500 years ago, and progressed forward to examining today's scientific research. My journey has changed my life. I hope that understanding it will give you ideas for impacting your life.

For most of us, the moment finally arrives that we understand that experiences on earth only bring us a continual stream of desires for greater opportunities, while avoiding disappointments. We realize that we are being enticed by a mirage where each solution results in a myriad of new expectations to be fulfilled and fresh problems to solve. We find that a sense of permanent peace and happiness is impossible in this world of flux and change. Finally, we realize we have to seek something beyond what life — with all of its complications — has to offer.

We want to be free. We seek a permanent peace and happiness because innately we recall our Souls' nature, which is free, pure and content. Clearly nothing can be done without a conscious decision on our part to become free. In time, our prayers are answered and God sends his Messenger. At that time, a Master or Saint in the image and likeness of God guides us in the process of returning to our God-nature.

I was fortunate in meeting such a Master. There is no measuring the ecstasy of meeting such an "Ocean of Love." When Sant Ajaib Singh would come to visit us in the U.S., in only a few seconds — as words and glances were exchanged — an eternity of love could be conveyed. Many people who had never before been in the presence of such a Holy One would come out of a meeting transformed. My mother wanted to learn to meditate after being in the presence of the Master only once. My father felt as though his life had changed completely after meeting the Master.

So I must write this story or I will feel as though my life is not true and complete. It would be dishonest of me not to share this journey, for this is not just my personal journey, it is the journey all of us must take. What belongs to part of the creation belongs to the whole. This passage represents something as critical as life and death. The truth is I *have tried* to distract myself with the mundane world, hoping that this journey would go away. I cannot immerse myself in work and forgetfulness to make this problem — this problem of life — go away. It must be faced directly with all truth and honesty. So my journey continues ...

Table of Contents

List of Tables

I. Logic of the Spiritual Journey

O God,
Please take pity on us
Your lost children
Who do not even know
Where to look for You.

First, there was only You!
Then there was the desire to admire You
Then You appeared as two
And then more and more.

In our admiration
Of the many forms,
We forgot You were always there
So we became confused.

Please show us your greatness,
So that we may forget
Our silly little dramas and
Wake up from this dream.

Only by your Grace will
Your children find themselves
Back in your loving embrace
Protected from this dangerous world
That shows no pity on our vulnerability.

Chapter One

Subjective Science of Spirituality

I started my spiritual journey with a question. Even though I was only nineteen at the time, I asked the most profound question of my life: *Who am I?* This one essential question elicited many other questions. My mind kept wondering at all sorts of puzzles. Why am I here? Where did I come from? Who is my Creator? How did it all begin? Why is there so much suffering and unhappiness on earth? Is it possible to be free from this pain and suffering?

Early in life, I discovered I did not care for the canned answers so easily espoused by my parents and church authorities. I could find no depth in them. I knew if I was going to find the real answers that I would have to investigate this concept of "God" for myself. In fact, if there was no God, then in the name of knowing the Truth, I had to find out. No matter how divergent from my upbringing my quest might take me, I had to find the ultimate answers. I wanted to know the absolute Truth. That was final!

"The universe and its inhabitants are as ephemeral as the clouds in the sky; being born and dying are alike a spectacular dance or melodrama. The duration of our lives is like a flash of lightning or a firefly's flicker."

— Buddha

So, understanding what life was about was never easy for me. I had to make it into a remarkable expedition. Although in my search I did take a physical journey to exotic lands, more than anything, my seeking was an inner one: a mental, psychological and intellectual expedition of Soul-stirring proportions.

When it comes to questions of a metaphysical nature, such as we are considering here, who can properly and accurately answer them? Who can we turn to? Who knows the basic Truth? I could see it was not to be a straightforward endeavor, since, in both the East and West, there is a massive body of religious writings that document the words given by God to mankind. The most important of these writings form the world's greatest religions. Based on these words given by God, all the religions claim they have the Truth — yet they say it differently.

"The Kingdom of God cometh not with observation; the Kingdom of God is within you."

— St. Luke

So, playing it safe, I began my investigation with a system that espoused no religious indoctrination — at least in the beginning. I chose to be initiated into T.M. — Transcendental Meditation. All that was required of me was an interest in the physical and mental benefits that meditation had to offer. Research was clearly affirming these claims. Several universities had conducted their own research on the physiological and psychological benefits of meditation. The results showed that, during meditation, not only did the body undergo a deeper state of relaxation than in deep sleep, but also there were other advantages, such as a sense of well-being, improved memory and physiological changes, particularly lowering the blood pressure.

After meditating the prescribed twenty minutes twice a day, I began to notice changes in myself and my life. I had a new sense of well being and my grades improved at the University. Further, I found meditation so enjoyable that I looked forward to doing it daily. Soon my whole family was initiated as well.

Even my father became enthusiastic about meditation. He said, "It's better than taking a good nap!" However, at that time, I did not equate meditation with spirituality. I meditated for happiness and self-improvement. During my early adulthood years, I used to find myself so frustrated with life that I would cry when life gave me a disappointment. The first year after I began meditating, I realized that a whole year had gone by and I hadn't cried. "Thank God for T.M., I would often say. I had found a state of happiness independent of the world.

"In meditation, go deep in the heart, in dealing with others be gentle and kind, in speech, be true, in ruling, be just."

— Taoist Proverb

So I had managed to take my first step into a spiritual life without having to deal with religion. Still, because of my religious background, I had to face the dilemma. Is religion based upon superstition and expediency, or upon spirituality and mysticism? If we examine the civilizing and educational aspects of any religion, we can find justification to classify it as a cultural development.

However, if we examine its spiritual aspects from the original sources of inspiration, we find numerous reasons to conclude that religion is spiritual. So, to answer the question, we find that some portions are culturally based, while other parts, given by Mystics and Saints, are spiritually inspired. These spiritual parts clearly come from subjective experiences. Interestingly, when we examine these experiences, we find many similarities, even though the Saints were living in different cultures and historical periods, and were identified with distinct religions.

As an anthropological study, it is interesting to ascertain the purpose religion serves in facilitating the efficient functioning of societies. Such a study would show certain consistencies between distinct cultures and historical periods. From this evidence, it appears that we humans need answers about our origin, our creation, our creator — and our death. Although the explanations may vary, they serve similar functions of providing philosophical answers and establishing codes of ethics, including the consequences of disobeying the rules — in this life and in an afterlife.

"Thy Beloved is within Thee,
And thou art ignorant of it.
He is the very Soul of thy Soul,
And thou art wandering without
In quest of Him."

— Magrabi Sahib

Chapter Two

Meeting a Christian Mystic

I suppose it was inevitable that I started my spiritual quest with a course given by a Christian. I had just turned twenty when a close friend from high school told me about an incredible Christian Mystic, who gave classes on spirituality. The mystic was a self-ordained minister who was psychic to a certain extent, so she could make predictions and perceive certain secret information about people. In addition, she was able to synthesize Eastern and Western religions and philosophies. I was fascinated with all these new perspectives on life.

In the first class with the Christian Mystic, we were asked to go into meditation and visualize a Master. Then we were to listen to what the Master had to say to us, perhaps a special message. Having become a total agnostic at that time, I could not visualize Jesus since I was no longer sure of His legitimacy or status. My perception of the hypocrisy of Catholicism had left me cynical about my own religious background. Since I did not know of any Master, I decided, out of respect for the process and acceptance of the intelligence of my friend who had insisted on bringing me there, to go ahead with the exercise as best as I could. I began by focusing on a Master's big toe, so as to move my inner vision slowly upward to see who would appear. In my mind's eye, an Indian Master with a turban and a white beard clearly appeared. I don't remember much else except that I was in such an altered state of joy and happiness afterwards that the teacher kept staring at me. I quickly left the room after the class, somewhat self-consciously.

As I left to drive home, a beautiful Hawaiian woman followed me out to the parking lot. She told me about an upcoming course with the Christian Mystic and talked me into joining her. I had no idea at that moment that my inner journey had begun. The rest of the week was filled with a wonderful bliss that was experienced both day and night.

"The Kingdom of God cometh not with observation,
The Kingdom of God is within you."

— The Bible

The subsequent classes included intriguing information about the paranormal, as well as the teachings of Christian mysticism. I learned about the "Master" Jesus to whom I had never before been introduced. During the "lost years," he had become God-realized after a pilgrimage to the Himalayas of India. I was fascinated to see Jesus in this new light, for his was a story of a prophet of extraordinary vision and powers. This class opened me to comprehend a process repeated throughout the history of religions; a process of seeking God in order to complete oneself.

At that time, I had no idea that my spiritual journey was to take me over such a varied terrain. I feel grateful that I have been able to come in contact with true sages of several different religions. I found that if we compare the different books of God, such as the Bible, Koran, Vedas and Buddhist texts, and we examine the tremendous body of knowledge reported by the

Mystics and Masters recognized in these religions, we find certain underlying themes.

Some of these consistencies between religious cultures can be explained by history itself. For example, the Sanskrit language is considered to be the mother of Latin and Greek. Since religion is often linked with superstitions that serve the purpose of providing answers needed by a particular society to face its daily challenges, it is logical that certain practices were passed along within a language group. Therefore, it is not surprising to see certain spiritual practices, such as performing rituals, fasting and maintaining celibacy, passed down from an older culture, such as the East Indian culture of five thousand years, to later cultures of Egypt, Greece, and Rome.

If we conduct a spiritual or mystical study, we also find certain consistencies. They range from similarities of the experiences of Mystics and Saints around the world, in addition to certain techniques used to arrive at these states of spirituality. In fact, *yogis* and Saints of all times have been known to practice withdrawal of their attention from the body and mind to subtler meditative states.

We could refer to these Mystics and Saints as scientists of the inner reality since they have focused their efforts on the inner subjective world to the exclusion of the external world. For most of us, their experiences are insurance that the amount of time and effort we devote to the inner world can influence the outcome of our spiritual journey. As we evolve, we receive more awareness of spirit, are more inclined to live aligned with spirit, and have a natural tendency to seek its source, God.

Similarities of mystical experiences are found in diverse cultures across the centuries, for example, between the writings of Saint Theresa in Spain and the writings of mystics in India. Even though Saint Theresa clearly had no exposure to the detailed descriptions of mysticism that are presented in some of the old Sanskrit texts or in other sacred scriptures, her descriptions of her inner experiences equal them in many details.

Additionally, an American Indian medicine man has reported out-of-body experiences that are described by meditators of other traditions. Research by an American doctor shows details of near-death and out-of-body experiences have many consistent elements. With the popularity of the paranormal, which is now documented and easily accepted by a wide audience on programs such as *X-Files*, we are beginning to admit that there is a whole new world: a subjective reality that gives us a new frontier. One that many feel is worth exploring.

Every religion has a series of practices that leads to an inner reality. Each step is purposeful in the process of purification and withdrawal. The body and mind must be prepared, for to know God is to know the most subtle and most pervasive of all — the One in everything.

"The paths are many, the Truth is One."

— The Vedas

Chapter Three

Discovering the Key to Happiness

The class on Christian mysticism changed my whole outlook about life. I knew I would have to go back and re-examine my concepts from start to finish. Using my new found information, I would have to sort out everything I had thought was true and was not true in my store of knowledge.

First of all, I had to ask, *"What are we doing here?"* In general, we are here working for ourselves and others with a sense of a vague purpose as we play out our dramas of give and take with others. Hopefully, we have fulfilled some of our needs and desires. Essentially, we are working on them either successfully or at least managing to collect a few fragments of happiness in our struggles. Each of us has our own definition of happiness. Each of us has our own path to follow. Each of us is unique.

"My plenteous joys, wanton in fullness, seek to hide themselves in drops of sorrow."

— William Shakespeare

Sometimes when I fulfill a desire, I may feel happy for a moment — until a new desire arises in my mind. When trying to please our minds, there is no end to its demands for fulfillment and happiness. Similarly, there is no limit to the mind's imagination of how to accomplish its desires. This is also true when trying to serve others. In one sense, we are continually battered about in our efforts to please ourselves and others. Our needs and wants just become more sophisticated — until a hundred different television channels, a hundred gourmet restaurants, and a hundred varieties of automobiles may not provide enough to satisfy us.

As Christians we were given certain rules for living. These rules were considered by the Church as a means to greater happiness and peace of mind — both in this life and the next. However, many of us were not really sure these rules produced the intended results. Some think that they may be based upon superstition, while others feel they are merely ritualistic. Let us take a look at the two most basic and fundamental rules.

The first one is *"Love the Lord thy God with your whole heart, Soul, and mind." The second is "Love thy neighbor as thyself."*

What happens if we were to live with this attitude? If every act is for God and every thought is on God, we are loving God wholeheartedly. With this devotion, we only have a relationship with God. We are no longer a mother or a father, no longer a friend or a boss, no longer a sister or brother. We are only in a relationship with God. What happens when we are solely in relationship with God? If God is the object of love and we only think of this love, then we are always loving. This state of love is to the exclusion of other emotions that could undermine our happiness.

The problem arises when I think of myself, for then I see my limitations. I see my inadequacies, then I try to fix myself. Even though I may go through a series of actions designed to overcome my shortcomings, my mind dwells instead on my sense of limitation. However, when I don't let my mind dwell on my limited self, but think in terms of the limitless God, my mind becomes expanded and feels limitless. So when I know and contemplate God, without limitation, I am happy. For example, the sight of the limitless water of an ocean or an empty expanse of a beach brings a certain peaceful repose to the mind.

Since I am not limited to my personal desires and inadequacies, I become happy. Consider the state of mind that comes with never thinking of yourself and your limitations, but always thinking of God with all your heart, mind and Soul. This practice brings great happiness. This love starts in the heart, consumes the thoughts of the mind, and becomes the occupation of the Soul.

This love goes to the level of the Soul. When we transcend our minds in the meditation of devotion, in that silence, we touch our own Soul. How can we know if such a love has gone to the level of the Soul? We have a physical body. We are in touch with it at the time of eating or running or doing manual labor. Likewise, we have a mind. We are aware of it when we are feeling an emotion or absorbed in thought. We can only know our Soul when we transcend the body and the mind. Because the Soul comes from God, it is only in relationship to God that the Soul finds its own happiness.

"A million speak of love, yet how few know, true love is not to lose remembrance even for an instant."

— Kabir

At some point, we just want the struggle to end because we become tired of trying, for we realize that the things in life never really seem to get solved. The completion of each endeavor brings new desires and challenges until, finally, we ask to jump off the hamster wheel altogether. We pray to God, "Get me out of this absurd cycle of birth and rebirth where nothing really seems to get resolved, where it is never certain that I can succeed in creating a perfect happiness for myself." At that time, our prayer is heard by God, and another process begins. Instead of walking toward death, we begin to walk toward eternity.

The Eastern religions specialize in practices that aid in withdrawing attention from the body, as well as from the mind. At such a time, we become aware of our Soul level. We also become aware of the longing of the Soul for God. Not only in the East, but all religious rituals and practices are designed to engage the body and mind, so that we can withdraw our attention to the level of the Soul.

"One who is able to withdraw all his senses from the attractions of the sense-objects, even as a tortoise withdraws all its limbs, he is a man of steady wisdom."

— Lord Krishna

The withdrawal process begins with the physical senses. We may start with the bells of a church with their ability to dispel the negativity of lower vibrations. Then we listen to chanting and prayers, an invocation of great intention. Progressing to subtler sounds, we may listen to the spiritual music of Gregorian or, perhaps, chants and music of Masters and Saints thousands of years old These soothing sounds cause the mind to turn away from thoughts of worldly matters and follow the sounds of a higher vibration. In India there are ancient scales called *ragas,* which represent different moods. Some *ragas* are spiritual in nature; therefore, they automatically entice the mind to follow these melodies. During a performance, the *ragas* become subtler and subtler in nature, thus carrying the listener to subtler levels of happiness. The *vibrations and harmony* rule of physics actually confirms how certain harmonies and vibrations attune to the universe which is why there is a principle behind the power of the word and the chanting of mantras used to precipitate a higher state of consciousness.

Then to be able to withdraw on the mental level, many saints chose a special object for devotion, which made concentration easier for them. Some were more attracted to Jesus, others to God the Father aspect, and still others to Mary the Mother, or the Mother aspect of God. This single-pointed focus and devotion initiates the beginning of the withdrawal process on the mental level. In the West, we are inspired by the profound examples of spirituality that the Mystics and Saints of the Catholic religion have given us. These Saints are remarkable in their demonstration of devotion to God and their ability to perform miracles attributed to love for God.

"But lay up for yourselves treasures in heaven, where neither moth nor rust doth corrupt, and where thieves do not break through nor steal: For where your treasure is, there will your heart be also."

—Jesus

Chapter Four

Law of Karma

If we examine our lives today, we are amazed at all the many choices that are available to us. However, we forget to consider that we must have earned these options in previous lifetimes through meritorious actions and devotion to God. When so many gifts of life are arrayed around us, we become forgetful of how this life is a result of the right choices we have made previously. At last we realize what we have is still not enough — never enough — we find ourselves forever wanting more choices. "Seek ye first the Kingdom of God and all else shall come to you." With these words, Jesus clearly states that by making God your first choice, all of your other choices will be manifest.

"We must make the choices that enable us to fulfill the deepest capacities of our real selves."
— Thomas Merton

One thing remains clear. All choices have consequences. The law of physics prevails. "For every action there is an equal and opposite reaction." This axiom expresses the law of *karma* of Eastern philosophies. The universe operates according to this law. Swami Vivekananda, an East Indian sage, illustrated the law by saying, "If you throw a rock into space and stand there long enough, it will return and hit you on the back of the head." In the New Testament, many references are made about the rewards in heaven for righteous action and the punishment in hell for unrighteous ones.

Consequently, we cannot escape the fact that along with our choices come results. As free as we may seem to be in our ability to pick and choose, to that same extent, we are bound to the consequences of choice. Therefore, we continue to return to a physical body to attempt to correct the consequences of our past choices. In spite of our best efforts, our dilemma is that we cannot foresee what consequences each choice will bring. There are so many variables and factors in time and space that it is difficult to know the future outcome of all the choices we make, and their connections with all the other choices made in other lifetimes — not only by ourselves but with others also.

The present becomes nothing more than a collision course of all the choices of the past and their consequences. Oh, how wonderful are the flavors of my favorite foods: chocolate ice cream, asparagus soup, eggplant parmesan, and fresh orange juice. However, when I combine all my favorite foods and beverages at the same time, I get a stomachache instead of happiness.

"We read the world wrong and say that it deceives us."
— Rabindranath Tagore

Likewise, our prospects for a perfect future become diminished by the mish-mash of combinations in the present. In the same way that perfect foods become imperfect in combination with other foods, so our perfect *karmic* rewards become imperfect when combined with other *karmic* consequences, since they occur at the same time and place. For example, you may have two children — old Souls who you have earned the privilege of parenting — whom you love and adore. However, they do not get along; so together with the love, there is pain. We are continually trying to get it right, constantly in effect, due to the consequences of all of our choices. Life becomes so complicated that we just don't know what to do. In short, our choices for happiness become a source of further unhappiness.

"Action, which springs from the mind, from speech, and from the body, produces either good or evil results; actions cause the conditions of men, the highest, the middling, and the lowest."
— Hindu Law of Manu

In the East, the sages suggest maintaining a certain frame of mind for survival in a world of action where making choices is inevitable; they call it, *karma yoga attitude.* As we go through life, we hold the attitude that we can choose any action that we perform, but we cannot choose the result. In other words, it is up to each individual to continue making the right choices in life, but not to be concerned about the results of the actions. The results are up to God. If we make conscious choices without worrying about what the world may do with that choice, we succeed in two things. First, we are true to our own nature, so that our individual *karma* is exhausted. Second, we have the peace of mind that comes from the acceptance that, in the greater order of things, God, the Higher Intelligence, decides how to manage our choice of actions and its outcome.

Understanding the role of God in one's life makes one a devotee of God. As a devotee of God even though we are performing our daily duties, we keep our attention on God. Eventually, God becomes the ultimate choice. In choosing God, no event, out-come or situation can stand between you and your relationship with God. And when God becomes one's sole goal and pre-occupation, one has made the final choice. This is the only choice that will permanently liberate us from the sea of disappointment and unhappiness. Only God and his liberated Messengers, a Master, can liberate one from the illusion that happiness is dependent on the things of the world. It is only with the choice for God that liberation, the final choice, can take place.

To accomplish this goal, we first embark on the process of "man making," as Master Kirpal Singh used to describe it. To become a true man or woman is to use all of the gifts that were granted us as human beings. The greatest of the gifts is inheriting the kingdom of God. With our body, mind and intellect, we make a conscious choice to accomplish what no other creature in the creation is capable of doing. We make a choice of knowing God in order to partake in the fruits of heaven on earth.

"A mind that has forgotten the past and the future and is awake to the present expresses the highest concentration of intelligence. It is alert, it is watchful, it is inspired. The actions of a person who has such a mind are exceptionally creative and perfect."
— Swami Chinmayananda

Chapter Five

What Is Spirituality?

After I completed the course in Christian Mysticism, my attitude toward Jesus, spirituality and mysticism totally changed. I learned so many new and relevant concepts in the classes. I was truly excited and overwhelmed with the reading of past lives, seeing auras and, especially, the concept of mastering oneself. I also gained understanding through my friendship with Piilani. Since she had been raised in the traditional Hawaiian culture, she was much more familiar with psychic phenomena. One day, she helped me perceive my inner guides. For weeks, everywhere I looked I could see their faces smiling at me — one right after the other. This experience made quite an impact on me. I was curious and ready to investigate further this phenomenon called spirituality.

Spirituality can be explained as an extension of the physical world, a world made of matter of a more subtle vibration. Both the physical and spiritual realms are made up of energy. These realms consist of a range of subtleness and vibrations, but they are all of the same reality. The difference is that the physical realm is perceived by the five senses of the physical body and is grosser in nature, while the spiritual world is perceived by the mental and Soul vehicles. Below is a graph to explain the two realms by level of subtlety.

Table 1. Five Gross and Subtle Elements

Five Gross Elements	Perceived By :				
	Nose (smell)	Mouth (taste)	Eyes (sight)	Skin (touch)	Ears (hear)
Earth	X	X	X	X	X
Water		X	X	X	X
Fire			X	X	X
Air				X	X
Space					X
Five subtle Elements					
Earth	Perceived by mental body apparatus, equipped with five subtle instruments of perception.				
Water					
Fire					
Air					
Space					

The instrument of the ears is highest, in that it perceives a greater range of perception, from the grossest element to the most subtle element, space. In the process of dying, we can observe how the creation is composed of five elements from the standpoint of our physical body. When someone dies, first the Soul withdraws from the earth element. The arms and legs begin to feel heavy and one's sight begins to diminish, so that surrounding objects appear as though in the distance. Then the element of water begins to dissipate and the mouth becomes very dry. Next, the element of air starts to withdraw and the breath stops. Finally, the last element of fire pulls out and the body turns cold. Similarly, when the Soul moves to the regions of subtler elements, it gradually begins a process of withdrawing from elements of these subtlest realms as it continues its spiritual journey. There are entire schools of *yoga* and Buddhist practices based upon this process of conscious withdrawal of the Soul from the body. St. Paul referred to this withdrawal as "dying daily."

To become what we call "more spiritual" is to become more aware of the realm of the spirit — from the mental domain on up to the domain of the Soul. Indeed, all beginning spiritual practices are methods for engaging the body, then focusing the mind on more and more subtle realms. Hence, the example is given in the Bible that it is as impossible for a rich man, who is encumbered with the material concerns of body and mind, to go to Heaven. The seeker must become subtle as space.

To be as subtle as space, we must concentrate on space with its quality, sound. As we know, sound has many different vibrational levels within itself. Prayers, chanting, and bells — all create certain vibrations in space that cause us to focus on this subtlest aspect of the five elements. Every church, temple and mosque has its enchanting sounds for this purpose. As the vibration becomes more subtle or pervasive, it reaches subtler and subtler levels or regions. Hence, if we wish to transcend to higher and subtler realms, we must listen to sounds of higher and subtler frequencies.

"In the beginning of the spiritual life we ought to be faithful in doing our duty and denying ourselves; but after that, unspeakable pleasures follow."
— Brother Lawrence

When we graduate from the realm of the gross world, we switch over to the sounds of the subtler realms. This is accomplished by prayer and chanting on the mental level. Mental prayers are said to be one hundred times more effective than physical chanting. The repetition of the inner prayer or *mantra* is a form of purification of the mind in its most subtle form. This connection to these subtler vibrations is important to the progress of purification of the mind and Soul. Thus the greatest spiritual gift is when a Perfect Saint gives an initiation with certain words or mantras that point one to their inner self. These subtle sounds actually purify and lift the Soul to higher and higher realms.

Recent research of the brain has indicated that the brain actually changes when one reaches a higher state of oneness with God. Whether examining the brain of a Catholic nun in the act of deep prayer or the Buddhist monk in the act of profound meditation, researchers have found that part of the brain closes down temporarily. The sphere of the brain that registers oneness is not in the part that registers differentiation between separate things. One thing is clear — regardless of the act — be it the dancer in deep trance in the African steppes, or the meditator in a monastery, or the devotee who is contemplating God, all acts come to a similar result. The sense of "small self" is left behind, and a subtle identification with God is experienced. All distinction between the "one who sees" and "objects that are seen" disappears and the mind merges into God consciousness.

"You live among illusions and in the world of apparitions, but you don't know this. If you awaken to this Reality, you will see that you are nothing, and being nothing you are everything."

— Kalu Rimpoche

This life is only a visitation. You and I are passing through this earthly reality. Along the way, we find numerous varieties of entertainment to distract us from wondering what life is about. In this human body, a Soul has many more choices than allowed in less developed forms of life. If born in a free country, we have many choices; the opportunities are even greater. The whole natural world and environment are here to serve in the process of collecting experiences. For what purpose is this process? We know our life is temporary, for death is certain in the end. When we examine the process carefully, we find death is a continuum — a part of a seemingly never-ending process. Rebirth will occur as surely as death.

Each birth is a chance to get it right again — a chance to satisfy unfulfilled desires and improve on relationships. Each birth provides another door to walk through, another avenue to walk down. Each Soul has to determine which way to go and with whom to travel. If life were a perfect and complete experience in itself, wouldn't each one of us be completely satisfied?

The truth is that, if we have accumulated any debts to repay, we are delayed in our process. This whole universe was established as a field of experience; it is supported by the efforts of all its many beings. So, while you and I may have had a moment of pleasure in time and space, it wasn't a free ride. It becomes our turn to help throw the party or our turn to help raise children, while it is another's turn to be fulfilled and be the recipient of their earlier service to others.

"Doest thou reckon thyself a puny form,
When within thee the Universe is folded?"

— Ali

When we ask where we came from, it is the story of the fallen Souls. Our real nature and identity are not of this physical world, or of the subtle worlds. We came from purer and higher realms. We, in fact, are not separate from the one limitless God. But as if in a dream, we have been caught up in the world and have identified with it as if it is real.

If I am in the world, then I am in it and a part of it and have to deal with it. The fallen Souls willingly or unwillingly are stuck in it. We have *karmic* debts to pay off that are registered in our Souls. At the same time, other Souls have debts to repay to us. As long as we remain in the dream, we must keep working, acting and reacting to the dreamlike material. How about the possibility of getting out of the dream life once and for all?

While spiritual practices are likely to improve our lives here on earth and in the afterlife, they do not necessarily free us from rebirth and may not change the fact that we have become a slave of the *karmic* rules and regulations of the lower three regions. In the East, they refer to a wheel of 84,000 lifetimes and endless transmigration. In this condition, no one can claim to be master of one's own fate. We cannot even remember one lifetime to the next. We have no knowledge of future *karma* or future consequences. What appears as great good fortune does not guarantee future success, for it can bring the fall of the Soul, who is ignorant of the *karmic* chains of the indulgences. In order to progress out of the *karmic* bondage, one must have a guide, a Master Saint, who is liberated and understands the way of the Royal Road.

As Souls, we were once all united in the One, but we fell into grosser vehicles for the sake of experimentation and seeking pleasure in the grosser realms. With the forgetting of our oneness with God, we were stuck, and therefore had to pay the *karmic* price for our false identification. But a time comes when our Souls tire of birth and rebirth, then we give a fervent prayer for help. At that moment, God answers our pleas by sending assistance in the form of a Master Saint.

"When the seed of the previous good karmas grows, one meets a renunciate Soul and, only then, one awakens from the sleep of ages; then the darkness is removed."

— Guru Nanak

II. Before Meeting a Master Saint

O Soul speak
Within its lonely entrapment
In cages of human flesh
Different and separated from all the rest
In isolation, darkness and deep night
Seeks out its maker of delight
Will reach the sky.

As sun evaporates the tears
In hopes of meeting in rivers
And merging finally in great oceans
'Tis emptiness and isolation
Which brings me closer to you, O Lord,
No longer falling out through senses
Of forgetfulness.

I seek you out in deep loneliness
The beginning of my journey is
Isolation and the night it must begin in darkness to
Finally find antithesis
The void into God's friendliness
Bright light and warmth and loveliness
Of beginning to no end

Chapter Six

Purpose of Spiritual Practices

In the 20th Century, our scientific exploration has been of an objective nature. We mastered exploration in outer space and on the molecular level, but explorations of the subjective realm have only been anecdotal in nature. Several famous physicists state that they no longer view time in a horizontal mode, just as we no longer view the world as flat. Hence, we begin to comprehend that there exists an inner world of subjective experience. The world of the mind and spirit becomes a whole new domain of exploration — not one dismissed as fantasy or imagination.

The philosopher Maslow described a ladder of human needs. East Indian philosophy reduces these needs to four levels. Actions are performed to satisfy needs in the outer world. As soon as these needs are met, actions are performed to satisfy our wants, both physical and subjective. After our various desires have been met, we begin to work to help others satisfy their needs and wants, both physical and emotional. Still, one is not completely happy and fulfilled since solutions to happiness for oneself, as well as others, appear to bring only temporary happiness and fulfillment. When fulfilled on these three levels, we reach our last desire — freedom. So finally, one reaches the fourth stage: the desire for liberation — freedom from the need to perform all types of actions. What does such a freedom imply?

This freedom is mentioned in many scriptures, but most carefully elaborated in Vedanta, the philosophical discourses written at the end of the Hindu Vedas. This freedom is only possible with a mind that knows non-duality. This is freedom for a mind that saw itself as separate from the world and, therefore, limited by that perception. This is a freedom born out of the *realization* that when we identify with the ego, we feel separate and limited. This ego or "I" sense sees itself as a body/mind complex. Since the body/mind complex is very limited, the ego also feels insecure and inadequate. Consequently, when the ego tries to make itself appear more or better, it only succeeds in causing all kinds of suffering and pain for itself and others.

"The mind is merely thoughts. Of all thoughts, the thought 'I' is the root of the ego. Therefore, the mind is only the thought 'I'."
— Ramana Maharshi

To understand this concept, let us examine the development of a child: its growth of sense of self and egocentricity. Two-year-olds begin to express a sense of autonomy and separateness when they throw tantrums, thereby asserting their own minds. By the time the individual reaches awkward adolescence, the sense of self and self-consciousness has become so acute that one may develop a tendency to withdraw and distance oneself with loud music, drugs, alcohol, sex and bizarre behavior. One assumes any identity necessary to cover up one's acute sense of separateness, self-consciousness, and sense of limitation. However, when one uses these avenues to escape from one's own awareness of acute limitation, maturation does not progress. The result is an immaturity in which one never stops being self-conscious and self-centered.

In fact, whenever we try to escape from the pain of the awareness of our own limitation and acute sense of separateness, we stop asking the right questions and stop pursuing answers. We stop our own development and remain stuck in the vicious cycle of feeling limited and inadequate, rather than trying to escape the sense of limitation. We can call this dilemma the *fundamental problem* of life. When we develop an overwhelming desire to solve it, the final stage of seeking liberation can occur. That is, after fulfilling both physical and emotional needs, and both physical and emotional wants, and trying to fulfill the wants and needs of others, something is still missing. We are still left with a sense of inadequacy, limitation and unhappiness.

At this point, we have eliminated the outer world as a true source of lasting peace and happiness. We have personally found that the objects of the world are limited and carry a burden, for we have to make a continual effort to acquire and maintain them. When everything seems *perfect*, the mind tires of them and becomes bored. Then it wants to experience subtler pleasures of life. For a while satisfying these emotions provides a subtler sense of joy and satisfaction, but still we are not completely fulfilled. Never have so many pleasures and distractions been offered on so many levels to all groups and ages of people as we find today in the U.S. Yet, if we ask the control group — of about 300 million Americans — "Are you happy?" the answer would be "No" — for the consumption and grasping continues. On a deep level, we are empty and lonely, trying to fulfill ourselves in any way the society offers.

The mass of men lead lives of quiet desperation… unconscious despair is concealed even under what are called the games and amusements of mankind…

— Henry David Thoreau

Truly, we long for a more lasting happiness. After all is said and done, we seek liberation from the whole system — with its inherent pleasures and pains. We begin to long for fulfillment and happiness of a higher nature and order. Then the real spiritual journey begins: our inner journey back to God, our source.

"The mind attains to the Supreme State by adopting the following disciplines: The duties of life have to be performed with detachment and as an offering to the Divine."

— Lord Krishna

Spiritual practices are specific techniques to withdraw the center of the psyche from the ego toward higher, subtler orbits of experience, so that we move away from the realm of the ego/mind complex into the realm of the spirit and spirituality. The spiritual teachings are created to free us from identifying with the egocentric consciousness, so we can experience and live the freedom of our genuine Self.

Now I could understand the purpose of church services. I remember when I was a child sitting in the church and being totally entranced by my surroundings. The colored glass, the glittering gold, the sweet sounds, the glowing candles, they all took me away from my normal world. I entered into a heavenly paradise where I felt safe and secure.

For withdrawal from body consciousness, many different denominations of churches, mosques, and temples use various methods to engage the five senses in sights, sounds, touch, taste, and smells. The idea is to switch one's focus from the world to God through symbols of God.

To entice the *nose,* there is incense that gives a vibrational smell to dispel the lower entities. The fragrance of flowers is one of the odors of highest vibrations, as is incense which has been used in temples throughout the ages.

For the *mouth* and its *taste* buds, we are given communion, or blessed food.

To purify the *skin,* or sense of *touch,* we have holy water that has been blessed to give it a special vibration. Water is used to baptize and bless, as well as purify, the devotee.

To please the *eyes,* we behold the *sight* of flowers, stained glass windows, serene faces of love and joy on statues and paintings, and the lovely glowing light of candles or ritualistic fires.

Again, to dispel negativity and negative vibrations, the *ears* hear the *sounds* of sweet melodies and chants or prayers of higher resonance, which have been established and passed down from the higher regions throughout history. These thought forms, chants, and prayers take on power similar to the hundredth monkey theory; they actually transform the nature of the physical realm. Additionally, the words of the prayers provide a conscious and subconscious impression, thereby transforming the mind's lower tendencies and acting as a springboard to the "higher mind."

Table 2. Comparison of Practices in World Religions

Religion	God Concept	Monastic Life	Use of Beads	Mantra
Buddhism	non-dualism	yes	yes	Om
Hinduism	non-dualism/ dualism	yes	yes	Om
Tao	non-dualism	yes	no	
Confucianism	agnostic	no	no	
Judaism	monotheism/ dualism	no	no	Shalom
Islam	monotheism/ dualism	no	yes	Allah, Ameen
Christian	monotheism/ dualism	yes	yes	Amen

Chapter Seven

Purifying our Inner World

When the physical rituals are completed, the participants may repeat the process mentally. Thus, the subtle activity of meditation begins. As the mind becomes more focused and less scattered, it becomes more subtle. This mind may begin to investigate the significance of the rituals and ask questions about their symbolism. As the mind becomes subtler, it begins to seek subtler and more refined depths of feeling. In the inner sanctum of the Hindu temples, often there is a stone symbol called the *Shiva Lingam*. This form represents the infinite aspect of God, the subtlest aspect of God to contemplate — God with no limitation. When we contemplate this aspect of God, we experience a peace and joy of the subtlest nature. We may even go into the place of limitlessness, called *Samadhi.*

"O man, outwardly you seem to be a small human form, but inwardly you are a great being with a whole world inside of you."
— Muslim Fakir

In fact the Sanskrit word for "limitlessness" is *ananta.* The word resembles the word *ananda,* which means bliss or love. In both cases, *ananta* and *ananda* bring joy and happiness of the subtlest nature. So whether a devotee focuses on the joyful or loving aspect of God or the limitless aspect of God, the result is the same sense of joy and freedom. As the mind begins to taste this joy and freedom, it naturally wants more and more of this joy. Eventually, one becomes steeped in this *Samadhi* state of consciousness, or oneness with God. This subjective state of mind is universal. It has been experienced by Saints of many distinct religious cultures in many different times of history. When achieved fully, this experience can bring about liberation from the things of the world. This quest of God-realization is the finest and subtlest pursuit known to human kind. This most glorious and noble pursuit is a natural result of our having fulfilled the hierarchy of needs and wants, if not in one lifetime, then over several lifetimes.

"Let us consider our place in sight of God and of his angels. Let us rise in chanting that our hearts and voices harmonize."

— St Benedict

The angelic forces and vibrations encountered in the synagogue, church, temple or mosque purify those who seek God's blessing. We leave the place of worship purified, uplifted, and happy. The vibrations assist our desire to withdraw to our subtler inner self. The sweetness of this withdrawal of our attention — from the world and back to God — brings a sense of very subtle peace and joy not felt before. Next we may ask ourselves, "What now? Is there a way to withdraw to an even deeper and more permanent sense of peace?"

All of the beginning practices relate to the physical, or grosser, realm. As we begin to withdraw from the world of objects, our attention is pulled up from the lower realms to the higher ones. The Soul receives relief when it dwells in the higher mansions of love, the region of the heart and above, if only for brief respites. We then begin to withdraw to subtle forms, depictions, projections and imaginings of the mind, that is to say, our mental worlds, which consist of these five subtle elements, the substance from which the five gross elements arise.

In order to feel God's presence even more profoundly, the ancient Sanskrit texts of a 5,000 year tradition assert that chanting and prayer in the mental realm are one hundred times more powerful than doing so in the physical realm. Further, they state that sound, being the subtlest of the five senses, is the most powerful and is likely to be antecedent to the subtle mental realm, which has five subtle senses. When withdrawal takes place, it is a journey from the physical to the mental realm. If the mental practice is ritualized, it facilitates the withdrawal of attention, which becomes steadier and easier. Again, all the religions of the world offer various methods of withdrawal from the physical to the mental realms.

Eventually, instead of external chanting, we begin to recite inner prayers and *mantras,* sacred words or phrases. Some religions advocate the use of beads to aid the repetition and to keep the mind focused on its task. Each bead represents a prayer. As each prayer is finished a new bead is held. The rosary beads and the prayers keep both the body and mind disciplined with a task. When we become adept at this practice, we no longer need to use the beads.

"If a man is so occupied with recollecting Me that he forgets to pray to Me, I grant him a nobler gift than that which I accord to those who petition Me."

— Mohammed

We then engage in continuous internal prayer, chanting or contemplation, until our whole mind becomes concentrated. Our whole heart, Soul and mind become focused on God — the more subtle the mind becomes, the more single-pointed it becomes. At this stage of practice, impressions, and thought forms appear in the mind's inner eye. Some are distractions, while others are signs of the mind becoming more purified and subtle. The subtlest of the five senses is the vision of light. Even subtler is the inner sound. A Master Saint can awaken this inner vision of light and sound at the time of initiation. Just as the outer world has an infinite variety of sounds and forms, so the inner world, the world of the mind and the world of the Soul, has infinite worlds of sounds and forms — all more and more subtle in nature — at increasingly higher vibrations and forms of bliss and peace.

"If we try to withdraw our Soul from our body all at once we will have a lot of pain. But if we gradually go on meditating every day, getting a little bit of pain, then one day we will become successful in withdrawing our Soul from our body. If we make the habit of sitting constantly on a daily basis, it can become a career."

— Ajaib Singh

Chapter Eight

Scope of Meditation

In order to free ourselves from the limitations imposed upon us by the body/mind complex, we must be able to either block them out of our consciousness, or to ignore them. We accomplish this every day when we go into a deep sleep, but unfortunately the mind remains unconscious at that time. So the challenge is to know this freedom consciously. The ideal would be to make the mind and body as quiet as in deep sleep, while remaining fully conscious, or absorbed.

We have all had the experience of being so absorbed in a movie that we forget about our bodies and our mental problems. Likewise, we all know the experience of being so absorbed in a piece of music or a sports event or a conversation that we forget ourselves. The goal would be to experience this kind of forgetfulness of ourselves, without having to resort to any entertainment outside of ourselves. This method is called meditation. Meditation is intended to enable us to transcend the body/mind complex while remaining totally conscious.

"This is certain: worship, incantations, and meditation are performed respectively with the body, voice and mind, and are in this ascending order of value."

— Ramana Maharshi

There are many different kinds of meditation. These different techniques are nothing more than methods of overriding the preoccupations of the body/mind complex to be able to experience a more subtle form of reality known as the Soul. The Soul is considered the subtlest of our bodies after the physical and mental, or astral body. The Soul is a reality separate from the mental realm. The Soul is attached to the mental body because of *karma* in the physical and mental worlds. The Soul becomes a prisoner. When the Soul becomes distracted by its body/mind vehicle, it forgets itself. In the same way, we forget ourselves when inebriated or caught up in an event or movie. These distractions of pain and pleasure, that is, the avoidance of suffering and the pursuit of enjoyment, keep us so distracted that we forget who we truly are.

The progress a person makes in meditation depends on many factors. Just as when we learn to ride a bicycle or any other skill, we learn at different rates. Some master it easily and quickly; others take longer and fall often. Some practices of meditation are more difficult than others. Many religions around the world offer different forms of meditation to their practitioners. Ideally, the *Guru* guides the disciples by giving them the technique that suits their temperament and vibrational level.

"When through discrimination the heart has become pure, then, in meditation, the Self is revealed."
— Mundaka Upanishad

Many religions have comparable prayers and chants to keep the mind busy, alert and quiet, yet vigilant. These are the beginning stages of meditation and withdrawal. Interestingly, I did not, until much later, correlate the similarities of meditation with the saying of the rosary. I found out that the Indian, Tibetan and the Muslim traditions used the repetition of a prayer with the beads to keep the mind focused on the task at hand. I realized later that, when St. Mary appeared to devotees and told them to say the rosary to ward off the threat of war, she was really asking the Catholics to meditate. If the rosary prayers were spoken mentally instead of verbally, the practice could take on a power one hundred times greater. Using the *mantra* of few syllables in the eastern part of the world produces the same results.

Mantras are short phrases pertaining to God, similar to the rosary prayer, but shorter in length. These *mantras* have an energy and power of their own, depending upon who has given them. Their repetition helps to purify the mind of its mundane preoccupations, while keeping it alert and focused on the task. Eventually, the mind begins to quiet down for a glimpse of the silence between the thoughts. This profound and enrapturing silence becomes the backdrop for the Soul's receptivity to God. This silence increases until the mind goes to what the Hindus call *Brahman,* thus allowing the Soul to continue its journey back to God.

What happens when we meditate? When we meditate all of the layers of our worldly and mental preoccupations are peeled away from our immediate attention. Using a method of meditation given by a Master, the seeker begins the inward journey. With practice, the mind becomes quieter. The withdrawal of the Soul from the body brings a whole new set of changes. The peace from meditation begins to spill into one's very life.

Another way of describing meditation is concentrated focus subtler and freer than thought itself. It is a way of synchronizing all the energies to perceive the inner vistas of the soul.

"It is meditation that counts most and should have the biggest priority in our lives."

— Ajaib Singh

Chapter Nine

Role of Subtle Energy Centers

All of our experiences, including spiritual ones, can be thought of as having distinct vibrational qualities. The Bible thus refers to the many experiences that comprise living in a human body: "In my Father's house are many mansions." During the process of my spiritual investigations, I discovered the *Autobiography of a Yogi,* which I found quite helpful since it added a great dimension to my understanding of the East.

One day, while praying to Yogananda, I asked him, "What colors should I paint the walls of this room?" It was a question my mind conjured up for some reason while meditating. I think it really referred to the walls of the inner room of my mind. Automatically, the thought came to me, "It doesn't matter what color to paint the walls, Yogananda will paint them with his aura." So dropping my concern for this mundane task, my mind became silent. Then I became aware that my Soul was slowly withdrawing from my body. Even my breath was about to stop completely. Alarmed with the fear of dying, I foolishly asked for my breath back. If I had not stopped the process, I think I could have experienced what St. Paul wrote, "I die daily." I might not have understood what this special event actually meant, but the event certainly made a deep, lasting impression on me.

In fact, Eastern religions have designated the possibilities of experience according to seven categories of vibration, called *chakras*. Each *chakra*, when focused on by the mind and Soul, brings a different set of experiences and feelings. It is as if we are taking a elevator ride up and down, opening our mental door to different levels of experience. Spiritual practices are designed to move awareness up to higher *chakras*.

"Sat Guru is present in the body, as well as in all the lotuses which are in our body."

— Tulsi Sahib

Each *chakra* is referred to as a lotus because it has a certain number of petals and a distinct color in the etheric or subtle form. The petals are composed of tiny nerve channels and emit a certain sound power.

These *chakras*, or centers of consciousness, are described as follows:

1) **Security Chakra:** Aligned with this basic energy, we are preoccupied with personal security matters, such as food and shelter. Its physiological role is related to generative function.

2) **Sensation Chakra:** When in sync with this center, we show concern with finding happiness in various forms of sensation, such as sex, food, music and entertainment.

3) **Power Chakra:** When acting from this center, we are concerned with dominating others, social hierarchy, manipulation and control in all of its subtle forms. Physiologically, it controls digestion.

4) **Love Chakra:** When aligned with this center, we begin to feel an unconditional love and acceptance of others. There is a compassion for those struggling at the lower centers. The self-centered ego is diminished at this center. The Heart Chakra is related to the function of the physical heart and circulation.

5) **Communication Chakra:** At the level of this center, all that is needed is provided. One is reminded of the Biblical passage: "Seek ye first the Kingdom within and all else shall be given." This *chakra* is related to the function of the lungs and the voice, including the ears, nose and throat.

6) **Consciousness Awareness Chakra:** Aligned with the energy of this center, we become an impartial witness to our body/mind complex and its dramas, without judgment or over-reaction. Vedanta refers to this center as being in the observer consciousness. It is related to the function of vision, the eyes, and the pituitary gland.

7) **Cosmic Consciousness Chakra:** At this level of consciousness, we transcend self-awareness and experience ourselves as pure awareness. In this state, we experience a sense of oneness with everything. We become love, wisdom, peace and effectiveness. This *chakra* is related to the brain, and especially the pituitary and pineal glands.

"The vast expanse of myself is so filled to overflowing with the fragrance of the Lord that the very thought of myself has completely vanished."

— Sufi Master

As far as the Soul is concerned, there are more and higher *chakras*. First, we will consider the lower seven *chakra* centers as presented in the following Table.

Table 3. The Seven Physical and Mental *Chakras*

Physical Location	Presiding Deity	Region	Associated Element	Function of Center
7.	Kal* Negative Power	*Casual Region* Soul		
6. *Ajna* (between eybrows)	*Atman/* Free Spirit	*Astral* Intellect and Higher Mind	Active Life Principle	All in All, Alpha & Omega
5. *Kanth* (throat)	*Shakit/* Mother	Higher Mind	Ether/ Sound	All-Controlling Power
4. *Hridey* (heart)	*Shiva/* Gabriel	Higher Mind	Air/ Touch	Disintegration Death
3. *Nabhi* (heart)	*Vishnu/* Israel	Lower Mind	Fire/ Sight	Sustenance/ Preservation
2. *Indri* (generative organ)	*Brahma/* Michael	Physical Body and Lower Mind	Water/ Taste	Creation of Species
1. *Guda* (rectum)	*Ganesha*	Physicak Body and Lower Mind	Earth/ Smell	Purification of Body

* The Dark Night of the Soul is experienced here when the Soul, once tied to the mind, must do battle with the mind to be able to progress to higher spiritual mansions.

The problem with operating from the energy of the three lower *chakras,* from which we live out our addictions, is that we are never satisfied with the results. From the Security *Chakra,* we are never totally secure, for we can always think of one more avenue to provide more and better safety. In the Sensation *Chakra,* boredom is the problem. We have to seek new and more exciting experiences. When our focus is aligned with the Power *Chakra,* we always have to deal with alienation and challenges from others, while trying to maintain our power and control in every situation. With this *chakra* energy someone always has to be at the bottom in the hierarchy. We are impelled to maintain a position of dominance. To do so we have to become increasingly forceful. Although we may be successful in the world outside, we are very poor in happiness within.

"I have learnt silence from the talkative, toleration from the intolerant, and kindness from the unkind; yet strange, I am ungrateful to these teachers."

— Kahlil Gibran

When we realize that we are all creating a world in which our addictions are lived out, we begin consciously to notice the hollowness and suffering that those addictions cause. Then we start to think about our actions, so that we begin to achieve insights that will help to free us of the unconscious behavior. As our addictions become upgraded to preferences, we eventually find we can emotionally accept those things that had been unacceptable previously. As our addictions are reprogrammed, we find that the ego has less and less to do. Also, the ego will alienate the egos of others less and less often.

The limitations of these lower *chakras* keep our egos in a perpetual state of unhappiness, even though the clamoring for happiness remains constant — whether the desire is for a better house or wardrobe or status in life. Since we have a tendency to want to repeat certain feelings, we end up stuck at a certain level with a set of addictions, which come with their corresponding emotional problems. Anytime these addictions are not met, an ego-driven negative emotion occurs. As one visits the mansions of higher consciousness, negative emotions give way to a wide range of insights and intuitive understanding. The ego's negative feelings and reactions, which serve as its protective mechanism, are no longer necessary since the sense of self is no longer limited to the perspective of the lower *chakras*.

Chapter Ten

Aligning with the Heart Chakra

As our consciousness expands, we begin to experience more peace in our lives. This calmness is a quality useful in the world of humanity. One is in a natural neutral state, instead of one of struggle and hardship. With this state of mind, one can use discrimination to steer past the desires of the lower three realms, or *chakras*. One begins to develop a general compassion and love, along with understanding, for others. This energy is in balance with the heart *chakra*.

The problem with being in a state of illusion about our true identity is that we continue to identify with all of the *chakras*, or energy centers, of the body. Because of this false identification, we become subject to the rules of action and reaction. Therefore, one becomes a sinner and a victim. To bypass this trap, Jesus said that we should operate only out of love. He said we should "Love the Lord thy God, with thy whole heart, whole Soul, and whole mind." Also, he added a second practice: "Love thy neighbor as thyself." Through love we can get out of the whole mess represented by the lower *chakras*. Maintaining this level of love is not easy. Mental alertness is necessary to observe the mind's programs and addictions for security, sensations and power. A strong will is essential to switch from an addiction framework to one of understanding and love. This task is infinitely easier if one practices selfless service and meditation.

Meditation is a method to get past our old tapes and to get in touch with the higher mansions of joy and peace. An angel, after all, is nothing more than a being whose *Heart Chakra* is so open that light pours out, making it appear as though she has wings. As a mother loves her child unconditionally, we begin to love others as we grow into higher consciousness — regardless of what others say or do to us.

"Love, by its nature, is a resemblance to God, insofar as this is humanly possible. In its activity it is inebriation of the soul. Its distinctive character is to be a fountain of faith, an abyss of patience, a sea of humility."

— John Climacus

Even when others attack us, we understand that they are acting out of their addictions of isolation, separation or paranoia. They are simply trying to get us to act differently, so that their addictions do not bother them. With understanding, we finally arrive at a place where no person or event can move us out of the Love Center of consciousness. Eventually, others find that being loved unconditionally is an experience worth remembering and repeating. They seek company of those who act lovingly toward them and not those relationships that bring them to identification with the lower *chakras*.

We can change our emotions by recognizing them as emotional traps, as programs created by conditioning. Then we remember love, and consciously reprogram each situation as we encounter it. We can use phrases such as "all gets dissolved into love," and "there are no others, just myself, in expanded form, experiencing all of this suffering."

One day long ago, it suddenly dawned on me that just about everything I did was motivated by ego. For example, I would dress and act to improve my image. In enhancing my image, I would find approval and an ego boost. Getting an ego boost would help me to forget myself and my sense of inferiority or limitation for a few minutes. I had this realization when I was younger, so at a time when I was free of the rigorous duties of raising children, working and running a household. Perhaps, when we are younger, when we have more time available, we become more self-centered and are concerned with presenting a certain image. However the case may be, the thought form "I", which at one time had the duty of serving as the connector between the body and mind complex, became carried away with its identity. Who is this "I" sense called ego?

At one time, the ego was only the designated messenger of the mind/intellect complex. As the official control office's circuit breaker, it served to connect one department of the mind with another. As the saying goes, "power corrupts and absolute power corrupts absolutely," the messenger started to take charge.

"If we divert the mind towards the One which is the source of all these variations, we can derive perennial Bliss."

— Sri Chandrashekara Saraswati

We do not have to wait to progress to the vibration of the higher *chakras* to have the viewpoint that there is only One. We can arrive at this understanding just by thinking that we are already there. Holding this mental attitude is called the "path of contemplation." Certain sects of the Buddhist religion and Hindu Vedantins practice this type of contemplation. The Buddhist *Nihilists* simply refuse to think of themselves as separate from the whole. The attitude is that there is "no individual self."

If we analyze this concept, we find that the genes come from the gene pool. The body comes from the parental body and food bank. Minds create thoughts that are donated by other minds. It is in acknowledging that this creation is one big pulsating whole unit — giving and taking from itself — that one realizes the idea of separateness is totally ludicrous. In this sense to say there is "no individual self" is an act of devotion to the whole, and avoids the lie that there is anything separate from God. Great peace arises from this viewpoint and one begins to discover a whole new sense of being and freedom.

In the East and West, selfless service is considered a way to come to know God and selflessness. Selfless service, or *karma yoga,* is effective in freeing us from the grip of the three lower centers. When we do only tasks that are pleasant, unavoidable, or enhance our security, sensation, or power, we let our ego keep us trapped. Whereas the performing of selfless service to our fellow human beings, without thought of future rewards, is a characteristic of the Love Center, or fourth *chakra*. When speaking of acting without ego, Jesus said, "... let not thy left hand know what thy right hand doeth." With this attitude, of not getting caught in the ego trap, we live in a world where there is always enough of everything and love is unconditional and unlimited. In the realm of conscious-awareness, we are all the same.

"Cultivate boundless heart toward all beings. Let thoughts of loving kindness for all of the world radiate boundlessly... just as a mother for her child."

— Buddha

Chapter Eleven

Eight Simple Ways to Begin your Inner Journey

1)   **Let your attitude toward all living beings be that God is in and through all ...** so that when you greet, relate or serve someone, you keep an awareness that you are greeting or serving God. In India the first greeting one hears from another is "Namaste" or "I salute the God in you."

This attitude is not an imaginary spin in order to get along with others, but a fundamental truth that all Souls once knew and embraced before their fall into separate bodies of experience. If you have a problem with someone's behavior, remember to focus on the action as the problem, not the person.

2)   **Meditate daily:** If you have no teacher, as yet, pick a prayer or name of God and repeat it in a sitting position with eyes closed for at least 20 minutes twice a day. Ask God for protection and help before you begin your daily meditation. You will see an improvement in your attitude towards life and your performance in your daily activities.

"An hour of meditation is better than a month of ritual worship."
— Rumi

3)   **Keep a positive attitude of gratitude,** remembering the old saying, "My cup is half full, not half empty." Think of all

the blessings that God has bestowed upon you, rather than feeling as if you are a victim. In this way, you attract positive thoughts and things when your energy is no longer constricted or blocked by the negative. Understand negative events as positive in your growth and karmic payoff.

4) ***Daily, ask for God's will to prevail in your life,*** so that your life's purpose may be recognized and enacted. Remember that everything that occurs in this world is by the grace of God. The only thing blocking your happiness is your choice either to embrace what is negative or to enact that which is positive. Ask God to help you to choose what is positive for you — and others.

"When you arise in the morning, think of what a precious privilege it is to be alive to breathe, to think, to enjoy, to love."
— Marcus Aurelius

5) ***Keep a daily diary of "Self-Introspection.*** Whenever possible, record your behavior that is negative, so that it may become spotted and stopped. The mind is tricky and can cause the downfall of the highest of all beings until the person has reached a stage of perfection when all of the five enemies have left for good. Until that time, one's mind should be scrutinized and held in check against lust, anger, greed, attachment, egoism and criticism against others.

"Love truth, but pardon error."
— Voltaire

6) ***Earn your own livelihood by honest means,*** for taking from others unfairly holds you in *karmic* bondage, while negatively hindering others.

7)   ***Know "Thy Self" by studying spiritual texts*** that help you to discriminate the difference between the Real and the unreal. The Real will free you, for your nature is pure awareness, existence, bliss and love.

Everything that is temporary deserves the same attention and preoccupation as a dream. So, don't get worked up over the passing parade of events and things. Instead act out of truth and love for God and God's beings not out of a sense of unhappiness and limitation.

"The more you learn and go into the scriptures, the more your angle of vision is changed."

— Kirpal Singh

8)   ***Know that God is Love and Love is you — always.*** Keep focusing on this truth and be happy. Give and share with others, in so doing you are giving back to God. In Jesus' words: "Inasmuch as you have done it unto the least of these my brethren, you have done unto me."

"Only pure love can empty the soul perfectly of the images of created things and elevate you above desire."

— Thomas Merton

Chapter Twelve

Vedanta: The Intellectual Path

In my hometown of Seattle, I began to find other sources of spiritual wisdom. I expanded my understanding of spiritual concepts with the philosophy of Vedanta, taught by Swami Chinmayananda, an Indian *Guru*. I was so intrigued with all the new information that I followed him to other cities in the U.S. I was learning totally new concepts. The Swami explained with meticulous logic that we are not the body, mind nor intellect, which perceives, feels or thinks about the objects, emotions and thoughts in the material and mental worlds. The reality is we are a Truth that is beyond all these means of expression. To understand this concept as a fact of life, we must change our perspective by becoming detached and purified through discrimination. In so doing, one becomes God-realized, or liberated. "Yes," I thought, "this is for me." At that time, I prepared myself to attend a two and a half-year course sponsored by the Swami. I would be able to study Vedanta, the philosophy and logic of God-realization, in an ashram setting near Bombay in India. I was determined, that with this understanding, I would have the wisdom and discrimination necessary for God-realization.

However, in the frenzy to finish my studies in anthropology and to earn enough money for the trip, I failed to listen to some profound guidance within. One evening while I was sitting in mediation, the face of the Indian Master, which I had envisioned in my first class of Christian mysticism, appeared to me. He clearly told me that I did not need to go to India to know the Truth. After this encounter, again I was catapulted into a very blissful state. But I would not listen, I had to go. I had to have answers right away. Even though I received further inner messages to guide me, I ignored them.

When the Swami was in Seattle, I made an acquaintance with Lorraine, an experienced and devoted person. I met her through the intervention of a friend, so we could share the ride to the Swami's classes. During these trips, we became the best of friends. She could not go to the study course in India because she had obligations of motherhood. But she gave me some interesting information. She had been "initiated" by a perfect Master. Besides giving her guidance in meditation, he was able to help and protect her. After the initiation, she meditated two-and-a-half hours every day and was a perfect vegetarian. She spoke of the absolute necessity of having a perfect Master to guide one's Soul out of the realm of rebirth. Unfortunately, her Master, Kirpal Singh, had left the body. At that time, his new successor was not yet known. It was only later that I found out that he was the one whom I had seen in my visions. I was, however, so impatient for answers that I could not wait. I pressed on to India. I did not, however, forget what she had said about a perfect Master. She insisted my standards for selecting a *Guru* should be high.

"When that yearning is created within us, then no doubt remains within us that now our soul is ready to meet the love."
— Ajaib Singh

And so the physical phase of my spiritual journey began ... In 1976, I had graduated from the University of Washington and went to India to learn more about God-realization. The ashram-school that I attended outside of Bombay was designed to provide students with a safe haven for the study of the ancient scriptures in their original language of Sanskrit. The texts of study were said to be at least 2,500 years old. These texts, or *Upanishads,* were from the end of the Vedas. Most of them were discourses between Masters and their students.

These students were not ordinary people, but were purified and wise through living a life of ritual, worship and study. Then, wishing to have God-realization, they went to the teacher seeking the final knowledge that would set them free from the bondage of the body/mind/intellect complex, including all rebirths. This liberation was considered to be the highest of pursuits, to be undertaken after satisfying the pursuits of fulfilling the worldly needs, desires, and serving others. This quest was the fourth* and final activity of life in traditional India.

"The man who rejects the words of the scriptures, and follows the impulse of desire attains neither his perfection, nor joy, nor the Path Supreme. Let the scriptures be, therefore, thy authority as to what is right and what is not right."

— Lord Krishna

Historians consider that the ancient *Upanishad* texts, the foundation of the philosophy of Vedanta, were compiled around 700-600 BCE from earlier texts dating back to 1200 BCE. The scholars of Vedanta insist that all of these texts had been preserved by word of mouth through the previous centuries. Therefore, the scholars affirm that the *Upanishads* have been in existence for more than 5000 years through this oral tradition.

---

* Four stages of life for a Hindu: student, householder, contemplative, renunciate.

Throughout all historical periods, many great *yogis* and teachers have been found in India. The Hindu tradition gives the highest regard to those who renounce the world and turn to the pursuit of God-realization. There are many levels of enlightenment and some of the spiritual traditions of the world have documented them thoroughly and beautifully. In Catholicism, we have the sacred teachings of Jesus Christ, along with the examples of the lives of the saintly mystics. The Jewish tradition embraces the sacred *Kabala* text for its mystical unfoldment. The Hindus speak of different systems of yoga for self-mastery: *Hatha Yoga,* a beginning practice for controlling the body, *Prana Yoga* for energizing the life force, *Karma Yoga,* which emphasizes right attitude and action, *Raja Yoga* for purifying and controlling the mind, *Jnana Yoga,* which applies Vedanta for the intellectual understanding, and *Bhakti Yoga* to develop devotion of the heart. Each system of yoga has a body of knowledge that gives incremental steps of practices.

In the Orient, we find many different forms of spiritual practices based upon the enlightenment of Buddha. Tibetan Buddhism has many aspects of rituals, prayers, practices of deep and profound meditation, and devotion with emphasis on love and compassion. Zen Buddhism, on the other hand, has its own series of practices aimed at mindful living through detachment, meditation, and contemplation. These practices lead to a series of enlightenment experiences. The general tenets of Buddhism, like all the world religions, begins with a prescription for right living, after which one becomes fit to practice the various forms of meditation. These tenets are called the Eightfold Way.

All of these practices are hierarchical and involve levels of cleansing and discernment or, as the Hindus would put it, detachment and discrimination. The author would say withdrawal and knowingness, while Christianity refers to purification and receptivity. The Buddhists describe various levels of experience is a hierarchy of ten worlds or realms of experience: hell, hunger, animality, anger, humanity, rapture, learning, realization, *Bodhisattva* nature, and the Buddha Nature. Another way to refer to the process is education, purification, concentration, elevation and assimilation. Yet another system refers to the process as the rising of awareness through the body's *chakra* system of higher and higher vibrations. The Path of *Sant Mat* (with which we will become familiar) states that the process culminates in an ascent through the inner regions.

"The human is present within nature as part of an unbroken continuum. So, too, is the embeddedness of each of us within essential Buddha-Nature."

— Master Mu Chi

Spiritual practices are a mechanism to withdraw the center of the psyche from the ego and its preoccupations, then to turn it toward the realm of the spirit. The spiritual teachings are created to free us from identifying with the egocentric consciousness, so that we can experience the consciousness and freedom that is our genuine Self. This intellectual understanding serves in the process of purifying the mind and intellect. As seen in the following Table, *pride* is the greatest pitfall of all spiritual aspirants. Its enormity can wipe out the positive benefits of any spiritual practice.

Table 4. Spiritual Practices:
Physical, Mental, Intellectual

Practice	Positive Results	Pit Falls
Physical: Any practice that enhances physical health and strength	Incredible control of the physical body and sense of physical mastery and well-being. New found energy for spiritual pursuits.	Preoccupation with physical body. Ego-centric about appearance and superiority over others. Limited to the physical body.
Mental: Any practice that improves concentration.	Tremendous clarity and efficiency: mental powers, sense of peace and well-being, contentment and love.	Over-inflated opinion of self. Manipulation and abuse of power to exploit others. Limited to the mental body.
Intellectual: Vedantins, philosophers and students who study the Truth.	Understanding that one is not separate from God. Attain peaceful disposition, detachment and discrimination.	Egocentric, thinking that they alone "can see the truth," that others cannot understand and are less for it. Limited to the intellectual body.

When I finally reached India, I settled into a small ashram with a tropical setting, for there was a pleasant park with a lake nearby. Life in the ashram was a full day of activities and classes. We began with meditation in the early morning. The concept of meditation was not new to me since, before accepting God and religion back into my life, I had been able to enjoy the benefits of Transcendental Meditation.

I really took to mediation in this new environment that I considered so sacred. Afterward, we attended lectures on Vedanta and had classes in Sanskrit throughout the day. Because of the rigorous schedule, some of the students had difficulty keeping up with the required studies. Piilani, my Hawaiian friend, who was attending the course, had trouble with her health and could not attend all of the classes.

For myself, I was absolutely thrilled to the point my heart and mind were on fire. The great and ancient secrets of the East were being unfolded to me. Nothing else mattered. I felt life was perfect. However, one evening, during the daily *satsangs* with the resident teacher that illusion was shattered.

During the discussions, I happened to mention Yogananda. The teacher explained that Yogananda had not achieved the highest enlightenment, that his way was not the highest path. I was stunned. Afterwards, I sat out alone under the stars. How could this Swami dismiss the holy Yogananda? I had had such a special experience while praying to him. If Yogananda was not valid and true, then who was? My frustration was so great that I began to cry. Who could I trust?

The next day, the Swami asked me how I was doing. I said I was fine, for I had resolved not to trust anyone easily. Even though this Swami was my teacher of the *Upanishads*, I would take nothing for granted about his — or anyone's — realization.

Surely he did not understand everything if he could discount such a saintly person as Yogananda (whom he had never met). My friend's words came back to me about the importance of finding a perfect Master. I began to look for signs of the teacher's perfection. Further, I began to ask more of Vedanta, for I wanted direct experience, so I could know for myself.

As the days flew by, the teaching became more profound. We gradually switched to Sanskrit for the study and explanation of these ancient texts. English was no longer adequate. We were also learning to chant the Vedas with certain traditional rhythms. I began to notice how the words would come to my mind before the Sanskrit instructor spoke them. How could I possibly know these foreign prayers before the words were spoken? At other times, Sanskrit words would start repeating automatically in my mind. Words I had never heard before, but later, as our study continued, I found out their significance. Could this affinity with Sanskrit possibly mean that in a past life I had lived in India and done all of this study before?

"... His faith is only useful so long as he is veiled and has not obtained direct vision and evidence. When that which was hidden becomes evident, when that of which he was merely informed is directly seen, the Soul no longer derives any profit from that which it believes, but only from that which it contemplates and sees. The states, the intentions, the goals which he had during the phase of faith are transformed. This transformation should be understood as purely inner. As to the exterior of this being, it is not modified even an iota. He continues to behave in a way which is acceptable to the sacred Law and commendable according to customs and natural law, engaging in the activities which conform to his situation and his rank among his fellow men."

— Abd al-Kader

Chapter Thirteen

Himalayan Sojourn

One summer, Swami Chinmayananda, the Swami I had met in Seattle, took us for a retreat to the Himalayas. In those sacred mountains, I became sure that I had been in India in another lifetime. I had such an unmistakable feeling of familiarity. The vibration in these high ranges is extremely charged. Uttarkashi, the place of our retreat, was a particularly holy place for *Yogis* and Saints to go to withdraw from the world and immerse themselves in spiritual practices. In the vicinity of our ashram, we could see the orange robed renunciates walking to and from the Ganges River for bathing. Observing silently, we remained respectful of their presence and their ability to renounce the world for the richer inner world of meditation.

And we were reminded of the world — not far away, a gunshot resounded through the mountaintops. We were near the border of Tibet, which had been occupied by China. As we continued our study of scriptures, I had half of a mind just to withdraw from everything forever. The pull to go within was so great there. For thousands of years, students had trekked through these mountains in order to receive instruction from their *Gurus*.

However, our course was not in their traditional format, for our class had seventy students from around the world. Their teaching was on a personal, one-on-one basis. The instruction would come only when the *Guru* deemed the student was ready; in the same way a mother is careful to feed her child only when the infant is hungry. Whereas, in our case, we were treated like orphans who were fed en masse because it was time to eat. Our curriculum had been established well in advance. We were learning what was considered a twelve-year course of study condensed into two and a half years. The explicit purpose was to prepare students to pass this ancient knowledge down to others before the sacred teaching was lost to the allure of the fast encroaching Western value system.

In ancient times, when these texts were originally presented to the students, their minds were considered fit. The knowledge originally was given extemporaneously from the mouth of the guru to the students whose hearts were burning with the desire to know. When they listened to the *Guru,* each word became a significant pathway to God-realization. Because austerities and meditation had purified these students' minds, each gem of truth issued by the *Guru* created a ripple effect in the mind. Upon hearing this highest Truth, the mind and the words turn back, or "one goes to the place of no thought." At the very hearing of the explanation of the truth, they would lose the small "I" perception and merge their consciousness with a much subtler reality.

"He whose pure mind turns inward and searches whence does this 'I' arise, knows the Self and merges in the Lord, as a river into the sea."

— Ramana Maharshi

The result must have been the same as that experienced by the Zen student after the master presented a mind-boggling *koan.* But in our course, we did not experience the traditional *guru*/student relationship, for if was shotgun style, a fast moving unfolding of the knowledge of the sacred *Upanishads, Bhagavad Gita, Brahma Sutras,* and other minor texts of Vedanta by various Hindu sages. Nonetheless, it was the most incredible intellectual pursuit of my life thus far.

As I listened to these sacred words, I found myself getting glimpses of the reality on a level beyond words. The words would take an inquiring mind through the dance of questions and answers about the nature of the individual, the world, and God — without relying upon any preconceived notions. Nothing was assumed. No one was asked to believe a thing. This practice was a rigorous inquiry above all else.

If I am my body who experiences a waking state of consciousness, then who am I when I am dreaming or sleeping deeply? So I am not just a body. When I am a dreamer, who is the waker or deep sleeper? With discrimination, I see that I cannot be any of these three states, but I am a witness to these three states of experience. Therefore, I am not an individual object of my awareness — be it body, mind or intellect. I am the constant unchanging aware being — aware of nothing in deep sleep, aware of a myriad of thoughts in dream, and aware of the mind/body/world complex in the waking state of consciousness. The observing awareness never leaves and is never diminished. It persists as pure existence. It is the nature of the true Self.

"Spiritual unfoldment cannot take place merely because of an intellectual appreciation of the theory of perfection. Evolution takes place only when a corresponding change in the subjective life is accomplished."

— Swami Chinmayananda

Meanwhile, when we returned to the Bombay ashram, the analysis of life in all its aspects continued. In the quest of understanding ourselves, the world, and God, each *Upanishad* would give a different approach to the understanding of the Truth. Sometimes the lecture would be so powerful and profound that I found myself in an altered state of awareness. For days, I would be in a blissful state. Sometimes, I would feel very huge and my body would seem to expand larger than the size of the building and beyond. At other moments, my mind would spontaneously go into a great silence. I did not totally understand what these experiences were all about. The intellectual Vedanta spoke of universal concepts, not the specific individual experiences I was experiencing. I was left with some questions.

During my stay, I also came in contact with other aspects of Indian culture. I knew that astrology was a viable way to predict important events in one's life. I gave the astologer what I thought was the specific time of my birth. He said he would be able to verify its accurateness by checking it against the events of my past. Sure enough, several events matched my past perfectly. He told me the exact years I had traveled to Europe to study. He knew the size of my family and other significant events about my life. Actually, at that time, I was puzzled and did not understand how this information could be so accurate. In addition, a preoccupation with spirituality and the metaphysical turned up in my chart. The astrologer predicted that I would have a destiny to share this spiritual knowledge with others. No wonder I have felt so driven.

Later, it was explained to me that each individual comes to this world with a destiny or a *karmic* disposition. This signature is stamped at the time that the child's head is exposed to the magnetic pull of the planets. That impression becomes the child's disposition, which will perceive all future events through the filter of this magnetic imprint. Everything that occurs becomes relative to this imprint, just as if we perceive the reality of a sporting event from the viewpoint of our assigned seat. With this model, I have come to understand that everything, including the body/mind complex, is made up of varying levels of energy that are influenced and patterned by the magnetic pull of the planets, as well as other influences in this universe. Thousands of years ago, the sages of the ancient cultures in India, China, Egypt and the Americas had a grasp of this science and used astrology to gain insight and guidance, including for predictive purposes.

"Vedanta recognizes no sin, it recognizes only error; and the greatest error is to say that you are weak, that you are a sinner, a miserable creature, and that you have no power, and you cannot do this or that. In you is all power. Summon up your all-powerful nature and this whole Universe will lie at your feet. It is the Self alone that predominates and not matter."

— Swami Vivekananda.

Chapter Fourteen

Process of Spiritualization

Because the creation is made up of three different qualities, one can apply this understanding to comprehend the process of spiritualization. Since our mental and physical worlds are part of the creation, these three qualities, or *gunas,* make up our physical and mental realities.

Tamas is the quality of darkness, dullness, ignorance.

Rajas is the quality of activity, movement and anger that is spurred on by desire and intention.

Sattwa is the quality of brightness, love, knowledge, understanding, wisdom, serenity and joy.

As we move through the day, we oscillate between various states of *tamas, rajas* and *sattwa* because everything in creation has some of each quality in it. These three make up what we call *maya* or the whole illusion of this creation. *Maya* is called an illusion because, similar to a dream, the whole of creation is in a state of flux or movement. Creation is not constant; it is subject to disappearance and, therefore, is unreal, like a dream.

"He the first origin of this creation, perhaps he formed it or did not form it. He whose eye controls this world in highest heaven, he verily knows it, or perhaps he knows it not."

— Rg Veda

To experience what is beyond the three qualities of *maya*, the practitioner of spirituality must first make a choice for the *Real* — the changeless and permanent one, which is called God. In order to accomplish this goal, one has to work the equipment one has available: the mind and body complexes, which are always in flux.

All spiritual practices aim at taking a person out of the most slothful and ignorant state to the most sublime and brightest of states. Thus one works to replace the dull, ignorant, inert mind by a process of moving to the next state of action, for one can only move out of *tamas* by going into the *rajas* state.

This progression can be accomplished by all sorts of activities, ranging from singing, dancing, selfless work for God, chanting, praying and meditating on God or for God-Realization. Each religion has its own set of prescribed activities. Each practice has the intention of changing the qualities of the mind and body, so that one can prepare for the meeting with God. Everyone has to begin with their own disposition and slowly change to become less unconscious and more God-like.

Since everything in creation is made up of the three *gunas* in greater or lesser degrees and the human being is considered the most highly evolved, only the human being can choose to express *sattwa* in the process of getting to know God. So, although many practices require some activity because they start out as having the nature of *rajas*, the practices gradually move us to the quality of *sattwa*. This process of purification and transformation continues until one's very being begins to reflect the nature of God. Another term to describe this process is the shedding of one's lower tendencies and surrendering the "unholy" impulses for ones that are conducive to peace, joy, love and clarity. In the end, dropping the last of the lower tendencies, the personal self steps aside to merge into one's object of devotion — God or God-realization — *beyond all the three qualities.*

This process can best be described by a review of the spiritual practices, or *sadhanas,* of the religions around the world. The practices all begin with a conscious choice to live a life in harmony with spiritual values. The promised result is the most sublime and fantastic journey into greater and greater levels of inner wisdom, joy and freedom — realms beyond all imagination and words. The scriptures become true: By seeking first the Kingdom of God, all else comes to you.

Because we have different levels of *tamas* and *rajas* tendencies to overcome in order to increase the quality of *sattwa*, we are given different levels of practices to perform. The distinct levels of practice are reflected in the different *yogas.* In the *yoga* terminology, we are beginning a process of withdrawing our attention away from the world and back to God. In so doing, we discontinue the serving of the body, mind and intellect and its various *dis-eases* and begin to serve our higher purpose to know the Soul and its need — to go back to God.

In the process, subtle energy currents are gradually withdrawn as in the states of deep prayer and meditation. These currents are actual pathways of energy called *"nadis"* in Sanskrit or *"chi"* in Chinese. When they are withdrawn from the nine gateways*, or lower spheres of activity of the body, to what is called the Tenth Gate, contact with the Soul actually begins.

---

* The nine gateways, holes, in which impressions from the external world can enter the body or flow out of the body in the form of attention. The Tenth Gate is not a physical opening, but an entrance into the spiritual realm of experience located between the eyes.

Living out in the world, the currents of energy go through every cell of the mind-body complex, so they become polluted by the world. Spiritual practices are means of purifying the five bodies — physical, astral, mental, intellectual and causal, or the Soul body. If one finds it difficult to reach the Tenth Gate and to withdraw the attention and energy currents, then practice is in order. If *tamas* is a problem, one will fall asleep easily during spiritual practice. If *rajas* is a problem, one's mind will be very busy and chatter constantly. This means that the Soul must drop down from its throne due to its own pollution.

Spiritual practices are a means of purging the Soul, so that it may enter the Tenth Gate. One's attention drops to the lower *chakras* because the body, mind and Soul have been grossified by the experiences of the sensations of the world. But one can change one's habits and disposition by simply performing spiritual practices in order to purify or make the mind and Soul subtler. Since the Soul has fallen from higher subtle states into the gross world, it needs to shut out the gross impressions and focus on the subtle realm of the Spirit — this is Spirituality. The removal of stains, or sin, from the Soul is the purification of the Soul, so that it can make its way back to regions of subtler and higher vibrations to God.

Chapter Fifteen

Purification Techniques for the Body

Many practices of the world's religions help to purify the mind-body complex, bringing one from *tamas,* to *rajas,* to the *sattwa* state. Since we have five bodies*, they may, when pulling in different directions, create a sense of uneasiness, and present a lack of sense of self-integration or conflict. When in conflict, there is a sense of *dis-ease* and unhappiness. The idea of all spiritual practices is to integrate all of one's energy back into unity. Then, the sense of godliness begins to dawn — for God is one. For this dawning, practices are in order. The term in Sanskrit is *"yoga,"* or yoking, fitting together.

"A man is the facade of a temple wherein all wisdom and all good abide."

— Ralph Waldo Emerson

Purification of the physical body is necessary to take one out of a lazy, lethargic mode. To accomplish this dynamism, we have such activities as service to the poor and needy, service to a higher, unselfish cause, *karma yoga, hatha yoga, tai chi,* spiritual dance, herbal medicines, *kundalini* yoga and so forth.

---

* The five bodies are physical, *pranic* or etheric, astral, mental and causal or Soul. See page 101

Any form of physical exercise, such as sports and gymnastics, that focuses on the coordination between the mind and body can bring on a heightened state of concentration. Therefore, one has a sense of being fully alive and connected to all things. This state is a "lower form" of *Samadhi*, or sense of "at-one-ment." It is also referred to as a "peak experience."

Although this type is not a true spiritual state, it mimics the real *Samadhi* or experience of "at-one-ment" because the body is in optimal health and the body, breath, energy, hormones and blood circulation are fully energized and coordinated. However, this peak experience cannot be controlled and integrated into one's normal life.

The practice of martial arts can also lead to a mundane *Samadhi*, for it helps in concentration of mind and body control. Having the body and mind under control can result in Soul level experiences.

Hatha Yoga is the practice of control of the body, breath and mind, which helps to improve one's concentration or focusing power. This focusing power takes the many distractions and sublimates them toward the one purpose of withdrawing the attention from the nine currents and pulling them up to the Tenth Gate — the Seat of the Soul. The Soul searches for truth and light. While body, breath and mind coordination can never produce *Samadhi*, they aid in preparation for it.

All actions performed for the sake of others and God automatically bypass the lower *chakras* and the five enemies of the mind: lust, greed, attachment, anger and egoism. These preoccupations and addictions, referred to as sins, or missing the mark, in Chistianity, keep the mind and Soul complex so clouded that they cannot reflect the qualities of godliness. Some practitioners simply concentrate on engaging in the opposite quality as spiritual practice. Instead of greed, we are giving. Instead of attachment, we practice being detached. Instead of anger, we practice sympathy and understanding. Instead of pride, we think of God and of others. Instead of lust, we observe chastity. As we progress, our practices become more natural and rewarding. They also become more subtle and engrossing.

The Hindus prescribe *Hatha Yoga* as a preparatory mechanism and not a spiritual end in itself. The Taoist and Esoteric Buddhists prescribe some physical practices as well, especially, for those who tend to think too much. These physical practices, they say, aid on the "path of cultivation."

1) For purification of the physical body, there are many activities from athletics to *Hatha Yoga* to tai chi.

2) For purification of the Breath Body or involuntary activities, one has breath therapy, or *Pranayama,* of watching and controlling the breath.

3) For the purification of the mind, there is a whole myriad of practices such as prayer, devotion or *Bhakti Yoga,* visualization, watching the breath, watching the thoughts, listening to sound, dream *yoga,* meditation on the five elements, *Raja Yoga,* and the cultivation of virtuous behavior.

4) For the purification of the intellect, there is the study of *Jnana Yoga,* Vedanta, philosophical ideas from the scriptures of all religions, contemplation, and *abhidharma* analysis of Buddhism.

5) For the purification of the Soul, any spiritual practice that takes one's attention to the Third Eye Center and beyond the activities of the lower *chakras.*

Practices for the Breath Body, or *Pranamaya-kosha,* which comprises all the involuntary functions of the body, are numerous and varied depending on the spiritual culture. Breath, or *chi,* control is connected to many spiritual practices and plays a vital role in their focus. There are hundreds of variations of breath exercises. Using *Prana* and *Apana,* or watching the rising and falling of the breath, one reaches a state where the external breath slows to a halt. When there is a cessation of breath, the mind is controlled. Conversely, when the breath is irregular, the mind is unsteady. When the breath is still, the mind is said to behave as if it were salt dissolving in water. The mind becomes still.

As animals are controlled using leashes, the mind is restrained and absorbed by regulation of breath. This form of Yoga is a device for effecting absorption.

— Ramana Maharshi

The Masters say that when one reaches a state of true breath cessation, the subtle *inner* breath ignites, causing a state of *Samadhi.* This *Mahayana Samadhi* is supposed to be the beginning of real *chi, shakti* or *Kundalini* cultivation. This state is not one of dull *tamas,* a blanked out or sleepy condition, but the state of clear awareness, which is not reliant on thought or form. Although this type of *Samadhi* may not be the highest because it is "no thought," or the opposite of "thought," it constitutes an important stage of spiritual progress — controlling the mind through the practice of controlling the breath.

While one can gain all kinds of spiritual gifts as a result of this practice, such as improved health, long life, psychic powers, and *Samadhi,* it still just constitutes the beginning stages. For true enlightenment does not result in a preoccupation with either of the pairs of opposite states of thought, or even a state of "no thought." True enlightenment is beyond this duality of mind. It is a higher order of wisdom — beyond body, breath and mind. However, these practices that control the breath do serve to help the practitioner become more detached from the mind and aid in greater concentration.

"The Third Eye, or Tisra Til, is the battlefield. It is where we must fight with our mind. So no matter what happens, he, the disciple, should not leave that battlefield. He should stay in the Third Eye Center."

— Ajaib Singh

Table 5. Five Stages of an Aspirant

Education: Aspirant reads about the truth of human nature and God.

Purification: Aspirant performs practices and lives properly to purify the body and mind for spiritual receptivity.

Focus and concentration: Student emphasizes practices that bring the attention to the Third Eye Center. Concentration is a natural product of spiritual practices.

Elevation: Soul experiences higher and higher forms of spiritual reality and truth.

Assimilation: Soul merges into God Power and Enlightenment.

Chapter Sixteen

Purification of the Mind

The mind is a subtle aperture that automatically comes with every physical body that a Soul inhabits. The mind has its own instinctual equipment that operates with the body. In a human body, it progresses gradually in maturity along with the growth of the human body. Because of the pressing needs and demands of the human body/mind complex, the Soul becomes a sidekick. The Soul becomes like an ant before an elephant. Its needs, wants and intentions are easily crushed by the needs and wants and intentions of the body/mind complex. In assuming the human form, the Soul can very easily and quickly forget its good intentions and become helpless in the realm of the negative power over and over again. The negative power and the realms of the mind rules over the three regions, making the Soul play by the rules governing the body's and mind's survival. At first the mental and physical worlds were intended to serve the Soul, but they ended up governing it and bringing it down.

"We must do our business faithfully, without trouble or disquiet, recalling our mind to God mildly, and with tranquility, as often as we find it wandering from Him."

— Brother Lawrence

Consider that the very powerful mind, which has a great deal of energy, is normally dissipated in many directions, in the same way light is dissipated around a large room. The moment light is focused into a smaller space it becomes brighter and stronger. When attention is focused to a tiny beam, like a laser light, the mind becomes so powerful that it can actually cause pain, destroy or control any matter that it concentrates upon.

With its ability to concentrate and manifest, the mind is said to have more power than thirteen universes, which is equivalent to saying that it can control more than thirteen universes. When it is focused or directed, the mind is more subtle than physical matter and, therefore, is capable of controlling physical matter. After all, the mind is made up of the five subtle elements that pervade the five gross elements.

If we view the subtle elements differently, we can see the atoms that make up all of earth matter can become tremendously powerful when split, even having the capability of destroying most of life on earth. How can such a feat be possible? How can a tiny atom, not even perceivable to the human eye, destroy a whole city when split apart?

In the mythology and religion of ancient cultures, including Indian, Egyptian, Greek, Roman and Chinese, there existed a belief in powerful gods and goddesses* who had the ability to control the events that would take place on earth. These stories relate to beings who by many years of spiritual practices were able to gain control of their minds in order to direct them toward a specific purpose. The mind has an immense power and energy and can be directed when it is trained. However, to be able to control the mind is more difficult than climbing Mt. Everest.

The repetition of prayers, chanting and uttering of single or multiple-worded *mantras* give the mind a job to perform. When the mind is directed in this way, it may rebel, so it needs to be trained over and over to remain within the scope of the practice of repetition. If the *mantra* is given by a Master, it is charged with a certain power that makes it easier for the student to control the mind. If one is not fortunate enough to have access to a Master, one can choose a few words from the scriptures of one's own religion and sit quietly and repeat them sincerely. As one masters the *mantra,* one becomes better at controlling the mind. Some practitioners repeat a *mantra* throughout the day while performing other duties, so that, when they sit to meditate daily, the mind is already trained; therefore, their Soul can go right to the Third Eye *Chakra.*

Such a practice is meant to create a kind of friction, where the "rigid" part of the mind is juxtaposed against the "free-moving thought" part of the mind. This practice can create various experiences of light within. Later, upon leaving body consciousness, one can see the sun, the moon or stars. As one focuses upon the light, the scene may change, but the mind and Soul become purified to begin to make its sacred journey. The principal work for the practitioner is the training or controlling of the mind. Once this ability is attained, the Soul, in the form of attention, can withdraw to its Seat, which is the Third Eye *Chakra,* or referred to as the Tenth Gate.

The Soul, having reached the Tenth Gate, must wait for the Master Power to open the door to enter its journey through the inner regions. In other spiritual traditions, the mind becomes dissolved in Brahman or *Samadhi.* The attention is focused on the Soul's development and purification. To make its journey, the

---

* These gods and goddesses lived in earlier eras or *Yugas* when time was available for special practices, as compared to today in what is called the *Kali Yuga.*

Soul must be able to fit through a space that is subtler or narrower than a strand of hair, or the eye of a needle as Jesus would put it. In other words, a Soul is purified and so refined that it can enter into more rarified realms of subtle light and sound and bliss. The purer the Soul, the more subtle, rarified and expansive, the more luminous and enrapturing — the more powerful and Godlike — is the experience.

If we look at spiritual practices as a means of becoming more subtle, we can understand that in the physical sense, we are transforming the five elements of earth, water, fire, air and space back into their original nature. By working with one of the subtler forms, one tends to purify all the other elements because they are pervaded by air and space.

Air, being one of the subtlest elements, is considered to be one of the easiest to transform. When one works with the air element one is essentially affecting everything that it pervades. The breath exercises open up the tiny capillaries of obstructed energy and help in the practice of not only controlling the breath, but in the practice of controlling the mind by watching the breath. Many lower *Samadhis* are associated with the cessation of the breath. But again the spiritually enlightened do not attribute the ultimate *Samadhi* to mere breath control. *Pranayama* is only considered a purification aid along the way.

Interestingly, while the air element corresponds to the energy meridians of the body, or *nadis* (*mai* in Chinese), the water element corresponds to our nerves and hormones. Water is the next easiest element to transform. *Hatha Yoga* has its own system of purification with water, which relates to this transformation process. The fire element corresponds to our *Kundalini*, or the coiled serpent in our base *chakra*, while the earth element corresponds to our bones.

The normal sequence of transforming the air element, then the water element or energy channel, and then the fire element, and finally the earth element generally takes over ten years, but the time can be greatly shortened with the use of a *mantra*. This methodology of controlling the mind — with its monkey thoughts — is superior to practices controlling the breath because, while breath is one of the subtlest of the five gross elements, the mind is subtler because it is comprised of the five subtle elements and contains no gross elements. The most efficient way to get out of the influence of the lower *chakras* and to rise to the vibration of the highest *chakra* of spirituality is through meditation.

"The mind is all. If the mind is active, even solitude becomes like a marketplace."

— Ramana Maharshi

One useful practice that helps in quieting the mind is visualizing an object. In this case, the practitioner fixes the attention on an object at eye level, at a distance of three to four feet. The object must become the center of attention, so it must be one that makes the person feel comfortable. Certain colors are used for different purposes. Yellow may be used for balancing one's stomach area; green helps with problems of anger and restores the liver; red brings joy and tends to increase one's energy. Darker, calmer colors are used for people with quick minds. Black should not be a color for vision focus because it causes sorrow.

When one continues this practice, eventually lower *Samadhis* occur while focusing on the inner body. The result is to send *chi* or energy to any obstructed areas for internal healing. Other powers, such as the ability to see at great distances clairvoyantly, may occur as a result of the practice of this discipline. The purpose of this technique is aimed at attaining what is referred to in Buddhism as "the emptiness of *Samadhi.*"

Mantra meditation is generally one of the easiest practices. One can recite a mantra continuously until the recitation ceases, then one attains what is referred to as the "silence of *Samadhi.*" Practitioners who choose a *mantra* and recite it throughout the day, including a period of sitting with eyes closed, can experience many kinds of transcendental states.

Mantra meditation repeated silently in the mind is more powerful than with the body, that is, chanting aloud with the lips. Similarly, the most powerful practices are those performed not by the body, or the *prana* body, or even the subtler mental body, but eventually by the Soul body.

According to *Sandilya Upanishad,* the whispering or quiet chant gives a reward 1,000 times greater than chanting aloud, while mental chanting gives the reward a "myriad times more." This practice is one of the subtlest and most powerful processes of spirituality. As we shall see further on, the *Sant Mat* tradition is a practice that begins at the Tenth Gate, or Soul level. This practice truly takes place on the Soul level. Although the mind begins repeating the *mantra,* upon mastery, it is the Soul that says the *mantra* and eventually gets absorbed in *Naam* (the essence of the *mantra*). Since the Soul is the subtlest, its practice pervades and transforms all levels of the personality.

Through *mantra* practices, as with other practices, one is able to open up one's *chi* or *mai* or *nadis.* So, all of these techniques are designed to withdraw the vital energies that are shooting out through the world in all directions up into a central and powerful laser-like beam. This beam can be focused in one direction, propelling one into the experience of light and sound in the higher realms or *chakras.*

While there are many *mantras* given in many spiritual schools, some *mantras* are given with specific instructions, such as not to be used in foul-smelling locations, or not to be used with a non-vegetarian diet, or only to be used if one practices chastity.

There are other *mantras* that can be used at any time or any place. The *Zhunti Mantra,* a Buddhist *mantra,* is one such *mantra* or chant. It is meant to open the heart *chakra* and bring about an improvement in one's fortune and destiny. Other *mantras* are used for purification and transformation of the physical body, including one's *prana* or *chi,* as well as the tiny energy currents, also called *nadi* or *mai.*

Additionally, the *Kundalini,* or *tumo* fire in Buddhism, is purified along with what is referred to as one's bright points or drops of hormonal reserves in the pineal gland. The end result of purification from meditation is the attainment of *Samadhi.*

While many Buddhist and Tantric sects combine chanting with visualization, Master Sawan Singh discourages the use of visualization with the *Sant Mat Mantra,* or *Simran.* Since *Simran* is so powerful, when properly used, it has a tendency to bring the attention to the Third Eye *Chakra,* or gateway to the experience of the Soul, very easily. *Sant Mat* also discourages the intellectual exercise of visualization since this technique is limited to the intellect and not meant to contact the Soul at the Third Eye *Chakra.* All depends on the *mantra* and practice. If a *mantra* is not so powerful, other means used along with a *mantra* help to gather one's attention and to control the mind.

"Simran is All-Powerful. After repeating the Simran daily for a length of time, your mind will become fixed on God."

— Kirpal Singh

In many systems of *mantra* meditation, the repetition of the *mantra* a given number of times brings boons to the mind in the way of mental powers. The use of these powers, however, is considered to be distractions on the Soul's journey and can retard one's progress. One could say it is encountering the gold mines on the way to the diamond mine.

We are so caught up in playing our parts in our daily lives that we have forgotten that we are actors who have a relation to the play, but will eventually leave it at the end of the show. Similarly, we will leave this body/mind complex and assume our original nature — the Soul. We are only passing through this field of experience and must remember not to get caught up in it because in doing so our life becomes "too noisy," so fragmentary and distracting that the radiant Soul and its purposefulness become forgotten. The Soul takes on a subservient role and gets kicked and knocked around the stage of life in the arenas of the lower *chakras* of physical and emotional addictions. The Soul needs assistance to get out.

III. Human Search for Meaning

There is no melody
Enchanting enough, O Master
To call You to my side.
I have no special gifts to offer you,
My tears do not deserve your notice.

But there are many
Who are innocent and need your love
Please take pity on all of us
Both good and bad
Glance in our direction and shine
Your love upon our minds and spirits.

I know that it is not You
Who have forgotten me
But I who have forgotten You.
I want to look out at the Ocean
To see your boat crossing it.

For it is really You inside of everything
Don't hide any more
Let the joke be upon us that
You are all and everything
And we did not see You.

Come, come, come
Let this dance
With You begin forever.

Chapter Seventeen

How Did We Get Here?

We may reasonably question, if we are originally a divine being, why don't we just experience it naturally? In the process of creation, Pure Being became mixed up with the objects of experience. Subsequently, attachment to them arose, and then identification with them took place. If a four-year-old boy likes Spiderman, he starts to emulate and dress like his idol. He becomes Spiderman. That is, as long as he is not hungry or doesn't fall and hurt himself, then he switches back to identification with his child body. But what if he forgot to switch back to his normal self?

Vedanta, the wisdom of the Indian sages, states that at one time our Souls did not inhabit physical forms. However, when we began to enjoy the experiences of materialization on the gross level, we began to forget our divine nature. In a process of identification and attachment to our gross bodies, we became stuck on the lower levels. Then we found we could not easily move out of this physical manifestation until the death process took place.

So the Souls fell from the higher spiritual regions of oneness with God, the Creator, into the Causal, then Astral, and then Physical Regions. In these regions, they enjoyed the objects of experience, which were once created to serve these higher angelic beings. However, their attachment began to slowly rule, dictate and enslave the Souls to the rules and consequences of enjoyment. You play — you pay.

Once while attending the Christian mystic's course, we were learning about reincarnation. At that time, the proposition may have appeared pretty way out to the Westerners indoctrinated into the one life — one chance scenario. My Mother and one of her friends were visiting the class with me as they were open to exploring new avenues of consciousness. That evening we were shocked when the teacher brought out a lamp with a red bulb. Each one was asked to take a turn sitting under the red glow while the rest of the class looked on and commented on what they saw. Interestingly, my mother's friend, who was the biggest anti-war activist that I knew, took her turn under the lamp. In amazement we all watched her face rapidly change into the appearance of countless warriors, soldiers and generals. We called out what we saw and we were all seeing the same image at the same time. It became clear why she was being such an ardent activist. Remarkably, when we watched another person, the face turned into someone who looked like Mozart, then a Chinese man, then the face of an elderly woman.

So, identifying with all the realities of the ego/mind complex, the Soul became self-centered and self-absorbed with the objects of a grosser and more limiting orbit. Feeling separate and limited, the Soul lost its true identity of oneness with God. The Soul forgot her true identity as *Atma,* pure limitless Being.

What happens to an ever-expansive Soul of limitless nature when it has to conform to a small world of a limited body/mind complex? The result is a never-ending sense of *dis-ease* and a never-ending desire for fulfillment. Where does the Soul in the body/mind complex look for its fulfillment? It follows the mind. If the mind seeks fulfillment through the five senses of hearing, seeing, feeling, touching and tasting, then into the world of sensual objects the Soul goes. The Soul will follow like an obedient puppy. The only problem is whatever the world has to offer, the enjoyment is only temporary. Consequently, the mind must come up with another, and yet another, idea for happiness.

The Soul falls when it identifies with objects of experiences of mind and body. Who becomes identified? The philosophy of Vedanta traces the *sense of self* back to God. This sense of self or being is fundamental, for it is the essential existence of every creature. This sense of being never stops. It is the identification with other things that comes and goes. In the waking state, the sense of being identifies with objects and situations in our everyday world. This sense of self is always known in relation to the body/ mind complex of the waking state. In the dream state, this same sense of self identifies with the dreaming, or unconscious mental objects of the dream state.

A person who is God-realized does not identify with any circumstances in the waking or dreaming states. A Master knows that "I am," that is, the sense of self is separate and independent of objects and situations. Such a person also knows God and is considered one with God in that realization. This is the highest form of spirituality.

"I dwell neither high nor low, neither in the sky
Nor on the earth, nor even in paradise,
O beloved, believe me, strange as it may seem,
I dwell in the heart of the faithful and
It is there that I may be found."

— Rumi

Only through the remembrance of our true nature and in meditation, we can rise up out of this dream and awaken to the call of the Soul and its divine impulse. At this awakening, we become free of the whims and demands of the lower bodies and we experience a true sense of serenity. In this serenity — free of its activities of lower mind and body, one can remain in the aura of the Master. Without constantly making small demands to serve the lower bodies, one is able to attune oneself to a higher vibration and to drink of the higher energy of the Master's inner radiation. Although the Master may not be physically present, the aura of the Master encompasses the disciple in the same way a group of small birds remain under the warmth and protection of their mother in the nest.

Spiritual practices, along with careful and moral living, help to control the lower vehicles* by switching the focus from the preoccupation with these vehicles of lower vibration. For example, when one criticizes another, one remains in the lower mental vibration serving a lesser purpose and wasting time that could be spent basking in the radiation of the Master's vibration. Serving the lower *chakras,* one accumulates negative *karma,* whereas, with the attention on the higher *chakras,* one purifies the lower vehicles of its addictions and creates a clear channel for oneself to be receptive to the impulses of the Soul and the Master Power that influences it.

When we grow in spirit (as opposed to matter), our Soul increases control over our instruments of body and mind, so that they begin to serve our higher Soul purpose. For example, we shift to an attitude of love and its natural expression of service to others as we enter into the orbit of the Soul. Whereas, before this stage, everyone would operate in the lower mental capacity

---

* The lower vehicles consist of lower *chakra* preoccupations of body and mind in contrast to the higher vehicles which consist of higher mental activity and Soul purpose.

of fulfilling desires and the lower mental emotions associated with the fulfillment or lack of fulfillment of such desires. This attitude could entail a life of anger, jealousy, pride, deceit, passion, selfishness and depression, all of which only drags one down into an emotional quagmire of action and reaction. Contrast this misery with the freedom we feel when we are not serving the ever-changing mind, so that we are able to express the love and joy of God and experience the serenity that this love brings to our demeanor. When we are serene, we can receive the true wisdom of the call of the Soul and the impress of the Master upon the Soul.

The first effect of the inflowing force of the Soul is the integration of the personality and the bringing of all of the lower aspects of the person into serving of the Higher — the God power. When purified by spiritual practices, the Soul begins to feel pulled back to its Source. Even though water runs through different forms, whether rivelets, streams or underground rivers, it will always seek to return to its source, the ocean, by its own initiative.

"They [mystics] are not in themselves and if they are in themselves at all, they exist but in God. Their actions are held by God and their words are the words of God uttered by their tongues and their sight is the sight of God penetrated into their eyes."
— Llewellyn Vaughan-Lee

Chapter Eighteen

Problem of Ego

Each human being is made up of five bodies, or five levels of vibration. These bodies are separate entities that have a reality of their own. The ego is a sense of being called "I am," or *"ahamkara"* in Sanskrit. It is a mental concept that holds the five bodies and three states of consciousness together through its identification.

We are composed of five bodies, or coverings, which cover the Soul. These bodies are enshrouding sheaths, which are progressively thick and heavy. Each of the bodies is swayed by its own preoccupations. Each layer veils all the subtler bodies, yet the subtler layers infuse all of the grosser bodies.

Physical Body: The lowest level, but capable of achieving highest spirituality in the sense that it is a gateway to all twelve *chakras.* Its maintenance requires a vegetarian diet of pure high vibration, healthy practices, including cleanliness, rest and sunshine. For the body to become the temple of higher vibrations, these components are necessary to help the body make the sub-atomic changes to handle the cosmic inflow of energy at a very high vibration.

Etheric Body: The forces of light/heat and air/breath operate to translate sunlight and air to the physical body by using the spleen. Then these energies from the sun, planets and Soul flow through a refined network. The best tonic for the Etheric Body is "right thinking." This covering must be kept pure and open, for it acts as a channel between the mind and Soul and the Physical Body.

Astral or Emotional Body: This covering is like a mirror of impressions. It must be trained to take on only impressions from the Higher Self through the sub-atomic level. One must maintain a very calm and peaceful Astral Body by eliminating desires, so the Soul can transmit through the brain. Masters work with the Soul, not the Astral Body.

Mental Body: This covering uses energies to create and to understand. When purified by meditation, it can become like a clear pool or mirror to reflect the intuitions of the Soul. Acting upon these creative influences, the mind becomes a tool for focusing the higher world of the Soul.

Causal Body: This sheath is the temple of the Soul. It is reported to be made up of three permanent atoms in a mental encasement. The inner light, out of which the Soul is composed, uses the physical body as fuel in order to move up the spine. The Soul begins to expand in luminosity, seeking greater vibration and color intensity. As the Soul moves to a fully-wakened state, the causal body is dropped.

Table 6. Five Bodies

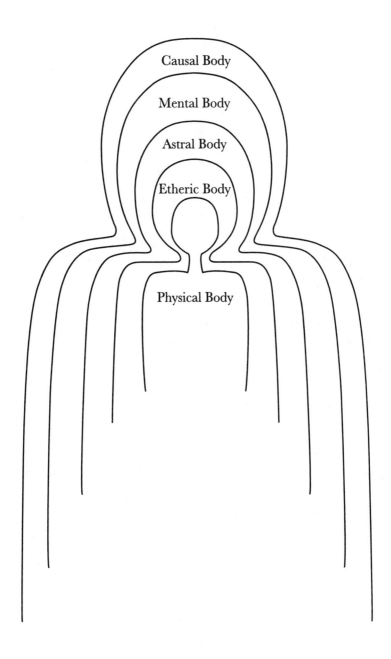

The ego holds the five bodies together under the theme of one unit. Ego, by identifying with each of these bodies, can use them for its own purposes. Yet, we cannot say the ego is exclusively any one of the five bodies. For these are five separate bodies with five separate vibrations. Since the ego cannot remain identified as any of the five bodies exclusively, but roams between the distinct realms, the ego cannot be any of them.

Further, the ego cannot be an awake person since it also identifies with the dreamer. Yet, it cannot be the dreamer since it is an entity that experiences deep sleep and awakened states of consciousness. So this sense of self is not in the three states of consciousness that the ego experiences while awake, dreaming and sleeping, nor is it in the five bodies that it temporarily identifies with to suit its current and changing desires.

It is as if there is no real self behind the ego. The body belongs to earth and goes back to dust. The mind and intellect are made up of thoughts of subtle energy. The sense of self is a fictitious concept, which can take credit for any thought which passes within the orbit of awareness and is attached to the five bodies that the self seems to hold together. In actuality, all belongs to God and God's domain. The sense of ownership or doership holds the events of the five bodies together. The self was designed to preserve the internal workings of the five bodies into one cohesive vehicle for the Soul's *karmic* experience. In actuality, the experience of the five bodies does not belong to the Soul but to the whole. When one understands this truth, the shame and ambition of life disappear, and there is only an awareness of the play of God within and without.

The Vedantin, or one who follows the Path of Knowledge, would view this world as a play of *maya* — an illusion which is always in a state of flux whereby the self is made up of three aspects: Truth, Awareness and Bliss

Because the sense of self does not understand its nature, it takes what it sees as real, what it is aware of as real. However, what is seen cannot be the self, for what is seen is an object of awareness, and not the aware being. But one thing is clear and true, this self is analogous to water looking for itself in all objects because it is looking for its true nature. Just as water will end up in the great ocean of the world, the self will go back to its source.

The nature of the ego is really not the ego — it is just a thought form. The ego is just a reflection of the sense of am-ness, which is the *Atma,* Pure Being. In fact, its whole nature is called pure existence, infinite awareness and bliss. Therefore, self is not located in the upper mental body as *"Ahamkara"*(ego), but in the causal body as *Atma.* This self is pure *"chit"* awareness, *"sat"* sense of Being and *"ananda"* blissful without the restrictions of subtle and gross matter all around it. The self has its own pure nature. When one removes this self from the other bodies — through understanding what it is not — one can better see what it is. While the Vedantins arrive at this conclusion by analysis, every religion in the world has a group of techniques for going beyond the mind. When one is able to perceive the Soul, the practitioner becomes a mystic. Especially when that Soul merges into God. Then God is known directly — not indirectly.

When we view life as temporary, ever-changing, an illusion, our attitude toward life changes. Whether a Vedantin of *Jñana Yogi* or an *Abhidharma* practitioner of Buddhism, the attitude towards ourselves, and the illusory world, takes a great paradigm shift. We see everything as in a dream. When we see life as an illusion or dream, we take our petty selves out of the picture. Thereafter, we don't buy into all the mental agendas of self-aggrandizement.

We are able to relax in our daily lives. The relaxation, resulting from maintaining this attitude throughout the day, helps the body to become full of *chi,* or vital force, a stepping stone for inner experience.

Physical body, or *anna-maya kosha,* is made of food, or the earth element.

Sense body, or *prana-maya kosha* (also referred to as the etheric body), is composed of voluntary and involuntary functions of the body, or the water element.

Mental body, or *mano-maya kosha* (often referred to as the astral body), is composed of emotions and feelings, or the fire element.

Intellectual body, or *vigyana-maya kosha* (sometimes referrd to as the mental body or higher mind), is comprised of thoughts and logic, or the air element.

Soul body, or the *ananda-maya kosha* (also called the causal body), is made of the subtle cause forms, or space element.

Table 7. Five Coverings of the Soul

Five Elements	Five Bodies or Coverings	Sanskrit Term	Personality Types or Characteristics
Earth Element	Physical Body	*Anna-maya kosha*	Wrestlers Body Builders Athletes
Water Element	Sensuous Body	*Prana-maya kosha*	Bold Courageous Enterprising
Fire Element	Mind-ridden	*Mano-maya kosha*	Strength Feelings Emotion

(Fire is associated with Heart Chakra: poets, writers, inventors, architects who engage in pursuits ruled by the heart.)

Air Element	Intellect-ridden	*Vignana-maya kosha*	Thinkers Intellectuals

(Air is associated with Throat Chakra: scientists, physicists, physi-cians, who must find the how and why of things.)

Etheric Element	Soul	*Ananda-maya kosha*	Give bliss preference above all else

(The Crown Jewel or Third-Eye Chakra)

The next step is the state of Nirvana followed by the inner regions ascension.

Chapter Nineteen

My Spiritual Journey Continues

When I returned to the U.S. at the conclusion of the two and
one-half year Vedanta course, I had to begin my life anew — in
a seeming foreign land. Fortunately, my degree in anthropology
helped me to secure a job in advertising, which was my father's
line of work. In addition, I fulfilled my duty to the Vedanta
organization in Bombay by teaching classes in the United States.
Wishing to preserve the ancient teachings of their tradition, many
of my students had financially sponsored the school I had attended
in Bombay. Therefore, the school gave back to them by providing
them a teacher since they could not attend classes in India. Since
my first interest was God-realization and liberation, my teaching
did not cause any conflict in that interest as I was sharing sacred
teachings. Further, both my teachers of Vedanta stated that one
becomes rooted in this teaching much faster by sharing it with
others.

Truthfully, teaching Vedanta was an exhilarating experience
for me. This period was, second to meditating, one of the happiest
times in my life thus far. Our course of studies had encompassed
the whole range of Vedanta texts from the famous *Bhagavad Gita*
to the major *Upanishad* texts to the *Brahma Sutras*. In a lesson
from the *Upanishads,* a student may come to see, by means of
intensive philosophical argument, that the world cannot be real

because everything is impermanent — everything is born and subject to death. Even our life, like our dreams, comes and goes. "How transitory we be!" Shakespeare lamented. But in the case of the student of the Truth, there is no lamenting. He understands that only permanent can be as real, for behind the transitory display of objects appears the backdrop of Truth.

What is the nature of this Truth? Truth is *sat-chit-ananda,* the all-pervading backdrop that consists of pure existence, awareness, bliss. If we have a purified mind, we need not hear any words other than this explanation from the *Upanishads.* The Truth becomes our reality. We are no longer soiled and dragged through the mud of the world and its *karmas.* We are no longer subject to sorrow, and no longer subject to death and rebirth. We no longer identify with the changing material world, but become absorbed in the subtlest of truths.

In Sanskrit, *"sat"* means pure existence. In the mind of the individual, the sense of beingness does not disappear — no matter what one sees or knows or does. This existence is also called "I am-ness," or the self. When the students hear this truth, the ones who are qualified identify with the pure Self, without their usual masks for acting in life: brother, sister, daughter, son, mother, father or student. After remaining in this pure non-dual state of beingness, we move a step further. Then the world disappears and there is the experience of *Samadhi,* or merging with the oneness of pure beingness.

"The desired result is what the old sorcerers called 'stopping the world,' the moment when everything around us ceases to be what it's always been. This is the moment when sorcerers return to the TRUE nature of man. The old sorcerers always called it 'total freedom.'"

— Don Juan

In the *Upanishads* the Truth is called *sat*, pure existence, it is also called *chit*, pure awareness. The awareness remains constant throughout all experiences. The awareness is the observer of pure consciousness, untouched by what is seen. Since the seer can never be the seen, we cannot be the object of our awareness. If we cannot be a thought, we cannot be the mind, for the mind is a flow of thoughts. When we become graced with this truth, we remain in the witnessing state of consciousness. We no longer identify with the objects of awareness as I or mine. We no longer have to wear a mask or play a role. Since we no longer identify with the external, we remain the pure aware being.

Another word for this Truth of the individual and the world is "*ananda*," or pure limitless bliss. Just as surely as we exist and observe continuously, we are also pure love or bliss. Here we find the key to why we are always seeking love and happiness — because it is our nature. We do not know our nature because of all the distractions, or illusions of distractions. It is similar to singing in a chorus. When everyone is singing, we cannot hear our own voice. Yet, as we quiet the mind in meditation, we become fully aware of the bliss behind the thoughts, which is constant. Since the mind is without limitation, or limiting thoughts, it becomes a mind of freedom, bliss and joy.

"Plough with truth.
Plant the seed of desire for knowledge.
Irrigate the mind with the water of patience.
Supervise your work by introspection and self-analysis.
And build the fence of right conduct and rules.
Nothing else is required to attain eternal bliss."

— Hindu Sage

The devotee of God experiences only love when all of the mind's attention is on the one object of devotion, the all-pervading, limitless One. God is love; love is God. We merge our consciousness with God as love. This love is the secret of the joy of the devotee of the Lord. All the riches of the Kingdom of God are poured down upon the devotee.

Although I was teaching Vedanta when I returned home from India, my journey was not over. I may have received many answers and I may have had spiritual experiences, but my longing was not satisfied. It grew greater than ever. It was now a heartfelt longing. Only when I was meditating or teaching Vedanta would my pain, caused by my separation from God, ease up. My sense of incompleteness was not going away with a mere intellectualization and some periodic experiences.

In Seattle, I found a Tibetan Buddhist Center, which I enjoyed visiting. The chanting of *"Om mane padme hum"* seemed vaguely familiar to me. I appreciated that, when we chanted, we were not only chanting for our own benefit, but to help the whole world. One time when we were chanting, I found the words coming faster and faster — a blur of sounds taking on a power of their own. An old monk was sitting in the front of the temple. As I watched him, he never stopped moving his prayer beads and never stopped chanting. I knew I could trust his devotion, so mentally I shouted out a prayer to him. As quickly as I had asked, he shot back an answer mentally. The wonderful energy of the Buddhist center demonstrated the commitment of the holy Rimpoches' devotion to returning to God and to helping others to return to God.

The chanting and the devotion of the Rimpoches had a tremendous effect on my being. I recall once I was sitting in a movie theater watching a trailer containing a Tibetan ritual. The sound of the chanting was so phenomenal. I remember the words flashed on the screen: "This worldly experience is not real, it is only fleeting. The objects of pleasure are like poisons, making us forget our true nature. Because of them, we must go through thousands of painful births. We have no control, just the pain of sorrow and the emptiness of the fleeting pleasures. Then we return back into the world of transmigration." It went on and on. "The only way out of this suffering is through liberation." Again, I experienced a great blissful state, while watching the ritual on the big screen, listening to the chanting, and reading the words. I was sure that I must have practiced those Tibetan rituals in another lifetime.

Through the Tibetan Center in Seattle, a group of us were able to have an audience with the Dalai Lama. The number of practitioners at the center was small, but the devotion to the teachings of the Buddha was very powerful. The Rimpoches had such sweetness emanating from their beings that we felt happy just to be around them.

I continued teaching Vedanta in the Seattle and Vancouver areas. One day, while leaving work to make my journey back up to Vancouver to give the bi-monthly seminar, a little music box went off in my mind. It began to play over and over again the familiar tune:

Row, row, row your boat,
Gently down the stream,
Merrily, merrily, merrily, merrily,
Life is but a dream.

The little melody was a reminder of the transitory nature of life and the attitude that one should assume when performing one's duties in life. Life is but a journey down a stream. We are only passing through as if passing through our dreams. I felt that my journey took me through all of the world's religions. First, it was my Catholic upbringing with early memories of incense and candles, with loving pictures and statues of the Virgin Mary, Jesus and the Saints. Then there were the stories of faith instilled in me by the nuns. After I returned from India, I attended a Christmas Eve mass with my family. Only then did I realize the same grace was pouring down on the congregation that I experienced elsewhere. I just wasn't receptive enough before my Asian journey.

"He that hath my commandments, and keepeth them, he it is that loveth me: and he that loveth me shall be loved of my Father, and I will love him, and will manifest myself to him."

— Jesus.

Chapter Twenty

Path of Devotion

Devotion is said to be the fastest way of dealing with the mind in the *Kali Yuga*. During these times, we do not have time for hundreds of years of chanting, nor are we able to renounce our many responsibilities. Although the mind is supposed to be more powerful than thirteen universes, it can be extremely deceptive. The mind belongs to the Lord of the three regions: the Physical, Astral and Causal Regions. Like all other aspects of these three regions, it is designed to perpetuate itself at the expense of all else.

We may wonder: With such distractions, how we will ever be able to control the mind and find the Soul? After lifetimes of prayer and devotion, God sends us into the right family with a spiritual vehicle that matches our previous experiences of various lifetimes. At that time, the Soul can continue its journey. However, in the *Kali Yuga,* our bodies and minds are not so strong; therefore, we do not live long and concentration does not come easily. That great big elephantine mind — with all of its passions of lust, greed, attachment, anger and pride — is difficult to bypass, let alone, to acquiesce.

It is curious that, at the time of the great Avatar Krishna, it was not the *yogis,* that is, the practitioners of austerities, who attained God-realization first. The *Gopis,* or devotees of Lord

Krishna, were the first to become God-realized. Somehow, it was the innocent lovers of God who could, in their ecstatic states of joy and longing, sidestep all of the nonsense of a big ego with its never-ending desire to prove they were great spiritual adepts or practitioners. "Unless you be [pure and innocent] as little children," Jesus said.

Devotion to God, whether in the form of the Lord Krishna or Jesus, Allah or Buddha, lifts us right out of ourselves without having to change any details of our life. You may be a mother or a child; you may be a farmer or a mechanic; you may be rich or poor — all that is required is your remembrance of God.

"Seek ye first the Kingdom of God and all else shall come unto you." We are no longer limited by the thoughts of fulfilling the desires of the mind. We are no longer running from our fears of the world. We are no longer in relation to the objects of the world, and subject to the demands that this relationship places on us. We act and think and pray with the One in mind. It is a simple thing to put God first in our attention. When we are only in interaction with God, God is seen in everything and everyone.

"Your Beloved is of such nature that He will not admit any other love, for He alone will have the love of your heart, and will sit therein as a king, on His proper throne. If you could empty yourself of the love of creatures, He would always abide with you and never forsake you."

— Thomas à Kempis

One scholar of religion referred to the difference between the East and West as the difference between the practices of the East and the use of imagination of the West. That scholar did not consider that in both East and West there have been devotees of God who, in their commitment to their sacred relationship, crossed over the great divide where differences cease to exist. Whereas the populace of the East is methodical and restricted, for they live according to the traditional rules, those in the West, with its love of freedom and individuality, may find it easier to be more spontaneous and creative in their expression of love.

"There were rules in the monastery, but the Master always warned against the tyranny of the law. 'Obedience keeps the rules,' he would say. 'Love knows when to break them.'"

— Anthony de Mello

If the person has chosen to love, the imagination can be used as a psychological exercise that takes her to the Infinite. The theory is comparable to the love of an adolescent girl who imagines her object of love is returning the love. She praises the boy for certain qualities, for being what she is not. Her love continues to expand until it knows no bounds and has nothing to do with the boy. As she expands in love, she gradually incorporates those qualities she was projecting on the boy. She loves for the sake of love. For in her state of first love, pure and simple and innocent, without conditions and complications, the young adolescent becomes the projection of expression of love itself.

As the devotee embraces the essence of love, the mental and astral bodies dissolve. As the devotee becomes more sophisticated in the process, an experience of pure enrapture occurs, as she merges into the object of devotion.

In this profound appreciation of God, the momentum builds, taking on proportions beyond the imagination. The pull of God on the Soul is so powerful that nothing can stop it. The mind vibrates at a higher and higher frequency, until it becomes fully focused with utmost concentration. At this point, having left the mind behind, the devotee embraces Godlike characteristics, so she reflects God's love back into the world.

To use an example from every day life, a mother wanted her small boy to meditate by repeating the name of the Lord. To encourage him she promised him a reward of a piece of candy. So each day, he would sit and repeat the name of God and his mother would give him a piece of candy. Finally, the day arrived that he was receiving so much joy and bliss from the mediation practice that he no longer wanted the candy. The boy eventually became a Saint.

In the same way, the Church creates an environment to entrance the mind. With time, transformation takes place, and grace takes over. So God actually meets the devotee on the path and God becomes the reality. Only God speaks in a language beyond analysis and words. When all attention is on the One — the non-duality of Vedanta occurs and the mind resolves into Brahman or God.

"And we have known and believed the love that God hath to us. God is love, and he that dwelleth in love dwelleth in God, and God in him."

— St. John

Chapter Twenty-one

Ch'an Retreat

After being a part of the Catholic community, then studying in India, Tibetan Buddhism had become another recognizable form of tapping into the grace that emanates "whenever two or more are gathered together in my name, then ye shall find the grace of God," as Jesus expressed. Whether in the temples of India or the mosques of the Middle East or the churches in our communities, the appeals for greater union with God are always heard.

In fact, I began to find references to higher states of mind experienced by mystics of all religions. In the graduate program that I attended at Tufts University, a lecturer spoke of the writings of Saint Theresa. Her words reminded me of descriptions of mystics of India. I became more curious to seek out details about the spiritual journey of others. I wanted to have an understanding of the common thread in divine experiences that was beyond what we have named: "religion."

Since I continually had a great longing for connection with the Divine, I pursued an opportunity to attend a meditation retreat in a Ch'an (Zen) Monastery in New York City. When a friend called me in Seattle to say that I could attend the retreat, I was elated. Since my background was non-dual Vedanta, I knew nothing of Ch'an. I prayed steadfastly that Shih-Fu, the Ch'an Master, whom I had never met, would prescribe the right practice for me. That evening, while falling asleep, spontaneously I began asking, "Who is this Self?" The answer was "the stick of a Tootsie Roll Pop." Then I was no longer mind or intellect. They were separate from me.

For the duration of the seven-day retreat, I knew that I would have to rely on mental prostration and prayer to the Buddha and the Bodhisattvas, just as Shih-Fu had performed many prostrations as preparation for practice in his early years. When I arrived at the Ch'an Center, I tried very hard to establish a connection with the Buddha before the Altar, which I felt was my only hope. The following morning I awoke with the feeling of "no self." I felt no connection with the content of any thought. This feeling increased my belief in the power of prayer and Shih-Fu's grace. Later in his lectures, he confirmed that my experience was valid.

"The best attitude is to understand and accept that it is the process of practice which is important, not the end result."
— Shih-Fu Sheng Yen

In the retreat environment, we were taught to be mindful of all actions. We were to be fully conscious while walking or eating, always remaining in silence. We were to be aware during the long periods of sitting in meditation, not letting ourselves succumb to sleep. If a practitioner's head would bob, he or she would give permission to a monk to slap him or her with a flat wooden stick on the shoulder as a punishment for losing consciousness during the practice. For one who is devoted to God and whose heart is on fire, there cannot be a moment of forgetfulness. One's attention is in devotion to God, the object of supreme love and joy. Even with all my enthusiasm and devotion, several times I could not sustain conscious attention during the long hours on the meditation seat, so I willingly consented to the whack on the shoulder by a monk to awaken me.

One afternoon during meditation, a verse came to me that best describes my overall impression of the retreat.

Much to do about nothing
Makes nothing into something.
Nothing to do with something
Makes something into nothing.
It's all in the mind.

Shih-Fu's retreat world was one of making the very small things in life very significant in awareness. Never before had I found that such simple actions as walking, remaining silent, eating, and chopping vegetables were activities that merited my attention. Usually, our focus is based upon likes and dislikes, but at the retreat attention was simply to be placed on "what is." Only the simple actions in the present mattered. What once had been something, for me, became nothing. All my concerns and ideas appeared as illusions. Shih-Fu held the mirror up to show that the vision of the self was backwards. It all became clear.

In the meditation hall, there was a huge statue of a Golden Buddha. My connection to the Buddha and the Bodhisattvas made me feel secure with this representation of them looking down on us in meditation. However, I was disappointed the next morning when I found they had moved the Altar out of its original place in the meditation area to make room for more meditation cushions.

"Bowing there is no separation between you, your act of bowing, and what you are bowing to."

— Zen Master

The following evening since there was no work in the kitchen, I used the time to sit in contemplation on the One. "There is no other" — this thought was ongoing in my mind. And then — *there was no other.* Tears flowed down my face. The next thing I knew, I was being shaken. Shih-Fu urged me to move my body to join the group, so I could listen to his lecture. Shih-Fu knew what had happened and perceptively commented on the enlightenment experience during the lecture. It's impossible for me to describe.

Thereafter, I would always come out of meditation with the thought that the Golden Altar was in front of me. It was always such a surprise to realize there was no altar there, just the blank wall. The golden and infinite light would gradually seem to fade with my eyes opened. I would have to remember that the Altar had been moved to overlook the street. Many times I went into meditation, taking refuge in the Golden Cave of Light, which was the Buddha's abode. It was solacing. Then Buddha had to go, along with all the other illusions.

The inquiry continued — "Who is this Self?" One day the practice was particularly difficult. The next day, she was shattered. All of life, all her problems, goals, trials and preoccupations became reduced to illusion. It became clear that something artificial called "self" was thought to be separate and independent. I knew this "self" was really just a concept born out of the coming together of the piano made of wood, the body made of food, and the music made of sound-thoughts.

Life had no meaning. It was embarrassing to think it had carried on as it had. I felt repelled. There was not even the Buddha to turn to. That concept, too, was illusory. I cried as if there were no tomorrow.

But who is the real Self? I remembered the sacred experience of the past evening, when I experienced there was no other. My life's activities had been so sacrilegious. I realized that all my life had only been in service to the imaginary ego, I was really serving the Buddha Self. Yet seeing the nature of things, I saw that the service was an offering of dead skull bones that garland the Buddha. Ordinarily we think the dream is insignificant, and the waking state is real, I realized that the Buddha was in both the dream and the waking states. So, one continues to go in and out of the non-dual state until stability in oneness occurs.

"Buddhism is to study the Self. To study the Self is to forget the Self. To forget the Self is to be enlightened."

— Ethei Dogen

Shih-Fu told me to keep asking, "Who is this Self?" As the days went by it seemed as though the pieces were coming together. At times there was an expansive peace. Now, as I reflect on the overall impact of the retreat, it was, up to that point, one of the most significant weeks of my life. After that retreat, it had been as though I was not participating in life as much as I was just watching the participation and being.

Despite my occasional struggles to stay alert, overall it was a wonderful retreat. At that time, I remember thinking that, in spite of all the long and difficult discipline, it really was the devotee of God in me that had the experience, not the dry practitioner of austerities, nor the student of logic. I knew my strong longing for God gave me my important experiences at the Ch'an Center. Or perhaps the rigorous practice in meditation gave me the God experience which fueled the fire of devotion.

I wrote about my experiences in the Center's newsletter. As I look back at that retreat report, the account is not as I remembered it. The practices were intense, but the highlight was my moment in front of the altar of God. It was my devotion that brought on the enlightenment experience. The devotion came easily and naturally, then the light that was emanating from the imaginary altar brought me into another state of consciousness.

All religious teachers and teachings state that the ego is the last to go. It has the strongest hold on the mind and imagines itself to be of such great importance. In actuality, all is really just God. Not long after the retreat, I was back to normal again. I was a human being who had been introduced to the love of her life, but was unable to spontaneously see that of infinite love, peace and bliss. How could I bear the pain?

"For the mind is nameless, the body is empty, and the dharmas are a dream. There is nothing to be attained, no enlightenment to be experienced. This is called liberation."

— Shih-Fu Sheng-Yen

Chapter Twenty-two

Culprits of Desire and Fear

In its pursuit of happiness, the mind has only two different categories of thought forms. One is desire, and the other is fear. One is attraction, while the other is repulsion. It is fear and desire that cause the Soul to drop down to the lower *chakras* of the body/mind complex and to degrade itself. The five thieves that tempt the mind are lust, greed, anger, attachment, and pride. The scriptures of all the ancient world religions warn us that the pursuit of these five sensations cause us to debase ourselves, and, eventually, cause us to fall into hell.

The problem with the worldly realm of experience is that the beings who want to find unlimited happiness are looking for it in a very limited arena. There are, after all, only a limited number of worldly goods and resources. Our selfish pursuits translate into selfishness and attachment, then the ensuing anger and violence arrive whenever the desires are not met. These results and their effects on others have been called "evil."

Similarly, the sense of self-centeredness can grow to be out of control in its pursuit of happiness through the medium of pleasurable objects, which are limited in number. Then we end up exploiting others, who are weaker than ourselves, for the sake of our happiness. An ego, which is out of control in seeking possessions and power, can wreak havoc on a society and create a hell on earth.

If we examine what happens to us when the mind is out of control, we need only look at any one of the thieves to understand. Take pride, for example. We have heard of a Napoleonic complex; an individual, feeling very small, attempts to make himself taller by cutting off the heads of others. We have to agree an ego that is out of control is potentially dangerous to others, as well as dangerous to itself.

"The world is the adobe of desires and fears. You cannot find peace in it. For peace you must go beyond the world. The root cause of the world is self-love. Because of it we seek pleasure and avoid pain."

— Nisargadatta Maharaj

In the region of the three realms of the physical, astral and causal regions, as earlier mentioned, one is held *karmically* responsible for one's actions, both positive and negative. One may be doomed to lifetimes of misery, pain, isolation and degradation because of an ego that rampaged out of control. Perhaps one would have to serve as a one-hundred-year-old oak tree, or live through countless lifetimes with no free will as various plants and animals. Visits to astral hells and purgatories are the results of evil deeds as well.

Just as surely as one finds oneself in situations that are hell here on earth, similarly one will find such places on the other side. Hell can refer to a particularly difficult life here on earth or to certain realms of the astral region where certain heavy *karmas* are worked out. If a Soul is extremely angry, there are regions where angry and frustrated spirits battle it out together. There are ways to vent here and ways to vent there. A part of the mental complex has its own self-judgmental apparatus. As we review our life at the end, we may experience remorse or regret over some of our deeds and wish to right our wrongs in another life. However, an ego that is out of control may not see this relationship clearly and will have to suffer in other ways to purify itself in one incarnation after another.

The general consensus is the laws of *karma* provide an exact system of self-correction, all the way up to the level of the Soul. In this way, minds, intellects and Soul bodies keep improving themselves by learning all kinds of lessons in the process of self-purification. The downside is that we are not aware from lifetime to lifetime of just how and why we find ourselves in certain predicaments. We have no way of knowing why our suffering must take place. If a person had managed to become famous by exploiting the talents of others and then stealing all the credit, the person may be born to be exploited for his talents over and over again, thereby receiving no recognition or gratitude.

"Follow all virtues. What is the definition of evil and virtue? In the terminology of the Saints, virtue is that which leads you to God, and evil is that which takes you away from God."

— Kirpal Singh

Further, such people are cursed with an over-inflated opinion of themselves as a result of having been arrogant and self-centered before. Thus, the lifetimes of self-correction go on and on, yet the poor Soul remains ignorant of how to get out of this correctional facility called birth and rebirth. After so many thousands of births — according to Hindu philosophy, it is eighty-four thousand — we make a plea to God for help.

God, taking pity on the Souls, sends a Master Saint to take each Soul out of the realm of the first three regions. Today we do not live as many years in the human body as they did at the time of Moses. The earlier spiritual practices of the ancient world religious cultures worked well for self-realization in physical bodies that were strong and lived for hundreds of years. The withdrawal process for the Soul was assured when so many hundreds of years of prayers, austerities and meditation practices were performed.* Now, with relatively short lifetimes, plus the divided and distracted attentions spans of our complicated lives, we need the help of a Master Saint, who has traveled the inner regions and is commissioned by the compassionate Lord. He is able to take the Souls back to their real home — the place of eternal peace, love and happiness.

Because the Buddhist refer to 84,000 kinds of human afflictions, they postulate that there are many teachings, or spiritual practices, available to human beings. They are designed for specific purposes. Although most of the practices benefit the student on several levels, they are usually preformed by one of the five apparatus of the human complex.

Generally, the more refined the practice the more refined the results. That is, any practice that produces profound concentration can actually take the individual practitioner beyond the lower mind preoccupations to higher realms of form and the formless into *Samadhi* states. Every religion in the world has Saints who have experienced different levels of *Samadhi* in the form realms of heaven and the formless realms. Individuals throughout time have been known to reach stages of Enlightenment, or what is referred to as God Realization, *Nirvana, Sattori* or *Tao.*

Once there was an ardent disciple, who was ready for God-realization, but could not experience it until his *Guru* told him

---

* Refer to Yuga Chart, page 174.

to move a pile of rocks from one location to another, without any inherent purpose. It was this action that brought on an "enlightenment" experience. So the student does not know all of the practices and events that took place in the person's life or lifetimes to purify the person and what further action was required, but the Master knew.

In the *Sant Mat* tradition, the initiate is engaged in many exercises to progress spiritually, from the watching of the mind and body for impure thoughts and actions, to the keeping of a diary for weeding out negativity, to the practice of light and sound meditation for the mind and Soul, to the study of scriptures or *satsang* for the intellect, to the practicing of dutiful action to offset negative *karmas* of past lives and *karmic* debts in this life, to the practice of a pure vegetarian diet, to the remembrance and devotion of the *Guru* to forget the ego, to the practice of repeating the *mantra* while in meditation as well as throughout the day to purify the mind and Soul.

In spiritual literature, there exist examples of devotees of God who could not progress because their energy moved up to the Heart *Chakra* and out to the object of devotion. The life of Saint Ramakrishna, who was devoted to the Mother aspect of God, illustrates this point. To sever this attachment at the Heart *Chakra*, his *Guru* ground a piece of glass into his Third Eye area to bring all his attention and energy to the *chakra* of non-dual enlightenment, or oneness with the object of devotion.

While the pitfall of devotion can limit progress to a higher non-dual state, similarly the pitfall of other spiritual practices preaching the non-dual theory may be ego, which is the last of the five enemies of the mind to leave and the most difficult to overcome. For example, although study and analysis of the intellect demonstrates that God is within and is absolutely critical for higher progress, a student may just be left with an over-exaggerated opinion of his or herself if the heart has not been purified.

"Pride is the mask we make of our faults."

— Hebrew Proverb

The result can be a personality aberration. The effect is that when outsiders, or insiders for that matter, go visit a particular spiritual organization, they may find that, although the scriptures and books and lectures are inspiring and uplifting, the behavior of the individuals promoting these high ideals can be poor demonstrations of human character. They may hide behind the membership of the organization to increase their pride, without doing the practices. Or perhaps, even though the aspirants may perform a lot of practices to be able to gain concentration and focus of the mind, they may not be paying attention to their total purification process. They are unconsciously serving their spiritual pride, not remembering the practice of the rudiments of all religions, which is non-injury or love for others. They might be forgetting to pay attention to an important fundamental truth: All Souls are equal and born in the image and likeness of God, for we are all one. Put in another way, God resides in all beings.

While certain practices enhance one's energy and power, if the heart is not purified, the power returns to the lower *chakras*. The problems of these *chakras* become exaggerated with displays of anger, lust, greed, attachment or pride. Therefore, with certain practices comes a word of caution, for as you gain greater power, you should practice more purification and give attention to moral foundation work or living the life of Christ's love.

Chapter Twenty-three

Five Enemies of the Mind

Most of us live in such a large and vibrant world that its distractions allow us to escape the awareness of our mind's nuances of greed, anger, lust, attachment and egoism. If we are made to earn our own living and perform the duties of a householder, serving family members and the community at large, we can pretty much ignore these petty characteristics of the mind, but if our world becomes small as found in a monastery, ashram or meditation organization, these five enemies rear up without life's camouflages and demand that we either serve them or renounce them.

Sometimes members of spiritual groups are busy serving one of the five enemies of the mind and can even be exploiting a spiritual organization for that purpose. Although practitioners, they may be serving the ego, trying to be better, or perform better, than other aspirants from the standpoint of service or spiritual practice. In some cases, these individuals could be spending more time demonstrating to others their spiritual advancement than working on their own inner progress.

"All religions, arts and sciences are branches of the same tree. All these aspirations are directed toward ennobling man's life, lifting it from the sphere of mere physical existence and leading the individual towards freedom."

— Albert Einstein

Additionally, because the task of conquering and controlling the mind is such a difficult one, spiritual practitioners may succumb to a lower activity of spreading gossip about others' faults and shortcomings and dwelling on the negativity within the group, rather than concentrating upon their own struggle and inner progress. Concerning this tendency in spiritual organizations, Master Kirpal Singh said very succinctly, "Reform is needed, not of others, but of oneself."

Unfortunately, such persons may work out their own ego problems by becoming very politically active in a group while as Ajaib Singh used to say, "Ignoring their own house which is on fire." He has also said that, for those who serve a spiritual organization, the biggest protection is humility. So, it is our challenge to remember that spirituality is an "inner path" of the spirit and not an outer path of public display.

Another enemy of the mind, besides spiritual pride, is greed. An example would be when spiritual organizations or ministers take money from others to support themselves. A true Master would never take from another. Wherever he lived, Ajaib Singh had a farm for his livilihood. Jesus was a carpenter.

Unfortunately, it is not uncommon to hear horrific stories of ministers, priests, *gurus* and disciples getting angry at their sub-ordinates. Anger is a result of not fulfilling one's wishes and desires, so it is hardly a demonstration of enlightenment or inner contentment or love.

I am sorry to have to mention the horrible injustices committed against acquaintances on the spiritual path who have become victims of a so-called teacher's or *guru's* lust. Any teacher who claims that personal lust can bring about spiritual progress or enlightenment has fallen prey to one of the spiritual paths of distraction of the Negative Powers. One cannot be withdrawn to the higher *chakra* and indulge in the lower *chakra* activities at the same time.

The other addiction of the mind, attachment, can also manifest itself in a so- called holy church or ashram environment when its members are living such an austere and restrictive life that one becomes attached to the smallest and least significant thing. A pettiness of the mind develops that is beyond a normal person's comprehension.

Spiritual practices are designed as substitutes for renouncing the five enemies of the mind. The spiritual codes of ethics are designed to curb them in the arena of life's activities, but each person is his or her own helmsman and is vulnerable, often substituting one negative quality for another or to the exclusion of all else because the battle with the mind is such a great one.

"The truth seekers' battle goes on day and night, as long as life lasts, it never ceases."

— Kabir

Little wonder that, in the *Kali Yuga* more often than not, the scriptures are about waging holy war against evil? The *Bhagavad Gita,* Koran and Sikh scriptures are intended as inspirational because the biggest of all battles is the one with everyone's personal enemy — the five enemies, or thought forms — in the mind. Clearly, for the practitioner, the mind is one's worse enemy.

It makes sense, therefore, to begin the battle where one is ... by asking for help from God and, whenever available, from a Master Saint, for this battle is the biggest fight of any Soul at any time in its long series of 84,000 incarnations. Of this battle, which may last for lifetimes, we must never lose sight of the fact that God is there to help in the efforts to bring our Soul back Home.

Chapter Twenty-four

Guidance of a True Master

When we make the choice to be liberated, it is similar to any other knowledge; we have to find someone who knows more than we do on the subject. Obviously, we can only rely on someone who is already liberated. Who is such a free being? In the East, they are referred to as enlightened Sages. In the West, they are often called Saints. In Sanskrit, the mother language of Latin and Greek, the term used to describe their state is *Moksha,* or liberation. Liberation from what? We seek liberation not only from our body/mind complex with all of the joys and sorrows inherent in such a system, but also liberation for the Soul from all *karma,* so that no further rebirths will occur and the Soul can go back to God, or infinite love and happiness.

For those who are identified with the body/mind complex, Master Soul is sent down to earth to liberate us because liberation by self-effort is impossible. Just as when we are dreaming, we cannot impel ourselves into the waking state. The dream material cannot create the wakened person any more than a body/mind can create the Soul or the experience thereof. This is even true of those extraordinary ones who have overcome the limitations of the body/mind complex, yet identify with subtler realities on higher regions. Unfortunately, as long as we take ourselves to be an entity on any level, we are still bound by the rules and regulations at that level of the *karmic* wheel.

"There is Someone, there is some Power, who has created this creation. And the things which are happening in this creation are not happening by themselves. There is someone who is controlling it. Mahatmas *[Sages] call that Power the* Naam *[Holy Name] or the Almighty Lord, and they came into the world to unite us with that Power."*

— Ajaib Singh

Since a Master is never allowed to interfere with the free will of another, our Souls can be freed in the highest sense only when we ask. When we truly ask for liberation, God, or *Sat Purush,* answers the prayer. A Master Saint is sent to show the way clear of bondage and to take our Soul back to its real home.

Then the Master Saint takes us on a journey through many kingdoms. We encounter many beautiful sights and sounds along the way to the real home of the Soul. Many Souls remain stuck in some of these regions, thinking they have reached the Ultimate. Only a great Master can help a Soul through all of these many regions to the great kingdom of *Sat Lok.* From there, *Sat Purush,* the Supreme Ruler, helps the Soul to its final destination.

In the course of practices given by the Master Saint, one enters a state of what Carl Jung refers to as "an ego-less mental condition or consciousness without an ego." St. Paul refers to it as a state in which "it is no longer I who live, but Christ who lives in me." This state is not to be confused with dissolution of the ego, for it is a state of an integrated ego that is strong enough to listen to the higher Self. The ego itself does not disappear, but the old functioning of the ego disappears. Then the ego is able to resume its intended role as the circuit board between all the data input from the mind and senses and Soul. In the *Sant Mat* tradition, this state is referred to as "when the five little boys leave the mind." These are the five thieves of the mind: lust, anger, pride, greed and attachment. At this time, one experiences Self-realization. That is, an understanding of one's Self, not as the egocentric entity, based on the mind and its antics, but as the "self-centric" entity.

"If one associates with the Sages, where is the need for all other methods of discipline? When there is a pleasant breeze blowing, of what use, tell me, is a fan?"

— Ramana Maharshi

If we could, we would create a world where all are happy and all is the expression of our limitless nature. We would experience an existence free of limitation; therefore, full of happiness. Down here on earth, the glimpses of happiness we receive only happen during the moments that we forget our small selves and our desires. Those moments are few and far between. We need someone to tell us that if we would just forget ourselves and our desires, we could get back in touch with our limitless nature. By desisting from focusing on the fleeting objects of pleasure and pretending that they are real and by knowing that in degrading ourselves to the illusion and our addictions to it — we come to understand that we have forgotten the truth of our reality and the personal freedom that this knowledge brings.

Whether one is a Buddhist, whose goal is enlightenment, a Vedantin, who seeks liberation, an Asian who seeks Satori, or a Christian or Muslim, who prays for salvation, the individual who seeks relief has often hit bottom with life and, therefore, turns to the Path of the Soul to go back to God. These paths form the

---

* This Region of Truth is the first completely spiritual region. After this region, *Sat Purush,* the Lord of All, takes the Soul further.

world religions. Some of the most mystical practices came from the direct inspirations of practitioners who suffered the greatest pangs of separation of Soul from God. All of them used practices and techniques to gain inner peace and God connection. The system was always a matter of withdrawing the attention from the physical body, then moving it up to the higher *chakras,* and to the Third Eye Center.

"The devotee finds no one is as dear a friend as the Sat Guru.
Then she accepts the inner Satsang (company of the Saint).
Her soul climbs the sky and she calls aloud,
The shy roars and the heavens cry in joy.
The mind sets on the throne becoming the intoxicated one.
The Soul has achieved the True Home
And has left the mortal world."

— Swami Ji Maharaj

**Table 8. Religious Practices for Purification of Body and Mind
In Order of Historical Appearance**

Religion	Body	Body/Mind	Mind	Intellect
Hinduism	*Hatha Yoga*	*Pranayama* *Raja Yoga*	*Bhakti Yoga* Prayer Meditation	*Jñana Yoga* Vedanta Contemplation
Buddhism	Eight-fold Path	Prostrations with *Mantra*	Prayer Meditation	*Abhidarma* Analysis Study of Scriptures Contemplation
Christian	Ten Commandments	Rosary Worship Service	Prayer	Study of Scriptures Contemplation
Islam	Tenets of Service Right Behavior in Koran	Prayer Chanting Rosary	Prayer	Study of Scriptures Contemplation

IV. The True Master Saint

Why do I say I meditate,
For it is you who are meditating.
When I say I practice,
It is you who do the work.
Although I say I understand,
It is You who are the meaning.

If I thought the doer
Was separate from the Holy Word
Then I did not know that those Holy Words,
Which I am to repeat, turn only into You.
The Speaker, Soul to Soul.

While I may say
I am walking with the Saint
It is really He who walks with me.
I can never be separate from You again,
For You have shown yourself to me.
I can no longer pretend that this reality
Is anything else but Thee.

While I may say I have eyes to perceive,
It is He who sees through me.
And while I think I have a mouth to speak
The words belong to Thee.
Where is there a place on earth
That You cannot be seen
When everywhere we go
There is only your Holy Being.

O Saint, your presence
Speaks only of God
You have shown me your Heart,
So my life is now a journey
Which my heart walks through
With only thoughts of You.

Sant Ajaib Singh

"When our previous good karmas help us to come in contact with some renunciante or awakened soul, we also awaken after sleeping for ages and ages. Normally we say that we are awake. Saints say, 'No, you are not awake. You are awake in respect to the world, but you are sleeping towards God.' Then what will we do? We will sleep towards the world, and awaken in respect to God."

— Ajaib Singh

Chapter Twenty-five

Who Is a True Saint?

Being fully enlightened, the Master Saint is aware of God in every moment. These rare God-realized beings are the most humble servants of God. They would rather run away from the world and stay immersed in the One than to be put up on a pedestal for others to praise. They have spent years of withdrawal in meditation and would never exploit another for tithing, fame, or lust. They are simple and humble, but their radiation can be felt for miles around, and the effect of their presence can dramatically change lives. There are no words to describe how an individual Soul benefits by looking into the eyes of such a holy Saint. One thing is sure — they have the power to liberate thousands by passing on the meditation techniques given them by their Masters.

There are a few sure signs of the true Saints and Servants of God, so one can know who can be trusted. They never live off of the money of others. They have practiced serious meditation continually for fifteen to twenty years. Such modest ones have already conquered the five enemies of the mind; therefore, they have no lust, anger, greed, attachment or pride. These culprits are gone forever. The Saints thus feel free of all fear and desires of the five senses, both subtle and gross. Most important, they are rooted in God-consciousness. They are no longer operating out of personal *karmic* obligation, but are free to serve others. These

Masters serve only because they are asked to do so by their own Masters. They accept the service with great reluctance, but do so with tremendous love and devotion to their Masters.

"Those who know don't speak and those who speak don't know."
— Lao-tzu

To take one example from the Sant Mat tradition, Ajaib Singh had no ambition to be anyone's Master or *Guru.* He had been a simple farmer in a village in Rajasthan in northeast India. When he was a small boy, he would not sleep in a bed at night because he said that the sleep might cause him to forget God. Even so, he suffered for years in his search for God, even spending seventeen years in an underground meditation cave. During that period, Master Kirpal Singh sought him out in the deserts of Rajasthan and initiated him. After the initiation, Ajaib continued his practice of meditation in solitude. He stayed away from the mainstream of the thousands who were constantly seeking initiation from Master Kirpal. Then Master Kirpal told Ajaib to sell his farm and to continue meditating in an underground cave. He said that he would visit Ajaib whenever necessary.

After the passing of Kirpal Singh, the disciple hid out in the desert. Even though Master Kirpal had selected him to be his successor, others had to find him and ask him to serve. Ajaib Singh's fragrance could not keep him hidden away for more than a few years. There was such an enthusiasm among the disciples of Master Kirpal to find the successor, while others were longing to receive initiation into the meditation practice of light and sound, that God heard their prayers. News of the authentic Saint, a farmer in Rajasthan, went flying around the world. He was sought out and convinced to come out of seclusion to assume the role of initiator in the tradition of *Sant Mat.*

The Perfect Saints do not tell us to leave our homes; they do not tell us to become renunciates. They tell their disciples to get up early every morning and meditate for two to three hours, to live a pure life, and to earn a living by honest means. By attending to these duties, plus their individual worldly responsibilities, and putting trust in the Master, the disciples reach their destination of liberation. Through connection to the Master, they are able to get out of physical prison and become liberated from all the worlds of death and rebirth.

"Only those Saints who have seen the beginning and the end will understand the glory and the light of the One who has created all the skies and the creation."

— Tulsi Sahib

A Saint does not really care about miracles; these phenomena are just a by-product of the power of love and concentration on God. When the mind becomes absorbed and contained, it gathers up so much power and energy that its own holy thoughts can manifest in the physical realm. Many *yogis* with supernatural powers exist throughout India. Often sincere practitioners get caught up in the gifts that come with withdrawal and concentration of the mind. These gifts can range from the capacity to read minds, to the ability to materialize objects, and to perform minor miracles. Because the mind is supposed to be more powerful than thirteen universes, many scriptures state anyone who learns to control their own mind gains control of other minds and the world as well.

This power is said to be much more common in earlier *yugas* or periods of time* when mankind had a much longer lifespan

---

* We are said to be in the fourth *yuga,* or *Kali Yuga,* where a lifetime lasts for some 80 years, as opposed to Moses who, earlier in this *yuga,* lived to be over 800 years.

with much fewer distractions. Today India is probably the one part of our world where there is the greatest concentration of *yogis* and spiritual practitioners because that culture encourages and supports individuals who seek God-realization. To the Indians, it is perfectly natural for even those who hold high positions in Government to practice meditation and to rely on the advice of their personal *Gurus,* or spiritual advisors.

While I was in India, I was fortunate to hear about and meet many spiritual practitioners who could perform miracles. Many *yogis* may willingly or unwillingly demonstrate certain powers using their mental energy. In addition, the history and culture are steeped in the practices of *yoga* for the control of the body and the mind.

One very famous *Guru* cured my girlfriend of a stomach ailment by placing his hand above her stomach and causing sacred ash to fall on her. Another time a friend and I were with a *Guru* who caused it to rain inside the room. My friend looked over at him with a startled look. He proclaimed, "That's Ganges water. You are an Indian now." I used to listen to this *Guru* speak to crowds as large as five thousand. His power was great; he kept thousands mesmerized with the Truth.

I met another *Swami* who had studied Raja Yoga and the laws of the five elements. In studying them, he was able to understand and use the laws of materialization. I once watched him make his picture jump up and down on a bookcase. I then understood that his subtle presence was the source of bliss that I had been experiencing for hours. His contemplation and focus was the element of water, the element that rules conception. Therefore, he was able to help many women who had difficulty conceiving to become pregnant by praying for them.

A priest of a south Indian temple told me that anyone who wanted the power to materialize objects could learn to do so in a few days, but the practice would shorten his or her life down to three years. This world is a place of give and take. All actions have a *karmic* consequence. To disrupt the flow and create circumstances different than the will of nature is to alter *karma* and to bring a consequence for altering fate upon oneself directly.

I learned this lesson for myself when I was studying at the ashram for Vedanta studies. A few of us came to know of a chant to Lord Ganesha from the Vedas. We were told that if we repeated the words a certain number of times our wishes would be fulfilled. Four of us did the chanting for the prescribed amount of time each day. At the end of the twenty-one days, Ganesha appeared to me. Everywhere I looked, Ganesha was present. My three wishes were also granted. Obviously, I was impressed by the results. However, my three friends, who also did the chanting, did not fare so well. One died, the other was stabbed thirteen times, and the third had to leave the ashram for personal reasons.

How is it that the gods and goddesses of legends, as well as the *yogis* of today, were able to wield incredible powers to manifest whatever they chose? The answer is in part due to the birthright of all humankind and their Soul connection to the all-powerful God Source. Today, only those who have a subtle understanding of the universe as innumerable of energies of different vibrations can see the basic principles of manifestation are really simple and easy.

In Sanskrit, the word for manifestation from subtle elements to physical form is called the *panchikarana,* or materialization. A *yogi* understands that thought forms are objects, but in subtle form. To manifest in the physical sense requires a certain level of energy projected into a thought form. Then, depending upon the *karmic* disposition of the universe, the thought form, or prayer, will either manifest quickly or take some time.

Everything in the Universe began in the Causal Region. Out of the Causal Region came the Astral, or mental, Region, composed of the five subtle elements. Similarly out of the five subtle elements came the five gross elements comprising the physical world: space, air, fire, water and earth.

The process of moving from subtle or astral form to a lower, or physical form, is called materialization or *panchikarana*. The description of this process is given in the elementary Vedanta text, *Atma Bodha*. It details the process by which the physical creation manifested from the five *tanmatras,* elements in an undifferentiated state of the Causal Region. The *tanmatras* are predisposed to transformation due to the three distinct vibrational qualities, or *gunas,* which comprise all of creation; therefore, they separate and divide, and then unite among themselves.

Accordingly, each *tanmatra* divides into two equal parts. One half remains stable while the other half begins to transform. For example, one half of space, the subtlest of elements, slows down to a lower energy vibration. With the fluctuation of the *gunas,* this half divides into four parts. These four parts, or one-eighth the original element scatter and merge with the four elements, finally creating the physical forms.

$$\text{Space} = \tfrac{1}{2}\text{ space} + \tfrac{1}{8}\text{ air} + \tfrac{1}{8}\text{ fire} + \tfrac{1}{8}\text{ water} + \tfrac{1}{8}\text{ earth}$$

$$\text{Air} = \tfrac{1}{2}\text{ air} + \tfrac{1}{8}\text{ space} + \tfrac{1}{8}\text{ fire} + \tfrac{1}{8}\text{ water} + \tfrac{1}{8}\text{ earth}$$

$$\text{Fire} = \tfrac{1}{2}\text{ fire} + \tfrac{1}{8}\text{ space} + \tfrac{1}{8}\text{ air} + \tfrac{1}{8}\text{ water} + \tfrac{1}{8}\text{ earth}$$

$$\text{Water} = \tfrac{1}{2}\text{ water} + \tfrac{1}{8}\text{ space} + \tfrac{1}{8}\text{ air} + \tfrac{1}{8}\text{ fire} + \tfrac{1}{8}\text{ earth}$$

$$\text{Earth} = \tfrac{1}{2}\text{ earth} + \tfrac{1}{8}\text{ space} + \tfrac{1}{8}\text{ air} + \tfrac{1}{8}\text{ fire} + \tfrac{1}{8}\text{ water}$$

Thus the whole of creation unfolds from the subtle realm to the mental realm, and then into the physical. This process implies that everything in the physical creation originated as a thought form. The more energy behind the thought form the quicker it manifests into the physical world. Is there any wonder that prayer produces miracles? Prayer is thought form combined with the supercharging angelic forces of the temple, church or mosque. Similarly, constructive positive prayer brings positive results, but if we have prayers — or even thoughts — that are harmful to others, the *karmic* consequences can be very heavy. The greater the concentration, the greater the energy is focused on a given thought form, the quicker it manifests. Hence, the miraculous powers of the *yogis* due to their prefect concentration.

In 1979, I met a renowned Swami of the Ramakrishna Mission in South Africa. We were discussing the political oppression in that country. He said it would take twelve Swamis with power at his level to be able to relieve the situation. Many years had to lapse until the system of Government changed to reflect the equality of races.

When the earlier gods or *yogis* had control over the mind, it meant that they had control over the energy on the level of the mind. This energy which converted from a subtler, mental format to a grosser format could be directed toward form manifestation in the physical reality. A mind that is scattered in self-indulgence cannot direct much power to manifest since it is like a light in a bulb spreading out over a large area. It simply gets dissipated. That same energy when directed to the level of no thought or single thought can, like a laser beam, create such a change that matter is no longer the same.

On the other hand, stories in the Hindu religious mythology abound with incidents of *yogis* losing their powers because of using it for self-centered purposes and indulgences. Those who are no longer able to climb the ladder into the Infinite are left with their insatiable appetites and struggles to acquire satisfaction from indulgences by "evil" or exploitative means of others. Hence, the fall of man and angels is all the same phenomena, the misuse of the laws of *Panchikarana*.

In Bombay several months after our chanting experiment, I mentioned it to a learned priest. He informed me that this chant was not an endeavor for amateurs to undertake. Further, he explained that the ancient chanting in the Vedic tradition was so precise that, even if a slight error in intonation was made, the power would reverse and negative things would occur. This truth I had witnessed for myself. Needless to say, I did not invoke the powers again. Perhaps the chanting worked for me because my wishes were for the sake of others as well as myself. Or, it is possible, that I had the protection of Sant Ajaib Singh even before I met him in physical form.

One thing is clear: the Master who comes to take the Souls back to the eternal heaven, called *Sat Lok,* is not allowed to exhibit miracles. The agreement with the Ruler of the first three regions is that, if Souls are to be taken out of the domain of the Negative Power, they cannot proceed due to the exhibition of supernatural powers. At the same time, the Ruler of these lower regions vowed that he would create such distractions that the Souls would not be able to recognize a real Saint.

In our modern world, we have as many distractions as possible to keep us tied to our physical vehicles. They include all the pleasures of a licentious society that offers more foods, entertainment and stimulation than any past king could have ever imagined. For the seeker of God, we have numerous preachers and *gurus,* including those with powers to distract us from our pursuit of God-realization. I have heard countless stories of individuals, such as myself, going off to India in pursuit of spiritual answers, only to be exploited and disappointed because of an encounter with a so-called "holy man."

I have listened to many sad stories of how these false *gurus* perpetuate the exploitation of their disciples by calling them "chosen" and "special." Just as clearly as there are many *yogis* in a culture that places the highest premium upon enlightenment, there are many of them whose character and intentions remain unclear. The greatest personal disappointment of my life is to have gone to one of these "holy men" with all the sincerity of my heart and to find out that they are less than perfect. If they were unable to forego their own desires for name, fame, lust or power, how would they be able to free me of mine? Seeing this kind of hypocrisy, I felt caught in a trap of disillusionment all over again.

There are many who claim to be a mouthpiece of the Lord. There are many who claim to be enlightened. There are many who take your money and personal power. There are even those who exploit women sexually. These *yogis* cannot be true Saints, for a true Master Saint is free of all desires.

"He is a Guru in vain who cannot turn the darkness, 'gu,' into light, 'ru.'"

— Kirpal Singh

Chapter Twenty-six

Meeting the Master

Without the backdrop of the life in an Ashram or a monastery to support my practices and to keep me in the flow of the spirit, I stood alone against the onslaughts of life. Yet, my longing for God remained. Back in America, I felt as if I were cut off from my own mother and was as helpless as a child.

"O Lord, of myself, I can do nothing. You are my only lifeline. At least let me turn to you with a prayer to save me. I am not able to shield myself away from my daily work in a private setting where I can perform intense spiritual disciplines and practices. I am not fortunate enough to be taken care of for the rest of my life, so that I am able to cloister away and immerse myself in God. I stand helpless before God knowing only what I am not and have not. O Lord, hear my prayer and have mercy on me," thus I prayed and prayed for months.

In my spiritual journey, I have found that the greater the heights of the glimpses of godliness, the greater are the depths of disappointment of not being able to hold onto the bliss. The greater the love abounds; the greater are the separation and the longing. It was indeed *Sat Purush*, the God of Gods, who heard my longing after so many years of bouncing here and there. After seeing so many *yogis* perform miracles, after having so many monks share their spiritual grace and insights with me, after performing so many spiritual practices of different religions, and after serving as a teacher of Vedanta for ten years, the Master Saint came into my life — near my home in Vancouver, Canada.

By the time I finally met Ajaib Singh, I was desperate. I had been working hard to support myself, plus I was continuing to teach Vedanta classes in my free time. The teaching was pure and simple, but I was not able to sustain its vision in my life. I went to Vancouver to have my first meeting with the Master Saint. In an ashram established by Master Kirpal Singh, I waited in a tent with 1,800 others. Then Ajaib Singh arrived.

The moment I saw him it was as if all of the searching, all of the longing, all of the praying, was inconsequential. In a moment, I perceived the depth of his purity. He was not one who traveled with an entourage. He was not one who lorded over a huge organization. Nor did he wear colorful silk robes like a king. In his simple white cotton, he presented a striking glimpse of the simplicity of Sainthood. He was visibly a Godman, surrounded with an aura of quiet humility — so much so that I was stunned. While he stood before us, his attention remained focused on each one of us. We felt as if we were as his children. His eyes displayed a look of compassion as he glanced into the eyes of the silent audience who were receiving his grace. This exchange through the eyes, called *darshan* in Sanskrit, is the avenue for communication between Souls. He was careful to look into as many eyes as possible on his way to the podium. Everyone who was receptive became blessed and blissful immediately.

On the stage, *Santji* (the name used by his devotees, meaning "respected Saint") was like a mother looking over all of her children. Full of love, compassion and humility, he was there to serve and bless his dear children. He had been commissioned by Kirpal Singh to take the suffering Souls back to *Sat Lok,* our eternal home. Only those who are commissioned by God can take on such a tremendous task of guiding the Souls beyond the realms of *karma*, then past the void region of tremendous darkness, then on to the higher region, called *Sat Lok*, the place of *Sat Purush*, the Lord of Lords.

Master Sawan Singh, the master who initiated Kirpal Singh, gives a wonderful description of the journey of the Souls back to *Sat Lok*. Even though *Sat Lok* is our true home, due to our interest in experience and experimentation in the mental and physical realms, we came to this earth region, only to be caught up by desire. So we ended up at the mercy of the laws governing birth and rebirth in these lower realms of grosser material.

While there are many heavens to reward the righteous, there are also many hells to purify the Souls. The Buddhists say there are 3,000 worlds. The Hindus calculate that there are 84,000 reincarnations into the various worlds. Although some of the lifetimes, spent as plants or insects, may be short lived, it is a long, gruesome journey for the Soul. Finally, out of desperation, the supreme Lord in *Sat Lok** hears the cry of the Soul. Then a Master Liberator comes to assist the worthy persons.

Many affirm that one glance from a God-realized Saint has the capability of liberating the Soul. Some say the power of the Saint is so great that he is able to liberate all of the worlds, heavens, and hells. My sincere prayer is that anyone who has begun the search for more than what their present life has to offer will find a Master Saint such as Sant Ajaib Singh of Rajasthan.

"I salute all the Saints because they donate such a high service. They come into this world to take Souls out [of the lower regions]."

— Guru Nanak

---

* *Sat Lok* is Sanskrit for *Sach Khand*

Chapter Twenty-Seven

Role of a Master Saint

Many initiates are not aware that, in order to be liberated from the first three regions, every *karma* must be paid back to the Ruler of these regions. By meditating, we are able to pay off the *karmas* much more easily and painlessly. For those who cannot or do not meditate, more of the burden falls on the Master Saint. Just as Jesus Christ had to hang on a cross to atone for the sins of others, so the Master takes on unimaginable suffering. Of the relationship of the Master to the disciple, Kirpal Singh has said, "If you knew just how much I loved you, you would be dancing up and down." Only this kind of great love can make the enormous sacrifices that these humble Saints make for us. Who would want to take on such a job? Only the most humble and grateful disciple can truly serve to repay the perfect Saint. The rest of us ever remain eternally indebted.

I have many regrets in life, but my biggest regret is not heeding Santji's words when he first made himself known to me while I was meditating in Seattle. I had seen him several times in meditation long before I met him in Vancouver. Although he would appear to me at critical times in my life, I was not clear just how significant his advice was, or who he was. First, he told me that I did not need to go to India for that two and one-half year course to get spiritual guidance. At that time, I was so anxious for answers that I did not listen, so I went on and pursued the intellectual studies. Little did I know that such a commitment would prevent my meeting with the true Master for almost ten years. My only solace is my lengthy search and subsequent suffering for answers can help someone else from making the same mistake of delaying such a propitious meeting.

Only because I followed the various extraneous paths back to God was I able to appreciate this all-encompassing path so dearly. I cannot say that I received no benefit from the study of Vedanta and from my sharing of its knowledge with others as a teacher. I found theory was nice for the mind and intellect, but it could never be enough to quench the thirst of my longing Soul.

Words fail me when I try to explain the experience of being in the presence of the energy field of one who is immersed in God-realization. The scriptures say that being in the presence of such a Master is equivalent to the burning up of thousands of years of *karma*. In other words, reading about Saints and having *darshan* of one is like the difference between reading the brochures about a Caribbean vacation and actually going on a Caribbean cruise. At the time we are in the presence of such a holy being, we get shown another reality. Thereafter, we do not wish to return to a world without God. How else do we explain the electricity around, for example, one such as Jesus? People would flock to hear his words. Because his aura could be felt as a radiance for many miles, the simple people would travel great distances through the desert to hear him speak.

When we are in the presence of these Saints and are able to look into their eyes, we experience such radiant love and joy that all other forms of enjoyment and pleasure are miniscule. The degree of the transformation is dependent upon the readiness of our Souls to receive the great gifts that such a glance by a Holy

One can bestow. "Just one glance of your nectarine eyes," one devotee expressed his devotion. Yes, this one glance could be the one that liberates, for the Master Saint has that capability.

I remember vividly when I first saw Santji in that tent, crowded with other devotees. I prayed that if only I could know that he was as great as Kirpal Singh, I would be forever devoted. At that moment, he turned his gaze from one side of the tent over to me on the other side of the tent. With one long glance, he filled me with such love and bliss that tears fell and fell. During the rest of the lecture, all that I saw was the form of Santji turning into all of the past Masters. It was truly remarkable how he heard my plea in that crowd of 1,800 people and answered my prayer by showing me a glimpse of his true nature.

"He Himself [Sat Purush] comes down, becoming a Mahatma. Sitting within the Mahatma, He Himself tells us, 'There is some Power in you, who is waiting for you, and who is the main cause of all of this creation. And if you obey me and follow me, I will make you go within yourself and make you see the one who made you.'"

— Ajaib Singh

The Saints want no personal adulation. For those who were devoted to Jesus, Kirpal Singh would say, "Go inside and meditate and you will be able to see Jesus, who is on the inner planes. Ask him about your initiation." Jesus had appeared to some of his devotees and told them to get initiated into meditation by Masters Kirpal and Ajaib Singh.

The true Masters understand, even though we Christians do not have the whole picture because so many of Jesus' teachings have been deleted from the Bible. Unfortunately, his secret journey to India was not revealed, so that Christians could have felt comfortable about meeting a living Master. When Jesus said, "No one cometh to the Father except through Me," he was affirming that only through a living Master like himself can anyone gain salvation. The genuine Masters have the wisdom to guide the Soul through the dark inner regions back to *Sat Lok,* or *Sach Khand* and to take on others' *karmas* in order to save their Souls.

I remember being in an audience of six thousand while listening to a respected teacher of Vedanta speak in Bombay. I looked up and saw a bright electric blue aura emanating from his body. However, the radiance did not compare with the light emanating from the body of the Master Saint Ajaib Singh. The bright white light radiating from him was of another region and of such intensity that I, in my unfit state, could not always keep my eyes upon it. The Soul, after traversing only the first three regions, takes on the intensity of twelve suns in brightness. This description does not even begin to touch the luminosity of a Master Saint.

Truly, the Master Saint, who has been commissioned by the Supreme Lord of *Sach Khand,* or *Sat Lok* to take the Souls back to their original home, does not come to start a religion or to provide new concepts and theories about God. This journey is not a pursuit of mental concepts; it is an engagement for the Soul. When Santji spoke before thousands, many initiates had the impression that he was speaking uniquely to them. The Master has the ability to manifest himself in many places at once and to perform tasks on many levels simultaneously. So even though he is not able to be present, the Master can help those in need. He may have to undergo excruciating pain for the sake of one of his dear initiates who is in trouble. A friend of mine once said that, although she was in casts up to her knees for several weeks, Santji told her that she would have had to endure the likes of the guillotine to pay off a *karmic* debt. He had helped her by lightening her suffering.

It is the job of the Master Saint to help the initiates pay off their *karmas* before leaving the earth plane, so that they never have to return. Once while in Rajasthan, my husband Philip was sitting near the platform where Santji was giving *darshan* when his whole body went into a tremendous trauma of pain and began shaking. Philip prayed fervently that the pain would leave his Master. Immediately, a bag of blessed food accidentally fell on Phil. On another occasion, a friend was in excruciating pain with boils all over his body without any known cure. When Philip introduced him to the Santji, he reached out and touched the friend. Philip cried out that Santji should not heal the man and therefore, suffer for it. Philip had merely wished for Santji to bless his friend. A few days later, the individual was healed forever of his incurable ailment.

We cannot comprehend the powers that are blessing our lives in so many unseen ways. The Master, upon initiation, controls all the *karmas* of his devotees. If one hand is laid unnecessarily on the initiate by the Negative Power in the afterworld, the Master Saint has permission, because of the agreement with Kal, to go into all the hells and liberate all of the Souls. This power is truly "protection" by the Master.

"Truth is the Supreme, the Supreme is Truth. Through Truth men never fall from the higher worlds because Truth belongs to the Saints. Therefore, they rejoice in Truth."

— Yajur Veda,

Not only do the Masters help individuals, the meditation of the Masters is essential to the welfare of the whole world. Meditation is badly needed here in the earth realm to balance out the negativity.

In 1963, when China was on the brink of invading India, Kirpal Singh stopped the impending disaster. Many Indians had believed that Kirpal Singh alone could accomplish such a task. When they asked for his help, he very humbly said that he would pray to his Master Sawan Singh (who had already passed away) to prevent the invasion of this holy land. Suddenly, without explanation, the Chinese turned back and did not invade India. Santiji has said of Kirpal Singh that he could stop canons from exploding in their targets.

Since Santji is no longer with us in physical form, for the time being, no one known to us can open the doors of initiation to the real inner highway home for new aspirants. Only a true living Master Saint can burn up the lifetime *karmas* by taking it upon himself. Santji is not with us for the same reason that both his teachers, Sawan Singh and Kirpal Singh, left their physical bodies early. The heavy *karmas* that these Saints must burn up when they give initiations are so great that their physical frames are weakened, so they typically do not live as long as they ordinarily could have. Santji said that the life of the Masters such as Kirpal and Sawan was shortened by ten to twenty years because of the taking on *of karmas.*

"The Sky is on fire and the fire is coming down. If there were no Saints in this world, then it would have been burnt."

— Ajaib Singh

Chapter Twenty-eight

Life of a Saint

Sant Mat means the "Path of the Saints." The path is based upon the principles of following of the inner light and sound through rarified realms up to the Fifth Region, called *Sat Lok* or *Sach Khand,* the eternal and original home of the Souls where the Lord *Sat Purush* resides. *Sant Mat* is based upon *Guru bhakti* or devotion to the living Guru Saint. The Guru Saint is what Jesus refers to as "the Word made flesh." He is God who has come in the form of a man. He is one who left the ego behind and followed the practice of light and sound to reach *Sat Lok* and beyond. By the power of such a God-realized Saint, who has been commissioned by his Master to take the Souls back to *Sat Lok,* the realms of light and sound are opened up by using the technique of *Simran* and *Bhajan.* This practice is often called *Sehaj Yoga.* The Sound Current of *Bhajan* and the *Simran (the holy Mantra)* act to pull the Soul up to more and greater rarified regions to the Soul's destination of origin.

Out of compassion for the fallen Souls who were caught up in the realms of experimentation and grosser experiences of the Causal, Astral and Physical Regions, *Sat Purush* sent His messengers. Their mission was to awaken the lost Souls from their bondage, free them forever from the snares of illusion, and guide them through the first five regions. Then *Sat Purush* guides the

Souls back through the remaining higher regions. To accomplish this extraordinary feat, *Sat Purush* sent the first Soul in a long lineage of "spiritual giants," beginning with the Soul of Kabir who has incarnated in each of the four *yugas* or major time periods. During each of these incarnations, Kabir inaugurated several lines of Masters. In the *Kali Yuga,* Kabir incarnated as a Muslim weaver in Benares, India in the 15th Century. Ajaib Singh is considered to be the eighteenth Master of this lineage.

Ajaib Singh's early life had one prominent theme: his search and preparation to meet God. Born in a Sikh family on September 11, 1926, Bhatindu, Punjab, India, he was adopted by a great-uncle and his wife after the death of his mother while giving birth. This unexpected tragedy was followed by his father's death only a few days later. His search for truth began at the age of five. Even at that young age, he would arise early to read the scriptures of Guru Nanak, the founder of the Sikh religion. Santji would dwell upon the book so much that he would dream of the scriptures.

Santji's first experience with a *Guru,* or spiritual teacher, was when he met a *sadhu* (spiritual adept) who could change himself into various animal forms. Although an interesting phenomenon, this power did not interest Santji. He was clear that it was only God whom he sought, so he left this teacher.

Santji's search took him to another *Guru* who worked many miracles, but again these phenomena did not interest Santji. However, the teacher gave him a *mantra* to repeat "Hey Ram, Hey Govind," so he practiced its repetition incessantly. Later, in an attempt to purify himself further, Santji performed a very difficult ritual of enduring the heat of four fires for forty days. Daily he would sit in the center of four burning fires while the blazing sun overhead reached temperatures of 130°. However, this practice, well known in India, did not help him find God.

Although Santji sought out many teachers, one by the name of Baba Bishan Das captured his attention because, as he described it, "I saw that he had something real." Although Santji tried for ten years to receive something "real" from Bishan Das, he only got rebuffs and slaps, which Santji described as "sweeter to me than the smiles of other *sadhus.*" One may wonder at the strange ways of such a *Guru,* but Santji's *Guru* did not wish to fuel the fire of the mind's biggest enemy, so he would not do anything to give the aspirant a reason for pride. On the contrary, Bishan Das would take Ajaib's money and send him away from the ashram that had been built with his donations. Santji knew this was a test of the teacher who was a true *Guru,* for he would ask his disciple to serve without any pride.

In the early 1940's, Ajaib Singh was drafted into the army and served for about seven years. During parade duty, Santji would repeat his *mantra* "Hey Ram, Hey Govind," until he was excused by his overseeing British officer who said Santji was "like a father" to him. Free from that duty, Santji was able to expand his spiritual practices. Since his regiment was stationed near Beas in the Punjab, Santji was able to meet the famous Master Sawan Singh, who initiated thousands into the *Simran* and *Bhajan.* When Santji made the acquaintance of the great Master, then in his eighties, he was told to wait because the one who would initiate him would come on his own to see Santji. Nevertheless, Santji would often go to see Sawan Singh and to hear his discourses. Later Sawan Singh would pass the lineage on to Kirpal Singh.

Upon being discharged from the Army, Santji returned home to work on his father's farm. At this time, Bishan Das, his first Guru, walked 25 miles to the farm to see Ajaib and to give him the first two of the five Holy Names. He told him that he would receive the other three names from one who would come to him.

Then Bishan Das proceeded to transfer all of his spiritual powers to Santji through his eyes since Ajaib Singh was the only initiate of Bishan Das. The next day he died. Because Santji saw that Bishan Das knew the truth, he always loved him dearly. In the end, he was rewarded for that devotion by receiving the gift of Bishan Das' spiritual powers.

"The wondrous and luminous form of the Master—only a true Master can make manifest to the spirit."

— Guru Nanak

After some twenty years, upon receiving inner orders from Bishan Das, Santji moved to Kunichuk in northern Rajasthan and built an ashram. There Ajaib continued to work on a farm and supported the feeding of many devotees who came to him because they felt the nectar emanating from his meditation practice. Although Santji was developing a reputation as a very holy man, he did not initiate anyone. In his meditation, he began to see the radiant form of his true master, Kirpal Singh. One year later in 1967, Kirpal Singh arrived at his door. Kirpal Singh initiated him immediately in a private room without giving any explanation of the practice of *Simran* and *Bhajan,* for Kirpal Singh stated that Ajaib already knew what to do. Further, he insisted that Santji sit on a chair rather than sitting on the floor during initiation.

Santji's relationship with the Master in the physical world lasted for seven years. Although Kirpal Singh had initiated up to 125,000 people and was exceedingly busy, he would slip away quietly from his ashram in Delhi to see his beloved disciple Ajaib. Without telling a soul, he would return covered with dust from the journey to rural Rajasthan. On one of those visits, in the spring of 1972, Kirpal told Santji that Santji would be carrying on the work of *Naam* initiation. In spite of Santji's protests, Kirpal had him conduct a full initiation for fifty people at the ashram at that time.

Kirpal told him, "Ajaib Singh, I am very pleased with you. I want to give you something." Then Ajaib describes, "Maharaj-ji passed His very life and power into my Soul through his eyes. I begged the Master not to do this, as I feared it would not be long before he would leave us."

"The Sat Guru is unreachable. He is formless. Even though He has a body, still He is bodiless. And with the grace I have reached there. I have also absorbed myself in Him."

— Guru Nanak

Then Kirpal ordered Santji to walk away from the Kunichuk Ashram, the farm, and to leave everything. He was to go full time into meditation. Santji went to another Rajasthan village, called 16 PS, and stayed on the farm of an associate in an underground room. He remained there for two years in full *samadhi,* only coming out for a light meal once a day. However, he emerged from his life in the cave a few days before the passing of Sant Kirpal Singh in August of 1974.

Upon hearing of his Master's passing, Santji went immediately to the Sawan Ashram in Delhi to pay his respects. because of all of the political carryings on of some ambitious disciples, Santji was not there long before he was escorted back to the train station. However, one disciple recognized that the eyes of Ajaib were the same as Kirpal's and told a Western disciple, who was prominent in the group. This disciple later sought out Santji, and, after great effort, persuaded Santji to come out of hiding despite his tremendous sorrow over the loss of the physical presence of his beloved Master Kirpal Singh.

The fully accomplished Master, Ajaib Singh, understood what a loss the passing of his great Master and Guru was. Having the inner radiant form of the Master is phenomenal, yet there is no measuring the tremendous experience of being in the physical presence of one such as Kirpal Singh. As the saying goes "it takes one to know one." Santji has wisely said, "Who wants to be a *Guru*? What is there in being a *Guru*, tell me that? Is it not better to be a disciple?"

For this reason, Santji insisted that his own disciples not give out his whereabouts to anyone searching for Kirpal Singh's successor. In spite of this admonishment, the Grace radiated out from that tiny village, so that thousands of initiates from around the world found their way to him. With their influence, Santji left his desert retreat many times to travel throughout India and to other parts of the world, including North and South America, Europe and Australia. Even as his fame grew internationally, thousands sought him out in Rajasthan where he conducted many discourses in 16 PS and a larger facility in 77 RB.

Both at home and abroad, thousands have become virtuous because they have come to know the Soul from the standpoint of direct experience. Santji offered many beautiful words to clarify the spiritual concepts during his discourses, but nothing would compare to the Grace which was transmitted from Master Saint to disciple. So that all the words of instruction came alive at the time of initiation. For during initiation, the Saint enters the Soul and reveals the secrets of the glory of God and his sacred Messenger. The language is beyond description, beyond time and space. The reality puts our earthly sojourn into another realm.

"We are given a taste of Truth. We are shown the way of love and we care not for all else, but for our sacred and holy Master had come to remove all pain and suffering. Offering his Self as a sacrifice to those who seek Him out. He has made the ultimate gesture."

— *Sant Mat* Master

Sadly, many years have gone by since the great Sant Ajaib Singh passed on in June of 1997. At the time, my daughter was only three years old, but she spoke of a dream about Santji. Upon awaking in wonderment, she exclaimed that Santji appeared to tell her that she should not worry, that he would take her home. A few hours later, we heard of his passing. The Saint had taken on so much *karma* of others, that he left his body too soon. He made the ultimate sacrifice by offering his life to those whom he had initiated, so that they too would become free.

Many initiates have visions that verify Santji's service to mankind. My husband Philip kindly shared a vision in which he saw a long parade of initiates walking behind Santji. They were all being escorted, by the thousands, into *Sach Khand.*

There is no way that we through our own efforts can achieve our own liberation in this *Kali Yuga*. Life is short and our lives are too distracted to accomplish much. Only the cries of suffering Souls—heard by the Lord of *Sach Khand* — bring the Saints down to us for humble service and sacrifice. Of all the *Yogis, Swamis, Gurus* and *Rimpoches* whom I have come to know and appreciate, there was no one who could come near to what my sacred teacher, Sant Ajaib Singh, has done for me. No other Master has ever shown me the true meaning of God's Love.

Chapter Twenty-nine

Where Did We Come From?

When we start out on the spiritual journey, we begin to question how we came to be in such a condition that we need to find a Master to show us our true nature. We begin to wonder just who are we and where did we come from? The various scriptures describe that we, as Souls, fell into these physical bodies to be able to experience the various enjoyments that the bodies have to offer. Then we became stuck, thus limiting our original sacred all-expansive consciousness. That is to say, we forgot our limitless state of oneness. In this context, limitless means without restraint, without restriction, and totally free. After becoming trapped and limited, we began to look for qualities of our true limitless nature in the finite world. Not finding them there, we became unhappy. Just how happy can we be when innately we know our nature to be total freedom, yet we feel so restricted?

The mind, senses, and body were designed to serve the Soul. Through the process described above, the Soul became a slave to them. The truth of the matter is that we belong to the One and are none other than the One. While identifying and serving the many, we have forgotten our true nature. Now we are stuck on a wheel of delusion, searching for the perfect world, trying to create a perfect life. We can never be really successful at the game of happiness since we remain *karmically* bound to play by the rules of the Lord of Matter. In this sense, we must be saved — saved from the ignorance of knowing our true nature, and saved from the *karmic laws* that dictate a payback to the Lord of the Physical, Astral and Causal Regions in which we inhabit.

The *Sant Mat* scriptures describe the fall of the Souls into the Causal Region, then the grosser Astral Region, then into the grosser body of the Physical Region. As something becomes grosser, it becomes more restricted, more limited. The more limitation, the greater the unhappiness. The All-Expansive-Conscious-One is trapped in a bottle — a body of nine leaking holes: the nine openings of the senses in the physical body, which are two eyes, two ears, two nostrils, a mouth, anus and genitalia.

In the descent from pure beings, initially, the Souls were caught up in the Causal Region, the first stop where Souls hang out if they have fallen out of the truth. Although this region is very subtle and refined, it is a place of complete ignorance, just as a seed does not know itself yet as a tree. The Causal Region is where the road map for the individual Soul is stored. The simplicity and purity at this level imply an experience of bliss. At one time, we identified with the bliss of this realm of existence and became separated from the truth of our nature. It is like a person who joins some friends for a party. Eventually, everyone in the group is expected to contribute something to the conversation, to participate. In the Causal Region, we mixed with the various subtle experiences to become an experiencer. Then we became a Causal Being.

As our Souls descended into matter, we eventually became grosser as we identified with the lower Astral Regions. Once again the experiencer becomes identified with the various experiences. In the same way, we identify with the characters and predicaments at the movies, then mentally take on their trials and tribulations.

We take the movie to be real. The problem is that the identification comes at a price, for we cannot be in a world without taking from it. Therefore, we are obligated to give back to it.

Eventually, we are born in a physical body to be able to live out the experiences in the Physical Region. This earth reality has its own eras, or cycles of time. The first *yuga* was called the *Golden Yuga*, the next was the Silver, and the third was Copper. The current age is the fourth, the *Kali Yuga*, or the Iron Age. The *Kali Yuga* began with the great battle described in the *Bhagavad Gita*. Each *yuga* lasts for eons, according to the calculations of the Hindu sages.

In terms of the number and intensity of challenges for the human being, each *yuga* is considered to be increasingly more difficult. For example, in earlier *yugas*, one lived much longer. In the previous Copper Age, for example, the life span of an individual was about a thousand years. Also, the Bible records cases of individuals living up to one thousand years during the *Kali Yuga*, back in the days of Moses. During earlier *yugas*, people were said to be "breatharians"; that is, they could live on air. Their bodies must have been much subtler at that time. The religious practices were more rigorous, yet easier to perform, since the beings were purer and closer to their godly natures. Evil, or separation, was supposed to have crept in about the time of what has been referred to as the Atlantian era.

Two factions are believed to have existed in Atlantis. The good group remembered their nature as one with God, while the other group began feeling more and more separate from God, and, therefore, took up activities based on a sense of separateness. The mind, feeling separate, took on the attributes of greed and ego. From this sense of separation, other emotions, based upon fear and desire, began to dominate the culture. A faction of the population, called by many psychics and teachers as the Sons of Bellallial, came into existence. Many scholars and psychics believe that these Sons of Bellallial were responsible for the demise of Atlantis and the sinking of that continent with nuclear explosions.

Likewise, in the ancient obscure texts of South India such as the *Siddhanta* tradition of Tamil Nadu, there is mention of an earlier culture that used flying machines and nuclear warfare. In addition, during a war, the soldiers would use *mantras,* or incantations, when they shot their weapons. This practice suggests they understood the capacity of mental powers to ensure a successful outcome.

So the last *yuga,* the *Kali Yuga,* is the only one in which liberation comes easily. Several Sanskrit texts say that at the *Kali Yuga's* height, individuals will not live past twenty. Further, the *Kali Yuga* is a time of chaos and pronounced evil, which rampages out of control. However, there is another point of view. One text describes the scene of an individual running through the forest yelling, "Hurray, hurray, it's the *Kali Yuga.*" Everyone looked at him in total disgust, questioning, "What could you possibly say that's good about the *Kali Yuga?*" The individual replied, "It's because in the *Kali Yuga,* it is so easy to get liberated."

Instead of spending many hundreds of years of doing spiritual practices, one may perform them in decades. If we are sincere, there is also no trouble finding spiritual teachings and even a personal spiritual teacher. In previous *yugas,* we would have had to perform austerities and meditate until a teacher would *accept* us as disciples for further instruction. The sacred teaching was on a one-on-one basis — not given before crowds of thousands, as I have seen in India.

Interestingly, the *Anurag Sagar,* an ancient text, states that the One who frees the Souls to go back to their real home in *Sat Lok* would only be able to incarnate in the *Kali Yuga.* The unusual power of this time is referenced in the Bible when Jesus said, "For every good action performed, it will be rewarded by God a thousand fold." The *Kali Yuga* is very intense, for good and evil are at war. The battle portrayed in the *Bhagavad Gita* was an unavoidable solution to the dangers of evil overcoming good. In this battle, Lord Krishna, the *Guru,* explains to Arjuna, the student and soldier, that, in this realm, *karmas* are swift and exact. Bad actions reap bad results, while good actions are rewarded with good results. The only way out is the path of liberation.

In earlier *yugas,* spiritual seekers performed many practices over hundreds, even thousands, of years. The mythology of India, as depicted in the *Puranas,* is full of references of beings who, because of their practice of austerities, were given positions of power to rule over others. Kal Niranjan had performed so many spiritual practices that he was given the authority to reign over the three worlds. The *Anurag Sagar* recounts that Kal, the Lord of Judgment, is as exacting in his *karmic* retributions as time. Incidentally, *"kal"* is the Hindi word for "time," also meaning, "tomorrow" and "yesterday."

Kal operates in the mind of the individual as *self-judgment.* He operates in his three regions, the Physical, Astral, and Causal Regions as the ruler. In these three realms there are varying degrees of heavens and hells, which are described by the Buddhists as the realm of 3,000 worlds — all existing simultaneously. Kal is the justice keeper, the enforcer of the exact balance, in whose domain every action begets an equal and opposite reaction. Each action is counted, so that rewards and punishments in the realm of Kal are swift and sure.

Table 9. The Four Great *Yugas*

Yuga	Meaning	Duration	Human Life span
1) Sat	Golden Age	1,728,000 years	100,000 years

The Age of Truth in which there is happiness and bliss.

Yuga	Meaning	Duration	Human Life span
2) Treta	Silver Age	1,296,000 years	10,000 years

The Avatar Lord Rama incarnated, his mission is recounted in epic, The Ramayana.

Yuga	Meaning	Duration	Human Life span
3) Dwapar	Bronze Age	864,000 years	1,000 years

The Avatar Lord Krishna incarnated and the Mahabarata War took place anywhere from 2,900 B.C. to 7,000 B.C. This may have correlated to the time of the floods reported around the world.

Yuga	Meaning	Duration	Human Life span
4) Kali	Iron Age	432,000 years	100 years and less

Lineage of Masters established for this "Dark Age" in which evil prevails.

Chapter Thirty

Reincarnation: Recycling of Life

Human birth is rare. In the book, *Tibetan Book of the Dead and Beyond,* it is stated that the chance of getting a human birth to be able to have the opportunity of improving one's lot is as rare as a tortoise swimming to the top of a 3,000 mile ocean, finding a loop, then jumping through it. Liberation is only possible with a human birth because the human form has the capacity for the greatest consciousness. The ancient texts of Asia and Egypt are full of explanations of the rarity and importance of human birth. Therefore, they emphasize the choices one must make to better oneself. These books also mention the journey of the Soul and reincarnation. The few passages about reincarnation in the Bible are not easily discernable because the Bible has been so heavily edited by the church fathers. During the Middle Ages, they removed most references about reincarnation in order to control the peasants. That is, teaching them that if they worked hard and were obedient to the authorities, they would go straight to heaven.

In 325 A.D. Constantine deleted references to reincarnation in the New Testament. This was confirmed in the Second Council of Constantinople in 533 A.D. Reincarnation was declared a heresy. The Gnostics, Clement of Alexandria, Origen and St. Jerome, among others, believed that they would live again.

Today, serious scientific research is being conducted at three separate and respectable universities to prove the phenomenon of reincarnation.

There are so many references to reincarnation in our modern body of literature that one need not look far to realize that we are not the physical cages that imprison us. We are a Soul that moves in and out of experiences in order to satisfy desires, to reconnect with loved ones, and to pay the universe back for any past mistakes and to enjoy the positive benefits of good actions of the past.. In many cases, individuals experience inexplicable feelings when they look into the eyes of a stranger. The mythological cupid is really a past life recognition of two Souls rediscovering one another. Many are unable to explain these attractions. These encounters seem to surpass our mental constructs of how to create and sustain a profound long-term relationship. The window of the Soul is the eyes. Such a relationship usually begins with one glance, if even across a room. Then a cosmic choice is made for that individual, the relationship of *karmic* give and take will begin again.

I remember so well the birth of my son, Matthew. At the moment he was delivered, I heard myself exclaim the words "orphan" and "teacher." Years later, a psychic, who had no prior knowledge of my life, explained that my son had been an orphan in India. At that time, I was a nun in a temple who took on the responsibility of mothering and caring for him. During those years, I had always wished that he could have a normal and happy life. The psychic also explained that I would learn a lot from my relationship with him. Perhaps I had this recognition of him because I did not take any mind-dulling drugs at the time of his birth. Also, I had done a lot of meditation over the years, which created a certain sensitivity, so that, when I looked into his eyes, there could be Soul recognition. The day he was born was one of the happiest of my life.

As a gift to our newborn Matthew, a dear friend of mine had his astrological chart done by a traditional astrologer in South India. Matthew's chart showed that his parents would move a lot. It has been over thirteen years since his birth, and Matthew has lived in nine different houses. My husband Philip is a developer/contractor; therefore, we have done a lot of house jumping, even living in rentals when our houses were not completed on time. The reading also indicated Matthew's innate artistic ability, as well as his talent in math and science. He has done very well in these three subjects. The astrologer also said that he would have a sister. Lo and behold, seven years later, his sister arrived in our household.

One need not meditate, however, to experience *karma,* or give and take, based upon a past-life relationship. Years ago, before I started meditating, I had a challenging relationship with one woman whom I dearly loved, yet she could not always appreciate my expressions of good will. I found out from a psychic that we had been mother and daughter in a past life. She, the daughter, may have been still trying to break away from "the mother" in this life. At any rate, I could not explain my feelings of love for her, nor the pain I would feel when she would not want to see me as often as I wanted to see her.

One thing is clear, words cannot express the grief of the loss of a dear one who dies, or the sense of regret over not having been able to convey our love or wish farewell to the departed. We think of so many things that we would have liked to have done for the departed one — if only we had known. So, it makes sense that, when we reunite in another birth, we are so happy to see one another again, on the Soul level, that we feel an instant bond.

Perhaps, after the novelty has worn off, we repeat the experience of sharing the mundane life and of taking each other for granted.

I remember hearing Santji tell a story about a *Sant Mat* initiate who was at the point of liberation, except he had one great attachment: his family. He could not leave the members of his household. Out of attachment, he even assumed the form of a worm in the family garden just to be able stay close to them. After death, his *Guru* had to show him what sacrifices he had made just to be near his family members. So after three different incarnations, the Guru was asking him — now have you had enough? Then the *Guru* asked him if he was ready to be liberated and move on.

If the world is in such perfect order in its workings from the molecular level on up, then why would that orderliness not apply in our own lives? Why must we assume that God is competent with the physical universe, but fails in matters of our private lives? No one could have told me that I would have found the loves of my life in my husband and children. Since I am one who gave up everything for fifteen years in my search for God-realization, I now have to say that I have been given everything — and more. I have a beautiful family, a beautiful home, and many wonderful friends. I keep thinking about the passage in the Bible, "Seek ye first the Kingdom of God and all else shall be given to you."

Many initiates have similar experiences in their lives. They all say that when they meditate everything that they want seems to come very quickly. When they don't meditate, life becomes more of a struggle. We all have our *karmic* obstacles to pay off. If this life is our last, the *karma* is often much heavier. In any event, meditation puts us into a peaceful frame of mind, so that we are better able to endure the blows that our *karmic* life has to offer.

No doubt, after thousands of these lifetimes, we become fed up and have such a longing for God that we think of nothing more than to get out of here and return to the source of love. This feeling is greater than any other feeling; it propels one through life to the feet of the Master Saint and beyond.

Chapter Thirty-one

Death Is Inevitable

A Master Saint can help us face the stark realities of life. In the realm of Kal, death is inevitable. Although we all know this fact, there is so much denial around it — especially in the U.S. It is as though we are pretending that somehow the people who are around us will always be there and that life is going to remain the same forever. However, everyone gets glimpses of life's uncertainty some time or the other, so we cannot remain in denial forever.

When I was living at the ashram in India, where I studied, Vedanta for two-and-a-half years, death was a visible fact of life. In the women's hostel, I witnessed the death of the doctor who lived two doors away and the near death of the beautiful young woman next door. Then there was the massacre of one litter of puppies by some wild dogs in the neighborhood. Six months later the same mother dog had to protect her babies by holding back a slithering six-foot green snake. After barking for hours, she finally won and the snake retreated. In that country, the elderly and infirm do not disappear into hospitals to do the unspeakable act of dying. In India, death is part of the process of life. They have a religion that assures them of rebirth. On the contrary, what do we have in the West?

At the time the Vedanta course was coming to a close in Bombay, I experienced another dilemma. Although my friend

Piilani had a liver problem, in a moment of weakness, she had eaten some meat outside of the ashram. She became so violently ill that she contracted cholera. She insisted that we take her to a naturopathic facility, rather than a regular hospital. However, as the days passed, she became increasingly ill. In the end, we had to make a decision to put her into a regular hospital because she was dying. Even though she was in a semi-conscious state, she fought the attempts to hook her up to intravenous feeding since she hated needles so.

Hoping to get some answers about the situation, a friend went to an Indian astrologer. The astrologer told her that if Piilani lived past 8:00 p.m. on Tuesday, she would live a long, but difficult, life. She died a few minutes before 8:00 p.m. on that Tuesday. It was such a sad evening for all of us.

The next day all the students at the ashram of Vedantic study gathered to chant and pray. Piilani had instructed us if she should die in India that she wanted to be cremated there. Since she was psychic, she must have had some premonition about her own demise. At her death, I told the resident *Swami* about her wishes, so all the details were carried out according to the Hindu customs for cremation.

A week or so later, while I was meditating, Piilani appeared in my room to give me an apology. She said that she was sorry that she had said bad things about me to a mutual friend, Georgette. Even though I was not sure who was doing the talking, I replied, "Didn't you know how much I loved you by the look on my face at the hospital?"

Later I went to speak with Georgette to find out if and what Piilani might have said about me. When I asked a simple question, Georgette told me the whole story. She told me that Piilani had been jealous of me because I seemed to be doing well, while she had been struggling with health problems and had trouble keeping up with the studies. She had grown to resent me and would complain about me to Georgette. I was so shocked. I felt like I had lost my dear friend in more ways than one.

At the end of the course of Vedantic studies, I went to South India because the ghost of Piilani was continuing to bother me. A temple priest who knew the science of rituals for special situations had invited me to South India so that he could perform a series of rituals to release her Soul from the earth plane. He had detected the problem while visiting our ashram. The long journey on an Indian train was quite arduous, for my health was declining. The poor diet and infestation of parasites in my intestines were taking their toll on my diminishing one-hundred-pound frame. I did not realize, at that time, I was also suffering from bouts of tuberculosis, which were weakening me more.

The rituals were phenomenal. They were directed toward the feminine aspect of God. I experienced my mind expanding to states of ecstatic joy and supreme peace. Afterwards, I traveled further south to a very ancient temple and ashram where I met several American students. At that time, I was experiencing great sorrow for not being God-realized. Feeling that I could no longer stand being separate from God, I was experiencing many different states of longing and withdrawal. Only God understood my pain. The *Guru* at the ashram said that I was very close to realizing God, but I found little consolation in words.

At that time, through the help of a close Indian friend, I was also able to visit the ancient monastery and center for the study of Vedanta at Shringeri in South India. When I met with the holy head of the monastery, he explained that my weak physical condition had left me susceptible to Piilani's apparition. He instructed me to return to the United States to get stronger physically.

Even though I was very disappointed at being advised to return to U.S., I do believe if I had not followed that advice, I would have died in India. There is no measuring the experiences of immersing oneself in that ancient religious culture. Yet I did not obtain a sense of completion in spite of all my wonderful experiences and connections. I remained disappointed that I had not reached a place of God-realization, or what is called in Vedanta *"nishta,"* being rooted in God-realization.

In the meantime, I had heard of the emergence of a perfect Saint in Rajasthan. The idea intrigued me, but I had no easy means of getting there. Many times, I regretted not just getting on a train and going there on my own to search him out. As satisfying as the profound explanations of the texts of Vedanta were, I had an equally profound longing for God that sometimes was so painful I could hardly walk without feeling a sense of separation from God. I knew I needed more than intellectual concepts.

Chapter Thirty-two

Negative Realms of Experience

There are numerous realms of experience. We can enter some realms that are awesome and frightening during near-death experiences and also during meditation. At these times, we realize what a blessing it is to have the protection of a Master Saint. Interestingly, because of modern medical techniques, death has been found to be an entrance into other realms. A well-known physician has been conducting extensive studies of near-death experiences. Hundreds of patients who were interviewed reported similar experiences at the time of death. They all describe that they saw their lives flash before them and that they saw a beautiful light, which some of them referred to as Jesus. They were also told that they had to go back to earth because it wasn't time to pass on to the other side since they still had duties remaining to be accomplished on earth.

I once met a woman who told me that she had had a heart attack and left the body. At that time, she had been declared clinically dead. However, she was not allowed to follow the light because she was told that she still had things to do here on earth. She said that she was "so disappointed" to have to return back to her earthly life. She remembers how buoyant and wonderful she felt without her heavy physical body. While out of her body, she had recognized relatives who had passed on before her. She also saw a luminous light, which she thought was Jesus. At that moment, she was resuscitated and brought back into her body. A few weeks after speaking with this woman, I saw four or five near-death patients interviewed on a television program. They all described events similar to hers.

In other ancient cultures around the world, there are books and treatises on the death process. One of the most famous is the *Tibetan Book of the Dead.* These ancient books explain the rarity of the human birth and the importance of making use of this opportunity to ensure a happy afterlife. In reality, the sum total of all thoughts, when flashed before one's consciousness, gives an overall summary that dictates where one must go to play out the next experiences. A guide is needed to help escort the Soul through the various *Bardos,* or regions, as described in the books. With the Master Saint there is no *Bardo,* the Soul is just taken out of these realms entirely.

Many religions talk about hell, just as they talk about heaven. Not all of the near-death experiences are positive. Some people describe being surrounded by ghouls just like Lord Shiva's entourage. We are familiar with states of mind and places on earth that correspond to our idea of heaven and hell. Some people experience places that could be considered heaven and hell after taking drugs. Often the influence of the drug can be an actual fracturing of the mind, breaking through to the astral world. These worlds are where the Souls get their just reward for good and bad actions on earth as a way of progressing and purifying themselves.

Once when I first began meditating, I had two amazing experiences of a type of hell. I don't understand how or why, but once I somehow fell into one world where people were beating up on each other. I had to say the name of a _Swami_ in order to get out of there. I conjectured that my habit of smoking cigarettes at that time had debilitated my _prana,_ life force, which connects the mental and physical body. This impurity had probably brought me to these lower astral realms.

Another time I was meditating and fell into a world where astral beings were climbing up a steep cave-like cavern with heavy loads on their backs in a very steamy, hot environment. No sooner did I see the scene than I was out of it again. A friend of mine, who also meditates regularly, described seeing a hellish world where everyone had to keep jumping to avoid stepping on snakes. Later, after initiation into a higher form of meditation, I no longer experienced these occasional glimpses into lower astral realms while trying to meditate. After initiation, I had a powerful _mantra_ to protect me.

In the _Bhagavad Gita,_ the student Arjuna was given a direct vision of God in his gigantic and frightening form. Although he expressed his appreciation at seeing the Lord in his horrific form, the frightened Arjuna begged the Lord to show his normal form again. This image was similar to the Lord of the Old Testament who extols, "An eye for an eye and a tooth for a tooth." This vision was of Kal, the Negative Power, who rules the first three regions.

Some spiritual books, in particular the popular, trendy, bestseller genera, state that the experience on earth is a journey of lessons and learning. Life is a righteous and positive sojourn where there is no punishment in the end — just Soul introspection. In my opinion, these books are popular because they provide "nicey nice" descriptions of the power and help of God — without any reference whatsoever to the obvious fact that most of the world is in a critical hell with absolutely no understanding of how to get out of it.

Plants and animals are serving time with no choice or chance of relief. Animals must endure 164 different varieties of suffering in this creation. This fact does not even take into consideration the intense suffering that animals must endure when they are used as milk or egg machines or when they are on their way to be slaughtered. Then there are the 84,000 births as humans in the three worlds of the Negative Power.

The tendency of young people to experiment to be able to experience other realities has become rampant in America today. The most worrisome is the consumption and addiction to mind-altering drugs. In our self-indulgent society where pleasure has become a reason for being, many children are selling their minds to the devil, so to speak. Television, radio and print advertising bombard us with advertisements pushing various types of pills for every imaginable problem. It is no wonder that our offspring think that drugs provide the answer to happiness. Thereby, the Negative Power is keeping these people from developing spiritually. Narcotics fragment and shatter the mind. Meditation brings the mind force together, strengthens and focuses it. How can young people learn the joys of spirituality if their astral bodies are blown out with chemicals?

Sadly, it is a very difficult time to raise children because they are taught to seek pleasure in life's experiences as much as possible. Their attention gets dissipated in video games, satellite television, Internet, chat rooms and MTV. The message of this ghetto culture is one of alienation and drowning one's sense of isolation in drugs, alcohol and sexual promiscuity. How can teachers expect a student to be enthusiastic about learning when they must compete for their attention over these temptations?

I am reminded of the words of a psychic after she had watched a play in a theater. She described how she could see the energy pouring out of the eyes of the viewers and being received by the actors on the stage. Thereby, the actors would get psychically energized and their performance would be enhanced because of all the energy given by the audience. Now I think of all the energy being siphoned from teenagers as they get dissipated in the world of stimulation and pleasure of drugs and alcohol.

It requires a lot of work on the part of those who are chemically dependent to rehabilitate themselves. For this reason, the Alcoholics Anonymous program is so powerful. Their basic tenet is reliance on the grace of God. A friend, who was in the program, told me that the amount of grace pouring down during the meetings was incredible. At the meetings, they invoke the prayer:

God grant me the courage to change the things I can change,
The serenity to accept the things that I cannot change,
And the wisdom to know the difference.

These words describe the dilemma of humankind. Not knowing what to do, in our confusion we try to escape the pressures of life with drugs and alcohol. We are godly beings cut off from God. Seeking to escape our condition, we turn to drugs and alcohol for solace.

Many young people have an important destiny to fulfill, but can easily lose sight of the urgings of the Soul when they have been fractured by drugs. Many fear that we have lost the war on drugs. Certainly, it is God's turn to wage the war with programs such as AA and other clinics, which help one to detox the body in conjunction with invoking God's help. AA and other programs, which rely on the powerful force of God to intervene and heal, are the only ones which actually have been successful in helping people come clean with their chemical dependencies. Once, an alcoholic said to me "You know, I even think that being alcoholic was a blessing, because it brought me to God."

In a sense, we are all addicts of one thing or another in life. Therefore, we all must, in one way or another, hit bottom before we turn to God and our salvation. It could be argued that the reason that religion and spirituality are a much bigger part of the ancient cultures around the world is life is not so easy there as we have it in America today.

When life is difficult, we are forced to give up things and to make sacrifices to control our bodies, minds and thoughts. When they do not get dissipated, the mind gets stronger and more disciplined. Is it any wonder that when we compare the test scores of students around the world that the students in the U.S. can compete with the best of them only up to the fourth grade? After that level, the scores begin to drop off. We have to question the toll that television, junk food, and the lack of moral upbringing and discipline have on the students' ability to use their minds. While younger, they still have respect for their parents and teachers. As parents we are losing the battle in having a positive influence on our children.

As a parent and former high school teacher, I am reminded of how far removed the children, and later as adults, can get from the true intentions of life for simple happiness and the joys of sharing and connecting with others. Our current cultural solutions to happiness have turned into a journey into astral hell. We need to about-face and get back to a relationship with our Creator and involve ourselves in service to the world.

Some may reason that meditation is just an escape or even a form of self-indulgence. While it is true that mediation does give one an escape, it is a revitalizing one. As far as self-indulgence, it is the most positive form. This respite from the world improves one's sense of well-being and recharges the energy system, which in turn, makes the person a more positive, productive member of society. By connecting to the Soul in meditation, the mind funnels its energy to work creatively in the world to enact and fulfill the Soul's destiny on earth.

Chapter Thirty-three

Story of Creation

We Westerners have a tendency to negate religion and spiritual life because we cannot see the logic in the spiritual pursuit. With our innate intelligence, we look around and we have to question what we see. If God is love and God created the world, then why is there so much hate, pain and suffering in the world? However, in the Eastern religions, particularly in *Sant Mat,* there is a clear explanation of how the world devolved to become the problem reality we see today — as well as the chaos seen through the centuries. There have been wars and pestilence and plagues since Biblical times. We are intelligent people; we are not going to settle for a canned explanation. We need to understand what is going on.

Thanks to Ajaib Singh, a commentary is now available in English on the ancient text, *Anurag Sagar (Story of Creation),* which describes the entire process of creation. Because the text was written in a pre-Hindi dialect, it is not well known; however, among the Masters, it is one of the most venerated esoteric books of India.

Of this *Story of Creation,* Master Sawan Singh has stated that, without studying this text, no one can truly understand the difference between the negative power Kal and the path of the True and Merciful God, nor can one truly grasp the teachings of *Sant Mat.* Following is a summary of the process of creation according to Santji's commentary on *Anurag Sagar.*

In the Beginning —

The story begins with Sat Purush *(All-Mighty God).*
He was in latent form. Nameless … Formless … Then, in His will he created the Souls, and seeing them, felt very happy. From the very first word, worlds and oceans were created in which He dwelt.
Where Sat Purush *sat, desire was created there.*
In the will of Sat Purush, *88,000 islands were created.*
In all the worlds, His desire exists, and is called very fragrant.

Sat Purush created sixteen sons — one of whom was *Kal Niranjan.* While Souls were the essence of *Sat Purush,* no one knew their beginning or end. In every region, the individual Souls were settled and their food was nectar. Endless happiness existed, for they were always in meditation on *Sat Purush.* All the worlds received light from *Sat Lok* (the Fifth Region) where *Sat Purush* resided.

Even the sun and moon shine with the Light of one hair of Sat Purush.

As time passed, the fifth son, *Kal Niranjan,* performed very difficult austerities. Standing on one foot, he performed devotions to *Sat Purush* for seventy *yugas,* * and thereby pleased *Sat Purush.* When *Sat Purush* asked Kal why he had accomplished such devotion, his son answered that he wanted some place where he

---

* *Yugas* range from 1.5 million years to around 500 thousand years.

might live. Therefore, he was sent to a place called Mansarovar, created by *Sat Purush,* located in *Daswan Dwar,* which is a place in the reaches of the Universe, known as the Third Region. Upon reaching this destination, Kal continued his devotion for another seventy *yugas*; therefore, he was given the ownership of this place where he lived.

Since Kal had distanced himself from *Sat Purush,* his pride became fully developed. Therefore, Kal was not satisfied with his kingdom, so he asked his father for a larger one. He was given the three worlds and told to develop the "void" region where he could create his own universe. The Void Region is the pre-existent state of the three worlds as we know them: the Physical, Astral and Causal Regions. The Void Region is extremely dark and dense and separates the Third Region (of the three worlds) from the Fourth Region.

Wondering how to develop these worlds for maximum benefit to himself he performed austerities of devotion for another sixty-four *yugas* by standing on one foot. Afterwards, he asked *Sat Purush* for the seed for the development of his universe. He was given the first seed of the individual Soul, named *Sohang.*

The seed was to be carried by the beautiful female form Astangi, who went to Mansarovar to create the dense universe. She was given the seed that would create 84,000 births and deaths. This incident was the first time a split between male and female aspects appeared out of the creation of the One. This split occurred because of the fall of Kal. Due to his self-centered nature, Kal swallowed Astangi.

As punishment, *Sat Purush* expelled Kal from Mansarovar and *Sat Lok.* He then ordered Astangi out of the stomach of Kal. Thus, Kal became the creator of sin and virtue, which was the beginning of the Laws of *Karma* in his universe. From the union of the two dualities (male and female), three sons, Brahma, Vishnu and Shiva, were born.

Also, the five elements were created. Each element was progressively grosser, starting with space to earth. Matter was also imbued with three modes of energy in various degrees. These modes were, respectively — *sattwa, rajas* and *tamas* — calmness, activity and inertia. Since every object is constantly in a state of flux and eventually dissolves in time, everything is subject to dissolution. All happens in the realm of time.

Time, in our creation, destroys everything. The word for time is *"kal."* In Kal's domain everything gets eaten up.* Therefore, again and again, the world gets destroyed and no one knows the secret of its beginning. For, in knowing this fact, the Souls would surely seek liberation from Kal's domain.

After giving birth to the three gods, Kal Niranjin instructed his wife to take the three children and rule the world, while keeping his existence a secret. He also instructed her to spread secrets in the world, so that no one would be able to know of *Sat Purush* and liberation. Kal Niranjan then went to reside in the Cave of the Void.

The *Anurag Sagar* further states that all individuals have the impression that Kal is the Inconceivable One, or Hidden One. Kal is referred to as the "negative power," as he involves the world in *karma,* that is, action and reaction. Therefore, individual Souls suffer the pain of birth and rebirth. Kal himself plays the trick of ensnaring them in duality, yet he is the one who gives the Souls the consequences of their actions, or *karmas.* Kal, or the ruler of

---

* In the Hindu text, the *Bhagavad Gita,* Arjuna has a horrific vision of the Ruler of the Three Worlds ferociously eating everything. After this vision, Arjuna asked Krishna about liberation from future reincarnation.

the mind, has become invisible, so one must understand that the mind serves Kal Niranjan. After defeating the mind, one receives knowledge of *Sat Purush*.

It is interesting to note that a tenet of the Biblical Old Testament is the concept of being held accountable: "an eye for and eye, a tooth for a tooth." Whereas, the philosophy of the New Testament centers on "turning the other cheek." In this statement, Jesus is suggesting that we get off of the *Karmic* Wheel by not engaging in a cycle of perpetual actions of revenge. Forgiveness is the way out of a *karmic* quagmire that otherwise could go on forever.

Continuing with the creation story, one of the first actions of Brahma, Vishnu and Shiva was to churn the ocean to bring forth the lower creation similar to the process found in the first chapter of Genesis. The first churning created the Causal Region, the second, the Astral Region, and, the third, the Physical Creation. Out of the churning also appeared three wives for each of the gods.

Out of the gods' lust for each other, numerous demons and gods were born. Out of these deities and demons, further creations occurred — up to a number said to be eighty-four *lakhs*. One *lakh* equals 100,000, so there are 8,400,000 species available for the Soul to experience in distinct incarnations. This figure includes a number of astral and non-physical forms as well. Thus the Soul rises up through a lengthy series of incarnations from minerals to plants, to animals, and finally to the human body — where liberation is possible.

After wandering in the four kinds of creation of minerals, plants and animals, the Soul gets a human body. Further, the Soul acquires the human body after wandering in the cycle of 84,000 births. The cycle is long because the Soul does not want to give up its habits of enjoyment of the world. Additionally, if there are any major transgressions, the Soul may experience the descent back down to the bottom of the ladder.

From whatever forms the Soul has incarnated, the differences in qualities are due to the impressions of other lifetimes, so that some may behave more like animals, whereas others exhibit the highest of human qualities, such as love and understanding, and find themselves contemplating God, rather than contemplating the world.

In the *Anurag Sagar,* the teacher, Kabir, further states that the human body is made for devotion to God. When the student asks the teacher how one removes the effects of one's past lives, the teacher replies that when one meets the *Sat Guru* and he gives the student true Knowledge, then he forgets any "beastliness," just as sandpaper removes rust from metal. However, some persons would comprehend the knowledge with just a little labor while others would require more effort. Moreover, the teacher explains that the student could go to *Sat Lok,* beyond the region of Kal, by using the Sound Current, the *Naam,** given by a Perfect Master.

The Vedas, the earliest books of knowledge, were said to have been given to Brahma, the lord of creation. In the Vedas, the original person is described as being in the form of light in the Void Region consciousness. Thus the Vedas are not higher than the Void Region, but also fall within the realm of Kal. Yet Brahma went on a search for his father. He went to the Region of the Void and sat in meditation, he went into *Samadhi,* but he was never able to meet his father.

So when Brahma returned from the Third Region, he claimed that he had met his creator. Astangi, his mother, cursed him for

---

* *Naam* is synonymous with *Shabda,* Word, or Sound Current, the primordial creative power of God. *Naam* is spoken of in the Christian tradition as well as the spiritual tradition of *Tao Te Ching.*

the falsehood, along with several others who had supported his lie. Because of this failure of Brahma, his creation became cursed with pain and suffering because of being devoted to false ones. Thereby, the devotees of Brahma and the Vedas got no spiritual wealth. His mother did not tell him about *Sat Purush* because Kal supported her and her world. In exchange, she supported and protected him.

Kabir, the First Guru, continued by explaining the dilemma:

"This world is such a play of Kal that not even the priests can understand it. They address Kal as the Lord and, leaving the nectar, drink the poison. Onkar is the root of the Vedas, and out of Onkar all the world is lost. Out of Kal came Brahma, out of Brahma came the Smritis, Shastras and Puranas [the Hindu scriptures and epics].

When Sat Purush saw the pitiful condition of the Souls, he felt mercy for them. Then Kabir stated, 'I was called by the generous, gracious Lord. He explained to me many things and ordered me to awaken the Souls.' When Kabir saw the Souls in the jaws of the Lord of Death, they called out for help. Kabir did help the Souls and explained that, when you come in the [physical] body, you will be absorbed in Sat Shabda, 'the essence of the sound current.' Only then will your Soul go to Sat Lok, the region beyond Kal's domain."

Kabir continued by warning the Souls that if they forgot *Sat Purush*, Kal would devour them. Using his skill, Kal had created many pleasures for the Souls, and no one could know a way to escape them. Birth after birth, they would be punished by him without recognizing the true *Naam*, or nature of God, and the way back to God.

Table 10. Lineage of *Sant Mat* Masters in the *Kali Yuga*

Master	Dates of Lifetime	Age at Start of Mission	Age at Physical Death	Location of Principal Ashram	Religion at Birth
1 Kabir Sahib	1398-1518	?	120	Kashi (Benares)	Muslim
2 Guru Nanak	1469-1539	?	70	Kartapur, Punjab	Hindu
3 Guru Angad	1504-1552	34	48	Khadur, Punjab	Hindu
4 Guru Amardas	1479-1574	83	95	Goindwal, Punjab	Hindu
5 Guru Ramdas	1534-1581	40	47	Amritsar	Hindu/Sikh
6 Guru Arjan	1563-1606	18	43	Amritsar	Hindu/Sikh
7 Guru Har Govind	1595-1644	11	49	Sri Hargobindpur	Hindu/Sikh
8 Guru Hari Rai	1630-1661	14	31	Sri Hargobindpur	Hindu/Sikh

9 Guru Hari Krishan	1656-1664	5	8	Delhi	Hindu/Sikh
10 Guru Teg Bahadur	1621-1675	43	54	Patna, Bihar	Hindu/Sikh
11 Guru Govind Singh	1666-1708	9	42	Anandapur	Hindu/Sikh
12 Sant Ratnagar Rao	no known dates			Poona	Hindu/Sikh
13 Tulsi Sahib	1763-1843	?	80	Hathras, U. P.	Hindu
14 Swami Ji Maharaj	1818-1878	25	60	Agra	Hindu
15 Baba Jaimal Singh	1838-1903	40	65	Beas, Punjab	Sikh
16 Baba Sawan Singh	1858-1948	45	90	Beas, Punjab	Sikh
17 Sant Kirpal Singh	1894-1974	54	80	Delhi	Sikh
18 Sant Ajaib Singh	1926-1997	48	69	16 PS, Rajasthan	Sikh

Chapter Thirty-four

Escape from Kal's Domain

Being a true Master, Kabir made his disciples aware of the Sound Current within by initiating them into this secret science. Thereby, their Souls could follow that glorious and refined sound back through the inner regions to *Sat Lok,* where *Sat Purush* resides. The initiates would also be given the five names of the Lords of the inner regions, whose vibrations would be so powerful that the Souls would be given easy passage through these regions without interference from Kal. The five sacred words, or names of the Lords, refer to the manifestation of the *Naam,* or Sound Current, on each of the five inner regions. Although they may vary in different times, regions or languages, they carry the powerful charge of the Master Initiator and offer protection to the Soul.

In his great compassion, *Sat Purush* promised Kabir that there would be other Masters in the following generation with the power to give liberation, thus insuring the continuity of the path. By this means, those who took the refuge of a Master were able to cross the *Ocean of Life.*

"If one gets a perfect Master, He shows him the Real Path,
And he makes one see the Truth and untruth.
Only He is the perfect Guru who shows the Truth.
Other Gurus are of no use. . . .
If one takes such a Guru, he never has

to take up the body in this world again.
He, on whom Sat Guru is gracious,
Never comes and never goes."

— Guru Granth Sahib

When Kabir first went down to the lower worlds to save the Souls, his name was *Achint*. There he met Kal, who wanted to know why Kabir had come to his region. At that time, Kabir explained that he had come to save the Souls because Kal had been very clever and had deceived them, causing them to forget their true maker and their real home. Therefore, Kabir would free them from the "Ocean of Life." Upon hearing these words, Kal tried to fight with Kabir, who exhibited the power of *Sat Purush* by using the weapon of *Shabda*, the holy Sound Current. Vanquished, Kal fell to his knees begging for a gift from Kabir. Kal said that *Sat Purush* had given him the gift of the Three Worlds because of his great devotion. However, he had also cursed him so that he must devour 100,000 Souls a day to survive. If all the Souls returned to *Sat Lok*, his hunger could not be satisfied.

"Please, in *Sat Yuga, Treta Yuga,* and *Dwapar Yuga* just a few Souls should go back to *Sat Lok*," implored Kal. "When the Fourth Age, the *Kali Yuga* comes, then may many Souls go back with you."

Honoring this request, Kabir agreed to send his incarnations primarily in the *Kali Yuga*. Therefore, in this *Yuga,* there are to be forty-two incarnations in the line of Masters founded by Kabir. These Masters dedicate their lives for only one purpose: sending the Souls back to *Sat Lok*.

With this agreement, Kal tells Kabir, "Even though you will only establish one path to send the Souls back to *Sat Lok,* I will create twelve paths in your name. In this way, I will delude the people." Then Kal planned to take up the body of a *sadhu* named

Jagannath [Lord of the world] and have a great temple built to
worship a false god.

Afterwards, Kabir said, "I will go to the world and bring the
Souls back with the support of *Naam* ... those who take refuge
shall cross the *Ocean of Life.*" Then Kabir went to Lord Brahma
who refuted him, saying the truth was in the Void. Kabir went
to Lord Vishnu who said he didn't need anything since he had
the four substances of *artha* (wealth and power), *kama* (desire),
dharma (service and duty), *moksha* (liberation); further, he could
give these substances to anyone who needed them. But Kabir
challenged Vishnu on having the ability to liberate anyone from
the insecurity of the Three Worlds. Upon hearing of this challenge,
Vishnu became embarrassed because of his lack of power.

In the *Kali Yuga,* Kabir began by establishing four authentic
Gurus who would initiate the Souls into *Naam.* One disciple was
Dharam Das, who Kabir asked to be an initiator of the *Naam,*
stating that the Souls of forty-two incarnations would receive
liberation by taking refuge in him.

"Be absorbed in the Shabd of the Sat Guru
And act according to the Master's orders;
Keep the attention in Naam,
Giving up all doership, illusions and dictates of the mind."

— Kabir

At the time, Kal, in order not to lose the Souls under his
control, created twelve paths, or distortions of the true teaching.
Each of the twelve paths would contain aspects of the truth, but
not all, just enough to keep the Souls trapped. For example, the
first messenger of Kal taught that the disciple was essentially one
with God, and, therefore, required no spiritual practice. This path
ignored the science of the inner regions and the existence of the

Negative Power. Because of this omission, the individual remains in the illusion that no effort is necessary except the knowledge of the unity of the universe with the Soul. Although ultimately the truth, this intellectual non-dualism does not free the Soul from Kal's worlds and the cycles of rebirth. One remains helplessly trapped. To become free requires the initiation in the Light and Sound Current, which, with the grace of the Master, pulls the Soul out of its entrapment and mental constructs to the regions beyond body, mind, intellect and Soul.

The messenger of the second false path will create a trap by telling certain true things. He will teach his followers to worship the sun and the moon and the techniques of astrology, thereby putting the Souls in the trap of *karma*. He will create a reading for all the lines of the body. Then, by creating sixty divisions of time and twelve months, he will create illusions concerning the body. He will tell about the use of the five elements, twenty-five natures, three *gunas,* and fourteen deaths. These qualities will all be called God by him. Following the path of the five elements, the individual perishes. Since the attention is on the elements, the student will go back into the elements. The emphasis on astrology, palmistry, dieting and physical healing are confined to the body. These practices ignore the Soul and keep one trapped in the illusion of *maya* of Kal's domain.

The third messenger is one who claims that "the Origin is with me." He will claim to have the "root *mantra."* He will have his disciples experience the sound current of the lower *chakras* only and create doubts for the individuals. He will claim that sensual experience is identified with mystical experience, thus dragging the practitioner down rather than up. In the "left hand" path of Tantra, the female organ is called the "philosopher's stone," but attention remains on the lower *chakras*. Other rituals using meat, alcohol and drugs are also aspects of this downward path.

The fourth Messenger will be like a Krishna who plays the flute with many female followers, who cannot see past the outer eye to the inner eye. Kal will speak of the shadow mind and call it the means of liberation.

Kabir forecast the challenges we would face in the future, "As long as you remain in the body, Kal will not manifest, but when you withdraw your attention in meditation, he will start his useless talk. Whenever you leave your body consciousness, Kal will come then." Kabir continued by saying, "Those who become helmsmen for the Messenger of Kal will become egoists. Because of their selfishness, they will not recognize the Lord and will mislead the Souls. ... Where there is ego, I am not there and one cannot progress to *Sat Lok.*"

Further, Kabir assures us, "In the *Kali Yuga,* the Soul will become free from Kal by the glory of *Naam.* Those who accept the *Naam* within themselves will become free from the traps laid by Kal. Kal will not come near to those who have faith in the Incarnations [the lineage of Perfect Masters]. Such Souls go across after putting their feet on Kal's head."

Thus the possibility of liberation with the assistance of the forty-two Incarnations began in the *Kali Yuga.* It is the author's sincere hope that *Sat Purush* provides many great Saints to accomplish the feat of helping the Souls back to *Sat Lok* and beyond because they are badly needed around the world.

"I will go to the world and bring the Souls back with the support of Naam. *... [T]hose who take refuge shall cross the Ocean of Life."*

— Kabir

Chapter Thirty-five

Evidence of Fallen Souls in History

Even though the theory of the fallen Souls (or angels) exists in nearly every religion, the concept is often relegated to the realms of myth. However, if we consider that these stories exist in the traditions of the Hindus, Greeks, native Americans, and even the Hebrews, we realize that they may be based on some historical evidence that at one time a paradise prevailed, such as the Garden of Eden and the Hindu Golden Age. As Souls began to materialize into physical forms they developed grosser appetites. With the populace degenerating, naturally, their societies took a wrong turn in development, so that other higher Souls had to come to earth to assist their lost brethren.

In modern times, with the use of scientific methods and the availability of ancient texts, evidence is being put together that indicate the existence of ancient advanced civilizations. So, the questions arise: Where did these advanced peoples come from? Why and how were they destroyed? Where did they disappear?

The existence of an advanced civilization of Atlantis, presumed to have existed somewhere in the Atlantic Ocean, is known from historical references by erudite philosophers, such as Plato and Francis Bacon. Bacon hoped to create a New Atlantis, in order to regain the lost paradise. Many legends of lost islands are existent which describe ancient cultures from the Greek Isles of Bliss to the legends of the Welsh about Avalon and the French about the Isle Verte. In recent years, remnants of Atlantis are believed to be part of the Americas, Bolivia, Cuba, Crete, Azores and Antarctica, particularly islands at the top of volcanoes.

In his dialogues *Timaeus,* dated around 360 BC, Plato described how Atlantis had been destroyed by earthquakes and floods about 9600 BC. He described the country as being greater in extent than Libya and Asia. Further, the kingdom had a fertile soil, an abundance of water, and an excellent temperate climate.

He described the citizens as enjoying such prosperity under the rule of ten princes that only a few inhabitants had to engage in physical labor for the sake of food. Plato gave credit for his information to the accounts of his great grandfather, Solon, who was an Athenian legislator. Solon reported that an Egyptian priest, who belonged to the group who kept these records, told him the tale (in around 600 BC).*

The most vivid descriptions of life on Atlantis were given by Edgar Cayce, who referred to Atlantis in the past-life readings of 672 different individuals. All of these references, which were received in a trance state, were remarkable in that they reflected very few contradictions in their descriptions of the way of life at that time. In these readings, Cayce described how the Souls of earlier times were not in a human body, but in subtle forms. The Souls had great concentration power and the ability to manifest thought forms into physical reality. Therefore, they were capable of participating in the co-creation of the earth kingdom.

In this realm, thought power controlled all things, in the same way a yogi can manifest in the physical using the principle of

---

* It is possible that these records were lost in the fire of Alexandria; however, some conjecture that they still may be found in the chambers of the Egyptian pyramids. These uncertainties remain to be solved.

"panchikarana." The Soul mind began to use the thought forms to seek gratification of the senses, evidently even imitating ways of the physical animals around them. Edgar Cayce went on to explain that "the Souls began to harden," as they sought physical pleasures and forms. In Hindu historical accounts, the powerful sage, Vaishista, happened to notice a couple of deer copulating in the woods. This scene impressed his mind, so that he had to spend a brief incarnation as a deer to live out that desire. As one holds onto certain thought forms, one becomes the forms.

There is evidence through legends and pictographs that certain Souls began experimenting by projecting themselves into bodies that were one-half human and one-half animal, such as the centaur, sphinx and mermaids of earlier times. Edgar Cayce states that this experimentation "caused certain imbalances in one's internal nature." Since the Souls could project themselves into whatever form they wished, the world became an arena of the will of one being trying to prevail over another.

After completing a three-year period of study in Tibet, Jon Peniel wrote the book, *The Lost Teachings of Atlantis.* The author submits ideas, similar to Edgar Cayce's readings. He found records that described how higher Souls felt compassion for the Souls who had become stuck in vehicles of experimentation and had forgotten their higher nature. So the compassionate Souls came down to help pull the fallen Souls back to the expansive state of infinite oneness with God. They were God-connected beings, like their brethren of early descent had been, but still were connected to their spiritual nature.

Peniel found this information while exploring Tibet, when he discovered a pre-Buddhist monastic order that had a library of old texts. The texts told of many ancient cultures, including teachings of Atlantis. He was told they had been preserved by Egyptians priests and they had moved the texts to Tibet. There they had established a spiritual monastery in an area with a name that sounds like "Shangri-La" in the Tibetan language.

Like Cayce, Peniel tells the story of the fall of a group of Souls in Atlantis; the division between good and evil occurred; that is, the Souls who remembered their connection to God and practiced the principles of being One with God versus those who, having forgotten this truth, became self-centered, exploitative and manipulative in their dealings.

Another source of information on Atlantis was the information given by a disembodied spirit named "Phylos, the Tibetan," who recounts in detail about his incarnation as Zalim Numinos in Atlantis about 13,000 years ago. He dictated his story to Frederik S. Oliver, while Oliver was living in the vicinity of Mount Shasta between 1883 and 1884. The records were published as *A Dweller on Two Planets* (1899).

Both Edgar Cayce and Phylos refer to a great crystal, which was called the "terrible crystal" or firestone. This stone was a source from which one was able to make both spiritual and mental contact. The eight-sided stone of light was the means of communication between the finite and the Infinite.

This stone was used for constructive purposes, for instance, laser medicine or power stations. However, many theorize that it began to be used for destructive purposes as well. Perhaps, the use of the stone caused the eventual downfall of Atlantis by enacting volcanic activity, which caused the final disappearance of the islands of Atlantis about 12,000 years ago. However, Cayce stated that the destruction of Atlantis into islands began as early as 28,000 years ago and was caused by the Atlanteans, who unintentionally overloaded the voltage of the power stations, causing a disaster.

But, the third and final destruction of Atlantis was due to the abject misuse of power by the wayward Souls who, becoming selfish and decadent, misused the power for selfish purposes and literally blew the islands up by causing earthquakes and volcanic reactions due to the misuse of the power stations. This group was referred to in Cayce's readings and the writings of Jan Peniel as the Sons of Belalial.

Even if we were not inclined to believe the existence of this civilization on the basis of ancient testimony, written records, and sources of channeling, in his book, Ignacious Donnally meticulously catalogued the similarity between many world cultures that suddenly appeared some time before 9,600 BC, the date Plato used as the time of Atlantis' destruction.

Many major events in world history appear to have occurred around the final beak up of Atlantis. Cayce and Peniel report that, having foreseen the final cataclysm, many Atlanteans dispersed to Egypt, the Americas, and the Pyrenees, among other places where they had already established trade and contact. One group was called the "Sons of Solitude." They had kept their connection with their higher Self; therefore, as they fled, they took with them the knowledge of the spiritual reality as well as material advancement.

After this time, there appeared similarities in ancient cultures which seemed to spring up overnight around the world. The existence of pyramids, similar to the Egyptian structures, located in Mexico, Central and South America, as well as China and Eastern Europe, is one example. The sciences of astronomy and astrology were mastered in China, Egypt, India, Europe and the Americas. Again, there are similar religious practices of worshipping the sun and the moon. Another case in point is the use of farming, which seemed to occur independently in seven different regions of the world from about 9,000 to 12,000 years ago, in the Near East, Central America, and South and North China.

Other clues that point to an extensive ancient culture are any number of "mysteries" around the world, such as the megaliths in Stonehenge, Carnac of South Brittany, Kashi Hills of India, Easter Islands, Ethiopia, and Madagascar. In addition, a site at the ocean floor near the Islands of Bimini is considered to be part of Atlantis. The purpose of these megaliths seem to relate to measuring the movements of the sun and other heavenly bodies, so astronomy would have been known by all of these cultures in diverse sites around the world. No one can explain how these structures were erected with the tools available at that time. These mysteries also indicate a common link of an advanced culture.

Interestingly, hundreds of ancient sacred sites around the world are now being found to have positioned themselves in alignment with the Old North Pole before crustal shifts of the great Atlantean break-up in 9600 B.C.E. These sites are in the Americas, Mesopotamia, Egypt, India and China. It is conjectured that movements of populations found these ancient sacred sites and being attracted to them — thinking that they were built by the gods — built around them and eventually over them. The advanced civilizations had sophisticated modes of construction and advanced knowledge of mathematics and astronomy, as evidenced by their precise position around the globe.

It is also difficult for linguists to explain how a large proportion of the Western European area and Southern Asia have a single linguistic family, which began to spread across Eurasia in what was thought to be the Neolithic or Early Bronze Age. The question remains as to the originators of this language. Not only do similar language groups crop up all over the globe, but many similar forms of vegetation appear on several different continents, as if carried there by cultural groups, either through migration or trade between themselves.

More and more evidence of a variety of fields from archaeology to new physics to near-death studies all support the ancient traditions and texts of the world's spiritual cultures. The Tamil epics of South India speak of an ancient tract of land Kumari Kandam with a great spiritual academy of yogic practices and and extreme longevity. This Kingdom was said to date back from 30,000 B.C.E to 16,000 B.C.E. Its ancient script is identical with the oldest culture and script of Easter Island and its megaliths.

There is underwater evidence as well of other ancient Pacific cultures linking countries and places like Japan, Polynesia and the Hawaian Islands with the Americas, thought to be the ancient civilzation of *Mu* or *Lemuria.* Recent underwater findings off Okinawa and the Easter Islands appear pre-Incan and to match the construction of a great spiritual center of the Andes Mountains. The tiny Malden Islands south of Hawaii have a road paved in stone which leads under water to 40 flat form pyramids.

Although carbon dating is often not possible in these underwater findings, undersea imaging equipment is now making it possible to find ancient ruins of the Pacific cultures with archways, columns and gigantic slabs with streets and drainage systems — such as found off the coast of India. The technology once relegated to more recent cultures pushes the timeline much further back on advanced and ancient civilizations and cultures making for a debate with the social scientists of today.

So we have archeological evidence that human civilization was not a process of slow evolution, but a series of startling leaps in regard to building, farming, and language. Therefore, we can conjecture that there were infusions of culture from outsiders who were more advanced.

Chapter Thirty-six

Clues in other Traditions

The legends of all the known religious traditions include stories of communication between mankind and gods. The most well-known are the "myths" of the Greeks. The Greek gods were not an almighty God, sitting on a throne. They had power struggles among themselves, and displayed other human qualities, such as jealousy, anger, revenge and lust, while others wanted to help the earthly mortals. The Titans, also referred to as the elder gods, ruled the earth before the Olympians. Cronus was the ruler of the Titans. His son, Zeus, overthrew his father and the other Titans and became the ruler of the Olympians, who were the new group of Greek gods to rule the earth realm.

Frequently, Zeus was in conflict with the other gods. Once Zeus was displeased with Prometheus, another god who wanted to help the earthly beings. When Zeus found out that Prometheus had given fire to the mortals, he punished him severely. Although Zeus was married, he was famous for his many affairs with both goddesses and mortals. However, he gave birth to his favorite child without a partner. Athena sprang full-grown from the forehead of her father.

Hera, Zeus' wife, was known for her jealousy and her tricks to revenge Zeus' infidelities. One myth describes how she manipulated and tricked Zeus. The gods wanted to assist a group in the Trojan War, but Zeus was against this idea and did not want the gods to interfere with the war of the mortals. Hera caused Zeus to fall asleep, so that she and the other gods were free to help those who they favored in the war.

Apollo was another god who liked to commingle with humans. He was often depicted as a handsome god who charmed many goddesses and mortals with his music. Known as a prophet and magician, several times he gave his gift of prophecy to mortals whom he loved, such as the Trojan princess Cassandra.

Speaking of magic, consider this story that illustrates the premise that the higher Souls used their powers to degrade themselves. Poseidon, the god of the sea and earthquakes, was another who had numerous love affairs. However, he fervently coveted Demeter, the earth goddess, but she refused him. To escape this powerful being, she fled to the countryside, assumed the shape of a mare, and hid herself in a herd of horses. Poseidon succeeded in finding her, changed himself into a stallion, and, thereby, succeeded in impregnating Demeter.

Certainly, all relations between the gods and mankind were not positive from the humans' standpoint. The Greeks worshipped and prayed to the gods for boons, but often the gods felt no obligation to help out the humans. They were more interested in the enjoyment of pleasures and power for themselves. These myths of communication between man and gods again must have been in a time when the Souls were of a more subtle nature, so that thought power was used and prevailed in many of their endeavors.

Intriguingly, the ancient Egyptians believed in an early paradise when there were gods in their land, followed by a time of god-men, then men who were kings but represented the gods, thus maintaining a link between earth and heaven. The Egyptians practiced *polytheism*, a belief in many gods. Their religion was based on service to these gods, since everything was controlled by the gods. A seemingly unusual aspect of their religion was the belief that animals were sacred. Thus, many gods were portrayed as animals or humans with animal characteristics.

Even our own religious heritage, passed to us through the Hebrew scriptures, contains comments on the intermingling of angels, or "Watchers," and men. The author of the *Book of Enoch* recounts that God sent legions of evolved Souls to earth in order to watch over and assist humans to begin civilization. However, these Souls taught man sciences that were forbidden by God, such as the science of the stars, divination and sorcery. Enoch goes on to say "but they chose husbands and wives from among the humans and led greatly debauched lives, neglecting their heavenly duties." Since God had sent these Souls to be "Watchers" to guide mankind, he was sorely angered by their insubordination and banished these "fallen" from his kingdom.

This account coincides with the verses in *Genesis,* Chapter Six. "And it came to pass, when men began to multiply on the face of the earth, and daughters were born unto them, that the Sons of God saw the daughters of men that they were fair; and they took them for wives of all which they chose. ... There were giants on the earth in those days; and after that, when the Sons of God came into the daughters of men, and they bore children to them, the same became mighty men which were of old, men of renown." The reason they became "mighty" was that they mated with were giants, so the Sons of Gods became great warriors, thereby, showing their new interest in earthly greed and strife. Again, God became angry and frustrated with his emissaries. Soon afterwards, he ordered The Flood.

Fundamentally, the original story of the "fall" in Genesis was not a fall of humans, but of subtle beings, for "they were naked and were not ashamed," living in a heavenly paradise in which God strolled around. God punished them: woman was to have pain in childbirth and man had to work to eat, "by the sweat of thy brow," so these physical realities must not have existed in Eden. Adam and Eve had simply desired the knowledge of good and evil. God had told them if they ate of that tree they would surely die. Since we can assume God did not lie, we can understand that the divine couple "died" to the experience of the subtle realm. Their vibration became too dense and dull to perceive the higher realms. Then they saw their naked bodies.

However, no group of humanity communed with the gods more than the Hindus. Their *Purana* epics and scriptures, particularly the *Mahabharata,* are replete with stories of gods using man, and man using gods. Actually, the *Puranas* are records of the lives of the gods dealing with earthly realities, sometimes to help, sometimes to beguile, and sometimes simply to have fun. For our purposes, suffice to choose one example from the thousands.

The principal protagonists of the great *Mahabharata* war, the five Pandavas, were born through their mother's union with various gods through the use of certain *mantras.* Arjuna's father was Indra, Lord of the Gods. In preparing for the war, Arjuna made regular trips to the heavens to receive advice and such practical tools as divine arrows, which converted into dozens of arrows once in the air. Arjuna was such a handsome being (half human, half god) that the heavenly handmaidens always wanted, even demanded, his services every time he visited Indra's heavenly palace. In the end, the righteous Pandavas did win the war, but not without intervention from Lord Krishna, who even had to resort to causing the sun to set early on one occasion to save Arjuna.

However, Lord Krishna's intervention was not appreciated by everyone. Gandhari, the blind queen of the vanquished side, was able to curse Lord Krishna through the power of her austerities, causing the untimely end of Krishna's life and of his dynasty. She told him he could have prevented the war, so it was only fair that he suffer the loss of his family as she had lost all of hers. And she was not the only one dissatisfied with Lord Krishna's behavior. Upon hearing of the Lord's deception in hiding the knowledge that Karna was his half-brother, the victorious King Yudhisthira lamented that he would not have fought the war if he had known this fact.

Other writings in Sanskrit of earlier cultures, including the oldest, the Rg Veda, describe many amazing machines of flight and nuclear power, as well as the use of psychic powers gained through *mantras* to be used to conquer the enemies.

Again we are talking about other *yugas* when Souls were more in touch with their subtle bodies and closer to their spiritual heritage. Just as the Atlanteans had a way of connecting the finite mind to the Infinite as members of the "Sons of Solitude," so that mind being the link between the Soul and the physical body has a way of directing itself back toward its source. And because the mind operates through forces which are higher than any physical force, it can control nature and recreate a heaven on earth by reconnecting or aligning itself with the Soul substance and the regions beyond. Not only can Paradise be recreated, but a means of reconnecting with the Soul can be given through the help of the most advanced Souls — the Saints and Masters of the Earth Plane.

Table 11. Major Events in each Yuga

Age or *Yuga* (approximate dates)**	Major Events
Pre-history	10,500,000 y.a. first advanced Souls appear on earth in *subtle form* only
Golden Age (3,890,000 years ago)	3,200,000 y.a. *homohabilis*
Silver Age (2,162,900 years ago)	Incarnation of *Avatar Lord Rama.*
Bronze Age) (866,000 years ago	250,000 y.a. cave sites and artifacts 500,000 y.a. Homo erectus 200,000 y.a. original Eve 180,000 y.a. Middle Stone Age 130,000 y.a. Homo sapiens 70,000 y.a. last ice age began 52,000 y.a. first destruction of Atlantis 50,000 y.a. world meeting 50,000 y.a. dispersal of humans 35,000 y.a. Cro-magnum man appears 30,000 y.a. artistic expression 28,000 y.a. second destruction of Atlantis 13,900 y.a. reign of Egyptian gods 12,000 y.a. break-up of Atlantis 6,000 y.a. Genesis, creation of Adam 5,200 y.a. deluge of Septuagint (possibly Noah's Flood) 5,113 y.a. first year of Mayan calendar 4,200 y.a. Noah's flood
Iron Age (2,900 - 7,000 years ago)	2,900 – 7,000 y.a. Mahabarata War* 5,240 y.a. First Chinese Divine Emperors 4,300 y.a. Egyptian, Chinese, Greeks

---

* The Mahabarata War, around 2,900 years ago, is considered the official beginning of the *Kali Yuga*. Recent archeological discoveries indicate the possibility of an earlier date of about 7,000 years ago.

V. Advanced Practices in Inner Regions

If I remember you
Then I may go
Don't you hide
I will hide
This is your world
This is all You
And only You, O Lord

Only You, O Saint Ajaib
Only your love remains
Let everything else disappear.
Your love is all that
We have.

We are instruments
You are the music
This is the symphony of love.
Yours is the love
Expressing in all
Traveling through the mind
The Soul had to fall

But your music it calls us
Back to our home
Letting us know
We are not alone.
Sound current of joy
For within
Shine brightly
Burning up all of the sin.

It is the Saint
Please let there be
So that I may hide
In the vision of Thee.

Chapter Thirty-seven

The Royal Highway

Unfortunately, we are not born knowing what brought us here and when we must leave. Only a few, who have esoteric religious instruction or remembrance of past life experiences, have a sketchy idea of this secret knowledge. Even those few may not understand a concept such as liberation. Those who hear of liberation and long for it are extremely few. Indeed, the *Anurag Sagar* states Kal does not want to lose any of the Souls from his authority in the three realms of birth and rebirth. Only through the grace of a liberated Master can we even know of a reality beyond the first Three Regions, much less think of the possibility of escaping from their snare and becoming liberated.

Only the Souls who have the rare privilege and opportunity of meeting a holy Master can hope to travel through the inner Astral heavens and Causal regions beyond these realms of rebirth. In fact, many remain stuck in Astral heavens, thinking themselves to be in the highest of realms. The gods and goddesses of Hindu, Greek and Roman mythology, just to mention a few, are included in this category. The Vedas describe the scene of their last day spent in their higher heavens when all their experiences earned by good *karma* have been used up. At that time, they have a glimpse of themselves in their fallen condition. Due to their accumulated stores of negative *karma,* they have to continue the cycle of birth and rebirth again, with total ignorance of their past.

Through all of my travels, I have been aware that my goal is to get off the cycle completely. All my studies did inform me of the possibility, but I felt myself no closer to that reality. Before I was initiated by Sant Ajaib Singh, I had found great solace, peace, love, joy and contentment in repeating different prayers or *mantras* given to me by the various teachers whom I had met along the way. Even so, my Soul kept longing for greater and greater connection with God. Finally, I was able to be initiated by a Master Saint from whom I received *Simran* and *Bhajan.* These methods would satisfy my Soul's painful longing for God.

"The journey is over an actual highway that the Saints and their disciples travel together. During the journey, they travel to higher planes through many splendid continents and worlds. It may require many years, but at last one reaches the end at the Highest Supreme Region, the home of the Saints and the Supreme Father."

— Sawan Singh

Normally, in our daily lives, everything we do is to please and to serve the mind. In contrast, in meditation one must do battle with the mind. This task is not an easy one. Once the mind is under control, and the Soul regains its connection with the Master Saint, its journey back to *Sat Lok* can begin. An initiation by a Master Saint is an infinite boon to one's spiritual progress. Although it may not be immediately apparent to us, the disciples, who have had to work so hard to do battle with their minds, ultimately receive the reward. We will realize the goal of our spiritual endeavors, if not in this earthly body, then in the afterlife.

The Soul must pass through the realm of inner stars, moon and sun. At that time, the initiate sees the inner Master and the Soul journey begins. Until one has passed the stars, moon and sun, thereby, manifesting the radiant Master within, one cannot say that they have completed the work of conquering the mind. The Soul is escorted to a lake called *Amrit* (nectar) where she is instructed to drink the holy water and is thereby purified to the luminosity of twelve stars.

Thereafter, the purified Soul can travel to subtler regions of experience. As our Souls become purer, our vibrations change to resonate with the vibration of higher and higher inner regions, or higher spiritual *chakras.*

To practice meditation, usually a teacher gives a *mantra* that approximates the vibration that emanates from a particular *chakra.* Words are sounds; sounds are vibrations. Just as everything in creation has a vibration, each *chakra* has a unique vibration that resembles a sound. On the spiritual path, the opening of each *chakra* is considered important, so that the Soul can travel up the energy centers housed in the physical body. After reaching the highest center in the body, the Soul travels beyond to additional *chakras,* and on to the Over Soul of the inner regions.

"The light of the body is the eye, therefore when thine eye is single, thy whole body is full of light."

—Jesus

The *Sant Mat* tradition, or the path of the Masters, uses the *mantras* of the deities who rule over the Third Eye *Chakra* and the five regions beyond it. Only a Master Saint who has mastered all of the five regions beyond the Third Eye *Chakra* is qualified to pass on these sacred words. These words carry the vibration of the Master Saint which gives the blessing and power that sets the

Soul on her inner journey. The initiation by one who is not pure or is not at a high enough vibration does not carry this power.

Further, anyone who initiates students, without being competent in taking on the responsibility of spiritually caring for the disciples, must suffer *karmas* that he or she cannot even begin to foresee. One scripture states that every false *Guru* is reborn as a snake with the angry disciples born as ants that eat the snake. Therefore, it is important to have a true Master who can take responsibility for the Soul of another. Otherwise, both the disciple and *Guru* suffer.

At the time of initiation, the Master Saint gives the student the *Simran,* the names of the rulers which represent the subtle vibrations of each of the inner regions. These words act as a passport through the inner regions. Also the Master opens up the world of inner spiritual sound by giving the aspirant the *Bhajan,** or the Sound Current. By listening to this inner Sound Current, the aspirant is able to purify the mind and Soul, thereby overcoming all hindrances and weaknesses on the inner journey. The vibration of the Sound Current is so sweet and delightful that the Soul is naturally pulled upward to further its spiritual journey. Further, the student is also given a vision of the inner light during the initiation.

Simran, the five charged Words, help to take the disciple through the five difficult regions back to the true home of the God, called *Sat Lok.* This kind of withdrawal is an important step in cleaning up our act and in detaching from the world, with its continual tendency to bring the Soul down. A subtle joy begins to be felt, which worldly objects cannot give. This is the joy of going back to God. This is the joy of the Soul returning to its

---

* The Sound Current *Bhajan* is not to be confused with the Hindi word "bhajan," which is the singing of devotional songs to God.

source. This is the rebirth that is spoken about in so many Holy Scriptures. Each Soul has the right to peace, happiness and infinite love. Each Soul is longing for that love, but has been dragged through the mud of the *karmas* of the body and mind; therefore, it has become so blinded that it cannot come out of this dream of the body and the mind.

"And what is the Simran? *They are the Five Basic Names of God, which are filled with the charging of the living Master. Master gives away Himself. And He gives away the Power in those Words. And the* Simran *is the Master."*

— Kirpal Singh

The world and the mind are like the bait of a fisherman. The poor fish mistakes a plastic worm for its food and gets hooked in the process. Forgetting its essential need of freedom to swim about in the ocean, it gets hooked. Likewise, the poor Soul is swimming along hungry for God, its source and true nature. When it sees the worm, or world, it mistakes the worm for its food or sustenance. In its hunger for God, the Soul reaches out in desperation for the world on the end of the nasty hook. The rest of its life is a struggle to free itself from this very painful hook. The more the Soul struggles, the more the hook digs in, until at last the Soul is exhausted and dies to one realm of existence. Finally, the Soul becomes so tired of the "getting hooked" game that it begins to look for an alternative, or a better source of nourishment or freedom from hunger. The Soul resolves to be free from the pull of the world.

Freedom from this struggle is not always easy. Sometimes the personal *karmas* of the mind/body complex are so strong that the individual has a difficult time meditating. Yet, for others, meditation and its rewards come quickly. In either case, there is no way to measure the benefit of meditation. Very often, people will use the excuse that they are not good at meditating to stop the practice. In meditation, it is the practice itself that is important. I remember at one meditation sitting in our home, even when I had an exceptional experience, my mind did not want to relinquish its control and created a very real impression of me vomiting all over the beautiful Oriental rug that I was sitting on. I opened my eyes in horror and fell out of grace. What a sham! My mind took one of my great attachments to bring me down. Yes, the mind will bring up anything - the most ridiculous and the most sublime thought forms - to bring us back in its control. *Santji* spoke of a very real and frightening image of a lion that appeared to him while in the seat of meditation to bring him out.

Regardless of what comes up during practice, don't get discouraged or use the mind as an excuse to give up meditation. See the practice as a game, if necessary, but never give yourself an excuse to stop the practice of meditation, if you are a meditator, for it is your soul's life sustenance. It is the job of the Negative Power, also located at the third eye area, to cut you off from this sustenance.

Meditation is a method to empower the Soul for its journey home. By not allowing the mind to focus on its own preoccupations, the Soul — with the help of prayer and chanting God's name — becomes empowered and freed from its preoccupation with the mind and the world.

The Master alone knows the Royal Highway of the Inner Regions. At the time of the initiation, only the Master can destroy the accumulated *karmas* of the Soul that keep us forever paying off debts throughout lifetime after lifetime. The Master Saint alone can attach a cord from the disciple to his or her real home in *Sat Lok*. Before initiation I had felt as though my Soul was just stranded out in space. During the initiation, I had a feeling of finally being connected to something tangible. I did not understand until later that a golden cord connected me to *Sat Lok*. During the initiation, the inner world of light and sound are opened up to the initiate. The Soul uses these two vehicles to purify its vibration to subtler and subtler realms of experience and to finally merge into God, its Source.

The sound meditations are vibrational signposts on the Royal Highway that enable our Souls to become accustomed to purer and more refined states of experience, thus purifying it. The sounds of the astral plane alone are tenfold, since the astral realms contain heavens, purgatories and hells.

Similarly, the Soul, once freed from the physical vehicle, is naturally attracted to the light. The Soul can become mesmerized and fascinated by various spectacles of light. These displays may cause greater feelings of love, warmth, joy and fascination. The many splendors of these inner regions may cause the devotees to think that they have arrived at the ultimate heavenly abode. A Soul may rest in some of these inner regions for years before moving on. It is ultimately up to the guidance of the inner Master to help the Soul journey back to its real home of *Sat Lok,* also called *Sach Khand.*

Once when I was staying in Rajasthan, I met a woman in the Master's home. She told me an interesting personal experience. During a retreat, she had been sitting in the garden reading a book that was describing our true home in *Sat Lok.* She told me that she was immediately whisked off and saw her place there. "It was as if my name was written there," she said. Upon realizing her real home, she couldn't figure out why she would have to return to the earthly one. Nevertheless, she found herself back in the garden again. Although we are not allowed to speak about our inner experiences once we are initiated, I was grateful that she shared this experience with me.

There are millions of Souls in *Sat Lok*. They look down upon the earth sadly as a place with no love. They also call this planet the red planet because of all of the wars. Furthermore, this planet has been referred to as a place between heaven and hell because both good and evil exist here. We must pay off some intense *karma*, but not quite heavy enough to warrant a trip into hell — yet. For here we can reap the rewards of our good actions and experience varying degrees of happiness as well as suffering.

Chapter Thirty-eight

My Journey after Initiation

After my initiation, I prayed to be able to serve Santji in whatever way I could. A couple of weeks later, I received a phone call from Philip, the person who was taking care of Millie, one of Santji's Western disciples. Due to Millie's advancing age, she needed a woman to help her in her home. Strangely, a few days before the phone call, I had the impression that I no longer belonged in Seattle. I felt I had to go, but I had no idea where I would be going.

I had met Philip and Millie in Vancouver where Santji gave a ten-day talk and meditation retreat. At the time, I was thrilled to meet this charismatic woman of whom I had heard so much, whom Santji referred to caringly as his mother. She had been initiated by Sant Kirpal Singh in 1955 and had spent many months in India, as well as accompanying him on his world tours. Both Kirpal Singh and Santji had spent many days in her home on many different occasions, thereby enabling hundreds of devotees to be able to meet these two great Saints of India.

When we were introduced in Vancouver, I only spoke briefly to Millie. I casually mentioned that I was happy to be there with fellow aspirants, and that I was looking forward to being initiated the next day. I also mentioned how hard it was to be understood in the world. Everyone was always trying to get me married off, even though I did not want to marry. My only desire was to go back to God. This expressing of my innate aspiration probably affected both Millie and Philip and, therefore, they called me to help serve.

"I slept and dreamt that life was joy. I awoke and saw that life was service. I acted and behold, service was joy."

— Rabindranath Tagore

Millie was remarkable in her love for the two Masters. Many aspirants of God were guided to seek initiation because of her inspiration and love. Philip had stayed with Millie to take care of her household and business affairs, and had worked for the spiritual organization for ten years. Dutifully, he arranged all of her trips to serve the Master Saints, including her trips to India. Because it was a household for the service of the Master, the environment was filled with an abundance of grace. One day when Millie was upset about something, Philip perceived the two Masters, both Kirpal Singh and Santji, standing beside her, looking on with concern.

I felt very fortunate to have the opportunity to serve Millie. On the day I arrived, I placed my things in the room that would be my home for six months. Then I looked into the mirror, in awe, I saw my face literally change due to all the grace pouring down on me. I knew it was a blessing to experience what it was like to do service, or *seva*, for the Master. One day, while helping around the house, I looked over at Millie and saw her whole body turn into light. Although she did have human qualities, she was a magnet for the Master's Power and had a profound effect on many who knew her.

Nevertheless, as most endeavors in the world tend to be, the service turned out to be difficult in many ways. Millie was growing older and undergoing some of the familiar symptoms of an elderly person. She had her bouts of forgetfulness and episodes of emotions. I quickly understood that I was to forget my personal concerns and just try to work with each situation to keep her content. Many times, I had to prepare her belongings for the trips that she took to visit numerous people in need. I knew intuitively that it was good for my ego to do this service. All of the years I had spent as a spiritual teacher had surely served to inflate my Aries ego.

While in India, I had been in the presence of many spiritual people, *yogis,* and *swamis* who had spiritual powers, so I knew that a teacher could be very advanced, but still not perfect. Because of her devotion to the Masters and to Jesus, Millie even manifested certain powers. On occasion, Millie acted as a healer, until she was instructed not to do so by Kirpal Singh because using spiritual powers for healing hinders spiritual progress. She had a natural gift of intuition which she used to help others.

Nevertheless, she, similar to so many other spiritual teachers, was also human. I began finding it more difficult to do service because of the challenges of dealing with an elderly person. Philip was also having challenges with her, but he could not end his service to her because of his devotion and the amount of grace he had received from the Master was so great. He also knew that Millie was dependent on him after so many years and he could not let her down. Even so, he realized that as Millie's condition was declining; therefore, his service would soon be completed. Since I was only the support staff, I was expendable. As much as I wanted to be helpful, Millie wanted me out of the house.

Several weeks later, when Philip delivered some mail to my new home, the dynamics of our friendship took another turn.

Here was a person who, like myself, had devoted over ten years of his life to spirituality. When he asked me to marry him, I did not know what to say, except that I knew that I loved him dearly. It was pure love, for we had never even kissed. When I felt some reservations about marriage, I received the answer from my higher Self that it would be foolish to walk away from love. This union was clearly God's will. I accepted.

If I had any idea that going to the Boston area was going to result in my marriage, I would have never crossed the country. But this relationship was different. I felt deep love and respect for Philip and his dedication to Santji. Three weeks later, we were married before the entire Boston meditation group. We all enjoyed this happy occasion. I am writing these words exactly fifteen years after our wedding on our anniversary day. On our wedding day, we expressed the vow that we had come together to serve God and the Masters.

"From Joy we came; for Joy we live; and in the sacred divine joy we will one day melt again."

— Paramhansa Yogananda

Interestingly, while I was still living at Millie's house, one day Santji happened to ask Philip if it would be feasible for a married couple to take care of Millie. Philip replied that he was sure that Millie probably would not approve. Little did Philip realize who Santji was referring to at the time, for only a week afterward, Millie asked me to leave.

I knew shortly after my marriage to Philip that I wanted to have a child. A Soul came to me and said, "Don't you want to have me?" I said that I surely did, but I would have to see if Philip wanted a child. I felt like crying for love of this being. I told Santji mentally that if the wish were His will, I would like to have a child.

Soon after, Philip and I were meditating. When the meditation was over, Philip said that we could have a child. I knew that this fulfillment of my wish was Santji's gift. I was aware at the moment of conception that this birth was to take place. Later, Philip had a vision of us together with the Master with a small child crawling on the floor. Santji said to Philip, "If you only knew the powers at work."

It is a blessing to have a partner who shares the same spiritual goals and aspirations. We have each other to celebrate and commiserate in the ways that life deals its cards. To be on the path alone in this world is not always an easy proposition, since many do not understand exactly what it means to be in the physical presence of a living Saint, to perform the higher forms of meditation and the ways that it can change one's life so completely.

Once while on the work site of the Federal Building construction project in Boston, Phil had a booklet in his back pocket about the Saint. One of the workers grabbed it and began to criticize the Saint. Another worker joined in, then one became quiet while the other continued ranting and spewing. Phil put his head down and shed a tear. It was a very calm, windless, hot summer day. Suddenly a gust of wind blew by and picked up a large panel 5 x 12 feet and weighing between 300 and 400 pounds and buried the critical construction worker. Phil looked up in the sky to see where this wind came from. The other workers ran around the site yelling "Witchcraft, it's a curse!" The critic ended up in the hospital for three days. Later the other man would ask Phil, "How is Sant Ajaib Singh?" with genuine interest. When one drives by the Federal Building, the large panels are seen covering the building.

Saints will never judge others or criticize anyone. They see all of the souls as the same. When one criticizes a *living* Saint, the Saints are indifferent. To send out a negative thought form, however, toward a powerful being means that it gets magnified, and by the laws of karma, it will be returned to the perpetrator. Similarly, to send a positive thought and prayer toward a *living* Saint means that it gets magnified also, and impacts one's life in a very positive and powerful manner.

"Dear One, you will never walk alone, for the Master's hand is on your back... through your journey called life."
— The Master

Today, I feel so fortunate to have a person in my life who shares so much in common with me. Phil and I both have such a need to meditate that our life together is not a normal one. Since our children go to bed early, everything in the day is about getting to bed early, so that we can wake up in the middle of the night to meditate. We are like meditation junkies. Some evenings either Philip or I, individually or together, are meditating all night long. I cannot measure the blessings of the Master that come through this daily meditation.

Chapter Thirty-nine

Journey of the Soul

The opportunity to meet a holy Master is a rare occasion. Even one meeting can change one to the core. An encounter with a Master is a meeting of Souls. It is beyond the scope of this writing to even begin to describe what the impact of meeting such a holy being has meant for me. I can only tell you that being with Santji was like leaving behind all of the religions of the mind and going to the realm of the Soul. My long and difficult search was over. The true journey, the journey of the Soul, had begun.

In order to move out of the body, out of the realm of the five senses, one must leave the baggage of lower vibrations behind. All of the exercises of concentration of the mind and personal purification aid in this process. The first step is to concentrate the mind at the Third Eye *(Tisra Til)*. We must pull in the wandering mind and hold it steadily at one point. In doing so, the individual spirit current is slowly withdrawn, first from the lower extremities of the body and then from the rest of the body. When this withdrawal happens, the body loses its feelings.

Although this process resembles the withdrawal that takes place at death, in this case, it is voluntary. The whole spiritual being gathers at the Third Eye *Chakra*. Its powers increase because of the concentration. Eventually, we are able to pierce through the veil, which is no thicker than the wing of a butterfly.

At that time, we open the Tenth Gate and step out into a new world. The body is left behind, but can be returned to at will. Its life processes are only slowed down.

In this state of consciousness, we are neither asleep nor unconscious. Instead, the being is super-conscious. We are now in a world that impresses the traveler as more real than the one left behind. The new world is "finer, more beautiful, and full of light." We are now operating in the astral body; the five subtle senses are used for communication, just as the five physical senses were used before. The practitioner has now gone from the "semi-dark" prison state to a whole new freedom. Space and time are obliterated and our world appears to be pitifully limited. We are now ready to begin the journey home.

Master Sawan describes these inner regions in order of increasingly greater subtlety. The heavens and purgatories are all located in the first region called the Astral Region. In this series of realms, the Soul becomes purified further, while receiving rest and upliftment. Passing this region, the second realm is referred to as the Causal Region. Because each region is subtler in nature, each region has subtler sights and sounds. The first region in the Astral Region has ten different sounds ranging from the sounds of purgatory to the sounds of the greater heavens.

Interestingly, the sound of the bell and conch are two of the principal sounds; therefore, they are used in the physical realm of temples and churches to dispel all lower astral vibrations and to help uplift the spirit. The sounds in the physical plane exhibit the physical qualities of sound, while the sounds of the mental realm are subtler and can only be heard with the inner ear.

While the first region — the Astral Region — is considered a mental region, the second region, or Causal Region, represents the initial step on the Soul level journey. In the Causal Region, the Soul receives *karmic* instructions. The *Akashic* Records of Time exists in this realm. These records map out all of the Soul's past and future, thereby, revealing the cause for its next physical and astral sojourns. The "I" gets destroyed in the body when we transcend the body. The "I" gets destroyed in the mind when we transcend the mind. Then one identifies with the Causal body which automatically wants to go back to God.

The Causal Region has everything *karmically* ordained for that Soul; therefore, its records keep the Soul in a perpetual cycle of birth and rebirth in the physical and astral realms. The Causal Region is referred to as *Trikuti* or *Brahma Lok,* for it is said in the Vedas that when the mind resolves in *Brahman* one begins the true inner journey of oneness with God called *Samadhi.* This region is supposed to be the region where the ancient Vedas of India originated. Immersing one's Soul in *Brahman* is going to the place where the mind and words turn back.

By virtue of the practices of *yoga* or meditation, many have reached this region. Although they have not tamed the passions, these *yogis* have subdued the mind. Because of excellent concentration of the mind and the ability to withdraw, they can, to begin with, penetrate into the lower Astral Regions. Unfortunately, many take these lower thresholds to be the final destination of heaven. Even many world religions consider these heavens to be the final destination.

When a Soul becomes very pure, the Soul travels beyond the Astral and Causal Regions to the Third Region, referred to as *Daswan Dwar.* Only by the grace of the Master Saint can one make the transition past the Causal and into the realm of the free spirit so that, thereafter, one is never subjected to rebirth again. At this time, the meditator experiences the subtlety of the region that is the center of creation of this world. From this center, the whole world emanates.

At this point of super-consciousness, the disciple meets the inner radiant form of the Master. No other teacher is required from this day forward. The Master takes command of the inner and upward journey along the Royal Highway to the higher regions. The student who has met the true inner Saint to guide him or her Home is truly fortunate.

"In the Nameless, Wordless State there is no Sound, no Light. But that is something in Itself. It cannot be expressed, that's all I can say."

— Kirpal Singh

Chapter Forty

Inner Regions Encountered in Meditation

The inner journey begins where the five subtle senses leave off. Not only are saints and mystics able to enter this doorway. Anyone who has subdued their passions and practiced according to the Guru's instructions to increase their concentration and power of penetration are able to enter the astral world. Some believe that this place of beauty and light is the final heaven. However, this region is the very lowest level of the expansive realm of heavenly worlds. Here space and time, past, present and future, birth and rebirth into the lower realms — all become nothing but a pitiful passing show. Here the student meets the Master who becomes the guide for the inner journey. The disciples who reach this junction cannot advance much further on their own, for it is only with the grace of the Master that one can travel further to the Region of Truth.

Each region has its own Lord and Ruler. These Rulers receive their powers from the Ruler in the region above. A spiritual aspirant may mistake any of these Rulers as the Supreme. Until one meets the radiant form of the Master, one does not realize the necessity to proceed further. Each region has various beings engaged in different occupations, most of whom are in concentration or meditation upon the Lord of that region. In these regions there are many beautiful continents, mountains, forests, gardens, oceans, rivers and streams, in other words, countless arenas of enrapturing sights and sounds to intoxicate the Soul.

The inhabitants of each region are completely unconscious of what is taking place in the regions above and below them, just as we also are unconscious of the realms below and above us. The ability to come and go from these regions is totally dependent upon the kind of lives we have led and their *karmic* consequences, as well as the assistance of the Master. We must qualify, or master each region, before graduating to the next one.

"When we rise above the body and go to the Brahmand, we come to the Prajagraj. This is the place where the three rivers — the Ganges, Jamuna and Sarasvati — meet. The Hindus think that this meeting place is a holy place, and they understand that by bathing in the holy waters then they will get liberation. But they do no know that the Mahatmas [Liberated Ones] saw those rivers within and that they named them outside.

"Mahatmas meant that they wanted us to go within and bathe in the rivers, in the holy rivers within, not on the outside, but the people did not understand that. PrayagRaj is the place in the Brahmand, above the physical body, when the three veins — Ida, Pingala and Sushuma — meet. That is the Daswan Dwar. There is a lake or river over there which the Sikh Gurus called Amritsar, or the Pool of Nectar, and bathing in it our Soul becomes pure."

— Ajaib Singh

Many of us wonder what the Soul experiences when it goes inside into deep meditation. Fortunately, several of the Masters, including Ajaib Singh, Kirpal Singh, and Sawan Singh have discussed what the initiate may expect to see and experience when they enter these inner regions. It should be emphasized that these regions are real; therefore, everyone, whether Master or initiate, sees them and experiences them exactly the same.

First, the Soul becomes aware of the manifestation of Light and Sound. The Masters say that when the Soul starts hearing the Sound Current, all sins are washed away. The Soul sees light in the form of stars, then the moon, then the light of the sun. Then the journey continues through the Astral Region or First Region of countless heavenly realms.

Afterwards, the Soul has to go through the *Bank Naal,* which is a very deep and profound level. At this point, the Soul has reached the Shore of the Inner Master and begins to hear the sound of a conch and the sound of *OM.* Next, the Soul travels into *Trikuti,* the Second Region. Upon reaching *Trikuti,* one has to remain in meditation for a long time to pay off the *karmas* that have been stored for ages and ages. *Trikuti* is a huge ocean which every initiate encounters inside themselves; it is impossible to cross without the "boat" of grace of a Master.

In time when the three coverings of the Physical, Astral and Causal are removed from the Soul, the Inner Master is manifested. When one sees the form of the Inner Master, the duty of the disciple is over. The Soul starts searching for the true essence of itself with the Master at the helm. Once the astral and physical shells of the dreamer fall off, the Soul enters a realm that is not affected by these grosser outer coverings, just as the physical person cannot affect the reality of the subtler dream world.

After meeting the Master, the Soul follows the Master to *Daswan Dwar* where there is a Pool of Nectar. The Master instructs the Soul to bathe in the nectar, which removes the slumber of the Soul. Thereby, the Soul is awakened and the Soul comes to know itself. In esoteric terms, the *Surat* (faculty of inner hearing) and *Nirat* (faculty of inner seeing) are opened.

Continuing on the journey, the Soul reaches place of *Mansarovar,* where it becomes a *Hansa,* literally meaning a "swan," a title indicating enlightenment. Here the many Souls welcome and praise the newly arrived Soul, saying, "You are a great Soul to have made the journey from the mortal world. You are a great Soul to have had the Grace of a Master to bring you here."

After luxuriating and enjoying this beautiful region for some time, the Soul prepares itself for the upward journey to an enormous city that is too beautiful to describe. One must experience it to comprehend its glory. In this region there are four very subtle and melodious sounds that are only heard by a few rare Saints.

In this region are supreme inner islands. On the right side is the island of *Achint,* where there are never any worries. Further ahead lies the gigantic island of *Sahaj,* where one enjoys an undisturbed, effortless bliss. Over to the left is the Isle of Contentment. Kirpal Singh says of this whole region, "The glory of these inner islands is supreme."

Since the *Surat* and *Nirat* (inner hearing and seeing) are opened, when the Soul goes to these islands, she perceives a unique waterfall. The Nectar of this water can only be tasted by the Soul with its subtle faculties.

In spite of the intrinsic beauty here, the Master tells the Soul, "You are not to get stuck here, for you have to journey beyond this subtle paradise."

The Soul must then cross *Maha Sunn* which means great region of void. The darkness is so dense and intense that only the Master Saint can help the Soul pass through it. The Souls of lesser luminosity cannot find their way through on their own. Then, accompanied by the Master, the Soul reaches *Bhanwar*

Gupha, the Fourth Region, where the Soul becomes intoxicated with the rarefied atmosphere. After crossing *Bhanwar Gupha,* the Soul arrives at the huge plane of *Sat Lok,* the Fifth Region, where she is able to see the Supreme Lord, *Sat Purush.* Upon seeing the Lord, the Soul realizes, "This is my true Father and God. This is my Master. I separated from Him to go to the mortal world." Some scriptures state that if you collect the radiance of trillions of suns, it cannot measure to the brilliance of one hair of *Sat Purush,* the Lord of *Sach Khand.*

When the disciple received initiation, the Master tied the cord of the Soul to *Sat Lok.* The Soul is overjoyed to return to its real Home and Father. From *Sach Khand, Sat Purush* takes over the duty of guiding the Soul to the higher regions of *Agam Lok* and *Alakh Lok.* The magnificence of these two regions cannot possibly comprehended by the human mind with its limited capacity. Of this area, Kirpal Singh says, "How can I sing the glory of it? It embarrasses millions and billions of moons and suns."

The next inner region is *Anami,* meaning "that without a name." Of this region, Guru Nanak has said, "Those who go beyond *Sat Lok* and rise above the *Alakh* and *Agam* Regions, find the true residence of the Saint." All the Master Saints reside in this indescribable region. In this region, the Soul remains forever peaceful and content, for there is no Sound, no *Shabd,* no Sound Current, no Light. There is only peace and bliss.

Once when speaking of these inner regions, Santji explained, "Now all these regions that I have mentioned cannot be seen by any outer instruments [senses], because they are all within us in their astral or spiritual form. We can see them only when we go within. The great artist God has created all these things and put them within us, but we cannot see and experience them unless we go within, into the inner regions."

Continuing, he gave an example, "In the same way, the worldly artists have written for and performed on television or film in which you see and hear people playing music, talking, singing and dancing. ... They have devised a technique whereby you can see all these things on the screen, but you cannot touch them. So all these things which I have mentioned are not material, they are within us in their astral and subtler forms and beyond. If any doctor were to say that by cutting open the body he would find the islands or inner regions, it would not be possible — because these phenomena are a matter of experience. All these things are present within us in their subtle form."

The Masters have generously shared this sacred knowledge of the inner planes with us. Upon hearing of the glories of the inner path, who will not want to follow the teaching of the Master Saint?

"The wave of the ocean of life is very deep,
The Perfect Master is the helmsman;
He is running the ship of Shabd,
And some rare ones who are brave get into it."

— Kirpal Singh

When a disciple is exposed to the vibration of the Master, the disciple may open, not only to the experience of the Soul, but even further, so that the Soul meets with the radiant Inner Master. Meeting the Inner Master is a matter of raising one's personal vibration through the purification that takes place from the exposure to higher vibration of more subtle sub-atomic particles.

From a physicist point of view, the initiation can be understood as the utterance of words of such profound power and electrical charge that their force is literally projected into the initiate's Soul Body, into the Mental Body, Astral and Etheric Bodies almost as if one is experiencing an electric recharge. The initiation has the effect of energizing all the bodies and their centers, and also purifying them. Effectively, a rearrangement of the sub-atomic particles is accomplished by the practice.

The *Sant Mat* tradition describes in clear detail the process of the purification of the Soul to the throwing off of its Astral Body in the First Region, its Mental Body in the Second Region, and its Soul Body in the Third Region to merge into the Over Soul. By examining the Inner Regions Chart, one can understand the five elements relate only to the lower *chakras*. The journey to higher *chakras* is best described by the Map of Inner Regions. With the grace of inner guidance of the radiant inner Master, the Soul is able to continue its journey through these inner regions.

"This is where the spirit currents collect and gain entry into the foxhole (called the hole of Brahman) and have a peep into the Brahmand or cosmic universe. This is the tenth aperture of the body, the only inlet apart from the nine outlets. This is the place where you have to knock and receive admittance into the realms more vast, more glorious, self-luminous and self-resounding with rapturous strains of celestial music. Music is unheard anywhere in the physical world which has been left below—now no more than a great slum fraught with miseries and tribulation."

— Kirpal Singh

Table 12. Map of Inner Regions

	Region	Sound		
8	**ANAMI** *Nameless, Formless State*			
7	Inconceivable		Agam Lok	
6	Indescribable		Alakh Lok	
5	Truth	*Bagpipe*	Sat Lok	
4	88,000 continents	*Flute*	Bhanwar Gupha	
3	**MahaKala** - *Free Spirit*	*Four Sound Currents*	Daswan Dwar	
2	Kala - *The Just* / Causal	*Drum*	Trikuti	
1	Anda - Astral	Heavens and Purgatories / *Bell & Conch*	Sahans dal Kanwal	
	Pinda - Physical	MASTER	Third Eye / Throat / Heart / Naval / Reproductive / Rectum	Paramatma / Shanti / Shiva / Vishnu / Brahma / Ganesh

Spiritual Regions (↕, levels 4–7)

Table 13. Summary of Inner Regions

First Region — *Sahans dal Kanwal* — is a vast and beautiful region named for its gigantic flower-like light, which resembles a lotus of one thousand petals. Many scriptures and mystics refer to this region. Master Sawan Singh described this region by saying, "The Master Guide has traveled this vast region countless times. His power and authority are recognized as one with the Supreme Lord. Under his protection, we are able to advance to Higher Regions. For, traveling alone, one cannot go to higher regions without the Master Saint."

Second Region — *Trikuti* — is a delightful region. This experience is so enchanting that it may take years to become purer and qualified to pass through to purer atmospheres. The Vedas originated in this region, so some believe it to be the ultimate region, called the *OM Region*. This is the region where Krishna, Christ, and Buddha are believed to reside only because this region acts as a link between the physical world and the higher spiritual worlds.

Third Region — *Daswan Dwar* — The very idea and feeling of this region are beyond the grasp of the earth dwellers concept or language. Here we leave behind the last of the three earthly bodies to become pure spirit, a child of the Supreme Lord. Thereafter, we do not return to the realm of rebirth because we are free from all the lower impurities. Here the Soul attains the brilliancy equal to twelve suns after drinking from the Lake of *Amrit* or *Mansarovar.*

DEEP DARK VOID REGION — Region where Kal Niranjan, the Negative Power, is said to reside. It is the arena where the

Soul asserts its dominance over the mind in meditation, so that it can finally be free of the influence of the mind, its first and last enemy. This region can only be traversed with help of the Luminous Master Power.

Fourth Region — *Bhanwar Gupha* — In the fourth region, there are vast and innumerable realms and worlds with numerous devotees living on the nectar of God's *Naam,* or holy name. Kabir refers to it as a region of 88,000 islands and continents, filled with beautiful scenery and palaces. Unfortunately, we have to pass through the deepest and darkest void regions to be able to enter the Fourth Region. This journey is only possible with the guidance and light of the Master Saint as an escort.

Fifth Region — *Sat Lok or Sach Kand* — is the home of all Souls and of the All-Mighty Father, *Sat Purush,* of such luminous nature that one hair equals the light of millions of suns combined. Although we reach this region with the guidance of the Master Saint, *Sat Purush* alone helps the Souls to advance beyond this region of such extreme brightness toward the three higher regions of indescribable love and joy.

Sixth Region — Indescribable

Seventh Region — Inconceivable

Eighth Region — Nameless, Formless

VI. Inner Alignment

May the One within all beings
Recognize God within all beings.
Let the dance of love begin now,
So that we never fall back into
The slumber of forgetfulness
Of your poignant love again.

Ancient stars twinkle your name
Moons and suns pale before
Your luminous rapture of
Good deeds and profound glances
Embracing all Souls who come near you
Your joy is our joy
Beyond all description.

Never again, can I ever think
That anything exists but You.
My mind cannot know this,
And I cherish it as true,
O, thank you, Holy Saint.

God is all there is,
God in God in God,
Like a single image
Reflected in many mirrors
Only God in God in God.
Through the grace of the Holy Saint,
There is God in God in God.

Chapter Forty-one

Science of Spiritual Practices

Everything in our universe can be viewed as energy-like forces that emanate from above and around us. In addition, everything in the universe is affected by the radiation, or magnetic influence, of these energies. The way a person reacts and makes use of these energies determines not only how his or her life will unfold, but also will have a significant effect upon his or her afterlife.

When a person does spiritual practices, two things occur. First, the vehicle of practice, composed of the five bodies, becomes purified. The result is the human vehicle (the highest form of conscious life on earth) becomes a receiving station for the higher vibrations of the subtler divine energies. Second, the individual is able to convert such energies into creative forces and become a transmitter of this energy in the forms of thoughts and divine actions for the good and upliftment of oneself and others.

"If your mind is empty, it is always ready for anything. In the beginner's mind there are many possibilities; in the expert's mind, there are few."

— Shunryu Suzuki

There is nothing inherently right or wrong with any of the energies in this universe. According to the way these energies are used or abused, we create a universe of negative and positive forces.

By existing in negative thought or conditions of hate, fear, anger or pride, for example, we do harm to ourselves, and to others. These negative emotions join other negative forces to bring great disasters to our planet.

The energy vortex associated with the negative emotions is the astral body center, or Solar Plexus *Chakra*. For example, when we become angry, we are taking astral energy and aligning ourselves with it. Continual use of this emotional energy results in a habit of relating from the Solar Plexus. Then all behavior is colored by the issue of anger; thereby, reinforcing the continued use of anger in the behavior. A person who does not consciously practice intelligent living becomes basically an emotional reality tank. At death, these negative emotions compel the person to be drawn into the Astral Region in places that reflect those dispositions.

The angry person will have a Solar Plexus Center out of balance from drawing too often on astral forces. This tendency causes the internalization of astral energies, which, in turn, causes diseases like cancer. A healer must balance the Solar Plexus Center. Thereafter, it is up to the patients to change their attitude to attract, integrate and assimilate a higher form of energy to themselves. They have to maintain an attitude that does not create disease, but generates an energy that affects the body in a positive way.

Similarly, persons whose thought energies are constantly directed toward sentimental emotions and desires are also creating and attracting corresponding force fields around themselves. These thought forms impel a sojourn to higher Astral Regions. These regions are built upon illusory astral energy, so that images of a loved one may appear. A loved one appears in subtle form in order to exchange emotions according to pre-existing attachments. These sentimental attachments hold the Soul back from higher, more refined spiritual experiences and cause further rebirth. When the mental vehicle is of a higher order, the astral preoccupations fade away or dissolve.

The human *chakra* systems and spinal cord are the network station and circuit board for the human energy system. The most important aspect of this circuit board lies protected in the spinal column. The three principal tubes are the subject of every spiritual scientist's concern. They are the *Sushuma* in the center, the *Ida* on the left, and the *Pingala* on the right. In normal breathing, the breath generally flows through the *Ida* and *Pingala* tubes alternately. When it flows through the *Sushuma,* the mind becomes steady.

The entire body receives its energy through the circuitry system of the central canal, made up of *nadis,* or energy currents in subtle form. When we perform spiritual practices, the subtle energy can be withdrawn from all of the *nadis,* which circulate throughout the body, and move up the three subtle tubes in the spine to higher spiritual centers.

Further, the body is made up of *plexus,* or points, where nerves, arteries and veins interlace each other. In subtler levels of the body, the *nadis,* or energy pathways, come together to form subtle plexus or *chakras.* The centers where all of these points converge total twelve in the human being. There are seven lower *chakras* found in the physical body and five *chakras* in the regions of the mind and spiritual body. The expression "as a man thinketh, so he becometh" explains that, the *chakra* at which we concentrate our energy determines how we act and interact, and who we are or will become.

In the chart illustrating the *chakra* system for the body, the seven *chakras* are likened to lotuses because they appear like a lotus with petals and stems, both of which emit energy. The higher

Table 14. Chakra Chart

Developmental/ Integration	Element	Sense Organ	Body Connection	Number of Petals	Chakra* Name	Corresponding Gland	Relevant Issues
		--	Causal Body	1,000	Crown	Pineal	Surrender, release, Higher will
21+ years	subtle elements		Intellectual Body		Third Eye	Pituitary	Inspiration, spirit, insight
15-21 years	space	hearing	Mental Body		Throat	Thyroid	Expression, communication
12-15 years	air	touch	Emotional Body	12	Heart	Thymus	Compassion, feelings, love
8-12 years	fire	sight	Astral Body	10	Solar Plexus	Adrenals	Assimilation, logic, reason, intuition
3-8 years	water	taste	Etheric Body	6	Sacral	Lymph	Empowerment, sincerity, secuity
0-3 years	earth	smell	Physical Body	4	Root	Gonads	Stability, acceptance self-preservation

* *Chakras, or energy centers, look like lotus petals with stems toward the spinal column.*

chakras appear to have more petals, or beams of energy, pouring out until the seventh *chakra* of the "Lotus of One Thousand Petals," spoken of by spiritual aspirants of many mystical traditions.

Each *chakra* is similar in that it is a vortex of energy, but each differs in the quality of energy vibration and its correspondence to the five elements from gross to subtle. Because the *chakras* represent different energy vibrations, they also take on different appearances from the perspective of sound and color. Many healers use light and sound to open different energy meridians and release specific *chakras* from being either blocked or overly stimulated. During the healing, all the psychological issues of the corresponding *chakra* get addressed, so that a resolution can be reached.

"In this body, in this valueless place, why remain imprisoned in the darkness."

— Kabir

While there are spiritual practices aimed at unblocking certain pathways to higher spiritual centers, some practices are more atypical, meant for achieving spiritual experiences. While some exercises of breath and concentration can force the *kundalini* energy up the *sushuma* canal causing a mystical experience, their practice may blow out, or otherwise harm, the circuitry of the delicate electrical system. If the person has not followed wholesome living in regard to diet and morality, as the energies are forced up the spine, they can over-activate lower, non-spiritual *chakras*. Then the energy can manifest in behaviors such as excessive anger or sexual drive and can wreck havoc in a person's life and those around. In addition, some practices can negatively affect a blocked circuit system to the point that they could even cause forms of insanity. If a practitioner wants to be initiated into some of these more aggressive forms of practice, the Master is very careful to consider who can, and cannot, handle certain energy practices. Therefore, the Masters are very discerning about who they initiate in order to be sure they follow the requirements of living a pure life, so these energies won't be abused or cause harm to the student.

"As a man works with his personality, purifying and bending it to the service of the spiritual, he will automatically raise the Centers in his body, up to the Center of his eyebrows."

— Djwhal Khul

Table 15. Activating Chakras with Sound

Element	Chakra	Deity	Buddhist Mantra	Sound
	Crown			
Third Eye	*Paramatma*		OHM	eee
Space (emptiness)	Throat	Shakti Mother	CHT	
Wind	Heart	Shiva Gabriel	Hung	ahhh
Five	Naval	Vishnu Israel	LAH	ho
Water	Reproductive	Brahma Michael	BEE	ooo
Earth	Rectum	Ganesha	AAH	uhh

The Science of Activating Chakras with Sound: Certain sounds correspond to the *chakras* and have been used to open the different meridians and free them from blocks. Each *chakra* corresponds to a predominant element and vibrates to that particular substance, so chanting certain sounds can activate them. By chanting, we are working on all the elements of the human body — including *chi* or the *prana* energy.

Chapter Forty-two

Alignment of Chakras

Most spiritual practices cause the activation of the energy centers, so the best approach is to go slowly and surely. By practicing love, the Heart *Chakra* opens; chanting and prayer activate the Throat *Chakra;* scriptural study and inspirational contemplation activate the Mental *Chakra.* Through the practice of meditation, the Third Eye *Chakra* opens. With a balanced and proper lifestyle, all the *chakras* become balanced. Then the "alignment of *chakras*" begins to take place. This alignment means that the instincts of the lower *chakras* that were used for self-preservation are sublimated by the higher energies of the upper *chakras.*

When this alignment occurs, the subtle energies from the practices create a pathway in the brain between the mind and Soul. This alignment causes the brain to subjugate the lower *chakra* impulses. Therefore, the result of alignment is that the Soul now dominates the personality from the higher spiritual centers while moving energy and awareness up and down the lower centers to participate in activity in the world. When the personality is brought into relation with the Soul, it is considered to be the first stage of the enlightenment process. The advanced stages of enlightenment are concerned with the Soul's relationship with the Master and with God.

The process of being a spiritual disciple or practitioner is one of learning how to direct the energies which are pouring down through him or her from the Soul, or later from higher sources of Master or God power, into realms of activity for spiritual practice and spiritual service to humanity. An adept is "in the world, but not of it." This person acts strictly from impulses of the Soul or higher sources.

"Truth is the Supreme, the Supreme is Truth. Through Truth men never fall from the higher worlds because Truth belongs to the Saints. Therefore, they rejoice in Truth."

— Yajur Veda

While the Soul has always been dominant, this perspective from the center of being shifts from body-orientation to the lower emotional astral levels of the Third *Chakra*. Next the Soul moves to the mental level of the Heart and Throat *Chakras,* then to an intellectual orientation. Finally, a Soul-centered perspective is reached in which the Soul identifies with the Self, the "I-center" — of the Sixth and Seventh *Chakra*. Next, as the Soul dissolves into the higher Over Soul, the Soul vehicle begins to reflect the wishes and intentions of the Universal Soul, for Divine purpose alone.

At this time, having bathed in the *Pool of Amrit* of the higher regions, the Soul no longer has its own *karma*. There is no longer a personal agenda based upon the ego, and no longer an ideology based upon attachment. The mind is no longer subjected to its enemies, but is subjugated by the impulses of the Soul and Over Soul.

Spiritual practices produce certain results that mimic the process of elements unfolding from each other in creation. The practices start by creating a condition in the body in which breath exercises, called *pranayama,* are used to open up the physical channels and subtle channels in the body. When this opening occurs the air element causes the fire element, located at the base of the spine called *Kundalini,* to open up and begin to rise. Although the *Kundalini* power moves like the wind, it must stabilize in each of the centers as it progresses upward in its journey. This practice could take months and years to perfect, until it takes the practitioner to the center of the Lotus of One Thousand petals. When this zenith takes place, the fire of life causes the water of life to become energized, creating psychological change brought about by the four physical bliss states or *Samadhis.* This change occurs when the hormones are secreted and descend back down the channels of the spine from the head center back to the throat and heart and navel centers.

According to the Tibetan esoteric school and the Indian school of *yoga,* the *chi,* or vital force, goes to the top of the head at the Crown *Chakra* for the first bliss. Then the hormones flow and descend to the Throat *Chakra,* which is "supreme" bliss. The substances continue to flow down to the Heart *Chakra* for the "special bliss." When the substances flow to the navel or fourth bliss, "innate bliss" is realized.

When we combine the bliss with the emptiness experience, or *prajna* wisdom, ultimately we can achieve the Tao, the highest Buddhist state, according to some schools. The bliss and emptiness are not enough — we must realize the one who is experiencing this bliss to merge into emptiness and to know the Reality directly, as the students of *Vedanta* would say. The Reality is no longer an object of theory, but direct knowledge. The *yogis* call this integration *Nirvikapa Samadhi.*

Again, the Tibetans combine the experience of four bliss states with practices of the four forms of emptiness, which uses the bliss experience to enhance concentration. So the concern is to avoid getting bogged down in the enjoyment of these bliss states by understanding the reality of enlightenment potential behind them. The wisdom of emptiness must be brought into our everyday life, so that this innate knowledge becomes a way of knowing and being. The Sanskrit term is *nishta,* or rootedness in the God state.

So the *Kundalini* practices are useful for purification of the five elements and as a springboard to "higher knowledge." Many spiritual practices can cause this physical reaction of *Kundalini* arousal, but the true awakening only occurs after we cultivate *chi* and *mai,* that is vital force and breath energy. Only with this preliminary purification can the fire aspect, which is the level of the next *chakra,* be ignited.

Once the body is pure, the *chi* and *mai* energy channels and the warmth (fire element) begin to rise to higher *chakras* because of *mantra* or other practices. At this time, one can expect that the *chi* or vital force to move up the central channel. This subtle energy is possible if the aspirant's energy circuitry of the *nadis* is already clean to some extent through using spiritual practices.

The *Ida, Pingala* and *Sushumna* channels intersect in four *chakras,* making them more potent. Therefore, some authorities say that focusing the attention on any of these four *chakras* draws energy back into the central channel *(Sushumna)* and will remove any blocks along the way. The two *chakras* most favored for concentrating are the Third Eye *Chakra,* the Heart *Chakra.* The other two potent centers are the *Sahasra,* at top of the head and the *Solar Plexus Chakra,* at the naval. Incidentally, these four *chakras* are the centers of the four *Samadhis.* There are also corresponding Sanskrit syllables for each *chakra* that aids in the clearing of the channels and the experiencing of bliss. So, correspondences do exist between the physical body and subjective experience.

Any drugs or intoxicants, even tobacco, cause damage to the delicate *chakra* system and its intricate electrical and subtle circuitry. After consuming these toxic substances, the delicate system can become damaged. The stems of the *chakras,* which open up toward the back, must remain open in order to purify the system. These open stems make the person psychically vulnerable to outside influences and forces. We become vulnerable to what the Buddhists refer to as the *"yin"* or receptive side of the mind. This "solitary shadow consciousness" can cause visions and strange impressions, bringing a state of mental illness. Drugs fragment the mental energies. This is the opposite of meditation which brings the energy and focus into unity.

The more powerful the drug, particularly illegal ones, the more vulnerable the individual is on the level of the etheric, astral and mental levels. The preliminary to spiritual practice is detoxifying the bodies and the circuitry of the subtle bodies, so that forces of higher vibration can easily move through the currents to revitalize, energize and even heal the seven centers of the three bodies: etheric, astral and mental. Only when these bodies are purified can spiritual enlightenment and alignment take place. This alignment occurs when all the bodies and their centers are rotating in unison.

Chapter Forty-three

Schools of Yoga

While India is a land of many *yoga* practices, it is also a country which accepts the possibility and importance of knowing God, not just indirectly through the mind or intellect, but through the Soul.* For the purpose of accomplishing this goal, many different practices have been prescribed, depending upon the quality of mind and physical nature of the individual seekers.

Yoga means "joining," or "yoking," into one, bringing diversity into unity. Therefore, all spiritual practices endeavor to bring all the different aspects of the mind and body into harmony and alignment. When this integration is achieved, our attention is no longer split into a thousand parts, but is able to focus on the one underlying Truth, the screen upon which all the daily dramas of life are projected. When all the aspects and the qualities become integrated into one, the seeker experiences the Soul. Only after this experience can the Soul expect to see God.

"To one who has destroyed himself (his ego), and is awake to his true nature as bliss, what remains to be accomplished? He does not see anything (as being) other than himself. Who can comprehend His State?"

— Ramana Maharshi.

---

* The idea of direct understanding or knowledge occurs on Soul level with merging into God or higher *Samadhi.*

Table 16. *Yamas* and *Niyamas* of Yoga

Abstinence from or *Niyama*	Observance of or *Yama*
1) Negation of God	Faith in God and God Power
2) Self Indulgence	Self-control; chastity
3) Using dishonest means to earn a livelihood	Earn living by honest means
4) Being impure within and without	Practicing hygiene and living in sanitary surroundings
5) Injury to others in thought, word or deed	Non-injury in thought, word and deed
6) Being deceitful, lying	Cultivating truth, sincerity and clarity
7) Impatience, greed, selfishness	Patience, contentment, selfless service
8) Self-assertion and ego-centricity	Self-surrender and humility

Righteous Living or *Karma Yoga*: *Karma* Yoga is the "yoga of action or service." In other words, it is a practice suited to everyone, but particularly those who have a restless nature with an inclination to be doing something continually. For others, the broad heading encompasses all kinds of purifying practices that assist in removing the dullness and sloth to make us receptive. These practices include pilgrimages, austerities, fasting, performing of charitable acts, reading of scriptures, and performing of one's duty according to one's own nature.

"With regard to excellence, it is not enough to know, but we must try to use it."

— Aristotle

In the *yoga* of service, we give up the fruits, or outcome, of our actions to the divine order of things. While we perform our duties in life, we remain detached, commonly referred to as "selfless duty."

Since all human beings are in the process of collecting *karma* during every moment of living, we are also in the process of experiencing the results. Further, we have taken rebirth according to our past *karma*. Therefore, our present behavior is a matter of concern. Virtuous behavior is recommended by all of the world's religions and spiritual practitioners. Every religion has rules that are concerned with rooting out of any desires that lead us away from harmony. All scriptures declare that to be able to benefit spiritually from the practices of concentration and withdrawal, we must live a moral life. Codes of conduct are the critical point of departure into the heartfelt experiences of devotional practices. Experiencing inner heaven is a direct result of creating heaven on earth. The Christians, Jews and Muslims have the Ten Commandments, the Christians have the Nine Beatitudes, The Muslims have the Koran, and the Buddhists have the Eight-Fold Path. The Hindus abide by Manu's Code of conduct and duties, and the Chinese follow the tenets of Confucius and the Way of the Tao. All of these guidelines can be summed up in a few words: loving and respecting our neighbors and loving God. The practice of these simple, but direct, words alone results in a peaceful mind and environment, conducive to devotion to God and spiritual practices. Nature abhors a vacuum: when you remove a negative, disintegrating tendency, you have to replace it with a positive integrating tendency.

"There is more value in a little study of humility, and in a single act of it, than in all the knowledge in the world."

— Saint Teresa of Avila

Many religions have created monastic orders to facilitate a moral life. Since visual perception accounts for 88-95 percent of our impressions, by living a simple life in monastic cells or *ashrams*, the student is able to diminish the external input of stimuli as an aid in gaining a clear mind. The benefit of this control over the senses is a clear mind that attains a state of revelry when applied to practices like prayer and devotion.

So, moral living is the very foundation for spiritual success and a peaceful life. Additionally, without virtuous practices, the *karmic* consequences are negative. Inappropriate actions cause the *chakras* and channels to be clogged or imbalanced, thereby, affecting the health and well-being of all the five bodies, preventing any possibility of transcendence.

By being virtuous, we become more conscious of what the Buddhists call "being mindful." As we become more aware, our minds purify; so that our thoughts and actions, which were once unconscious and emotionally based, become conscious and intelligent. We become more relaxed; therefore, we are able to meet the flow of life aligned with a higher purpose.

This practice is also a means of cultivating *Samadhi*. Countless Saints in all of the religious cultures of the world, who had no formal practice of meditation, exhibited all kinds of different super-powers and miraculous abilities because of their virtuous approach to life and prayer.

Devotion to God or *Bhakti Yoga:* *Bhakti Yoga*, suited to those of an emotional or devotional nature, is a practice of thinking of God throughout the day and repeating his name continually. In this meditation, God can be in the form of the baby or adult Jesus, or Mary, the Mother aspect of God, or God the Father, as well as a deity or Guru. The process of devotion proceeds in stages from wishing to dwell in the same region, or heaven, as the object of devotion, wishing to attain close proximity, wishing to become similar, then to completely absorb one's being into the form of devotion. At this last stage, "I and my father are One" has been realized, even though the devotee may still verbally refer to the object of devotion as separate, from the past level of understanding.

"We should know that a spiritual life without discipline is impossible. Discipline is the other side of discipleship. The practice of a spiritual discipline makes us more sensitive to the small, gentle voice of God."

— Henri J. M. Nouwen

As the devotion continues, the realization becomes clearer to the devotee until the form of the devotion, be it God or Guru, is seen in and through all things. Our sense of bliss and the vision of God expand to include all things and beings. The devotee of God loses all sense of self or duality and merges into God in *Samadhi*-like experiences until all that remains is the One. From this experience, a sense of "I am the doer" is superseded by the realization that it is God who does all things.

Some form of the *"yoga* of devotion" has been practiced in all the world religions and involves the constant remembrance of the object of devotion. The religions of Christianity, Buddhism, Judaism and Islam all share similar techniques and practices. While ritual plays a big part in keeping the imagination active, the repetition of certain prayers brings a subtler reward of a quiet, peaceful mind, with heightened concentration and awareness. This practice, however, may sometimes be limited in that it only brings experiences up to the Heart *Chakra*.

In the *Sant Mat* tradition, devotion is important, especially in dealing with the ego. The ego remains the last and most tenacious enemy of the mind to capitulate and let go. Devotion is a powerful antidote for the ego, especially when accompanied by the practice of focusing the attention on the Third Eye area to avoid being limited to the Heart *Chakra*.

Illumination takes place after mind and heart are merged.

— Alice Bailey

In all of the esoteric schools, devotees of God transcend the experiences of mind and heart *Chakra* and embrace the experiences of the Soul. This is when sublimation of a higher order occurs. True meditation is blending of heart and mind and the Soul takes its journey to a whole new level of love, far beyond the heart *Chakra* which lies in the domain of the mind. With the help of the Master Saint, the Soul journeys back to the true source of love, to the Lord of the highest spiritual regions of *Sach Khand* and beyond.

Why is the Third Eye *Chakra* so important? The act of concentrating in the Third Eye area causes the Soul and mind to battle it out for attention. This battle is said to create friction which ignites sparks, then fire and light.

Authentic practices generate energy that transforms the elements to the next subtler element. This conversion process gives power to the more subtle element, as wood gives fuel to the more subtle element of fire. This process creates a total change in vibration, similar to conversion from water to air in evaporation, or hydrogen and oxygen combining to make water.

The subtle and gross elements flow into elemental forms of higher vibration. Chinese refer to it as *jing* (vital fluid) folding into *shen* (spirit), which in turn folds into *mai* (energy). The Hindus use the term *ojas* into *prana*, which flows into the *Kundalini* fire, which dissolves into *bindu*, or subtle drops. Ultimately, the Soul feeds off this energy of conversion to become more subtle and powerful, as it takes command over the mind.

Consequently, the subtler the practice, the more powerful the effect. The small light of the Soul expands to the radiance of twelve suns, yet even greater is the light of the Master's. When the devotion brings on total God identification, the thought form is "God is the doer of all things — not I." In this experience, God can be seen everywhere with eyes open or closed.

Devotion works well as a practice because of its capacity to engage every aspect of our being — from physical devotion in serving God to mental devotion of seeing God in all things. This devotion is a form of concentration that can involve all senses and actions and thoughts — ideally to dissolve in God.

"The world is lost in reading scriptures, yet never comes to knowledge: But one who knows a jot of love, to him all is revealed."

— Kabir

When the object of devotion becomes visualized in the Third Eye *Chakra* at the start of contemplation, devotion can give an exceptional boost to spiritual progress. Here ego, the most potent of the enemies of the mind, becomes dissolved in the object of devotion. But we must still go forward and this progress requires devotion to a Perfect Saint or a Living Jesus for greater help and grace to break through to higher regions of inner experience.

To explain the physical process, ancient Chinese Buddhist and *Yoga* systems state that in order for the *chi (prana)* and *mai* energy to be developed, it is absolutely imperative that the practitioner develop chastity, so that the vital seminal fluid *(jing)* can transform itself into higher energy forms. With the practice of chastity, the subtle aspect of *jing* (*ojas* in Sanskrit) transforms into *prana* or life force. The resulting bliss is centering for the aspirant where the vital fluid and life force are transformed into energy (*mai*) and spirit (*shen*) to bring Soul experiences of God.

When using the techniques of ritual, prayer, singing or dancing for devotion, the spiritual practitioner should concentrate on the critical Third Eye *Chakra,* the center

Intellectual Discrimination or *Jnana Yoga:* The path of knowledge of Hinduism and the *Abhidharma* analysis of Buddhism is an inquiry into the nature of the Self, God and Reality through a system of logic.

Jnana Yoga is for those of us who like to think and need to have logical answers for everything. Scriptural inquiry and self-analysis are required, until by eliminating the "unreal" with intellectual discrimination, we arrive at the Truth and live it. This Path of Knowledge, or the Vedanta method, is like cutting the branches of the tree of the mind, and then destroying the tree itself by cutting the roots buried in the ego.

This path is designed for the most discriminating of intellectuals. For by using the process of elimination of what is not true, we can arrive at the Truth. When the practice of analysis is applied with an open, inquiring mind, it is possible to experience mental cessation (or a freeing up of the lower mind and its monkey-like tendencies). Buddhist texts state that to succeed in this path, we must also practice accumulating merit by regular meditation and sexual discipline.

Although this form of intellectual practice can result in elimination of all the aspects of the body and mind as "Self," and even bring about the annihilation of thought, the practice cannot take us past *Trikuti* region into the inner spiritual regions. The instrument of the intellect can only be used for self-contemplation and discrimination. To reach the inner regions, the intellect has to step aside and bow to the Soul. But who is to carry the Soul to the higher regions? Only a true Saint and Emissary of God can assist the Soul further.

"The three practices of reading the scriptures, contemplation upon its truths, and the shifting of attention from the sense of Self to the Eternal Self, the limitless awareness, requires one to have exceptional discrimination and an intense longing, which is difficult in today's time. However, in the past, Masters like the Buddha and Shankara took this short, but very steep, path."

— Kirpal Singh

In Vedanta, the Hindu Path of Knowledge, with the practice of rigorous disciplines and discrimination, the two — subject and object — eventually merge into One, which often creates *Samadhi*-like experiences as well.

As in all the other systems of *yoga*, "cessation" is not going to happen unless your *jing* or *ojas* (vital fluid) transforms into *chi* or *prana* (vital force). This *chi* then settles and transforms into *shen*, or etheric body energy. Similar to other paths, spiritual progress and understanding involve a physical transformation as well.

Even on the path of Confucianism, which has an orientation to practical matters, after investigating the world of phenomena, the students eventually discovered that the world had an inherent emptiness. The foundation of Confucius is, of course, based upon right behavior.

The key for all who travel the path of discrimination is to live one's life with the Truth in mind and avoid getting caught up in the limiting concept of being separate. The problem is that this system is only for the intellect and seldom goes beyond.

"Knowledge gives power. In practice it is very simple. To control yourself, know yourself."

— Nisargadatta Maharaj

Meditation *or* *Dhyana* *Yoga:* Meditation can enhance and deepen all other spiritual practices. There are two types of meditation, either on a form or on the formless. The student usually starts with the meditation on the form of God or saintly Guru or living Master. The meditator's attention is focused on the inner darkness between the two eyebrows. With practice, the dark spot within gradually becomes illuminated and assumes the Radiant Form of the object of meditation. If the Master is a Perfect One, his appearance means he will immediately take charge of the person's Soul when it rises above consciousness of the body.

Obviously, we must take care in choosing the object of meditation. First, meditation on Masters who are no longer in physical form does not bring desirable results. Only a Master in physical from can provide the grace that is the launching pad for the inner spiritual journey. Second, meditation on imperfect masters will not bring any positive results.

"When in meditation, the Godman appears within; one sees the Secrets of Eternity like an open book."

— Rumi

Even though meditation is a spiritual pursuit, this quiet respite from the world also can bring advantages in our daily lives. Through contemplation, we can have all desires met. Further, good concentration equals ability to manifest subtle to gross realities. All kinds of maladies like fear, shame, indecision and self-assertiveness disappear, giving way to fearlessness, confidence, firmness and happiness. We acquire an evenness of temper in all of the varying conditions of life. We are no longer obsessed with attachment or detachment, but, in the same way that the lotus blossom is untouched by the mucky sludge below the water's surface, we float over water. All of our actions become motivated by love and good will toward others.

Concentration techniques of the mental *yogas* result in eight kinds of *siddhis,* or powers. The *yoga* master, Patanjali warns the student, "give up *siddhis* and destroy the seeds of bondage." Further, he states "do not be allured by the winning smiles of celestials, who can steal one's powers."

"All types of miracles of the lower order, such as thought reading, thought transference, faith healing, particularly in cases of nervous and mental diseases, fall under this category. ... However, it is better to conserve whatever psychic powers one may acquire and use them for gaining at least the lower spiritual planes and regions which form the seat of the deities concerned in the spirit of selfless devotion."

— Kirpal Singh

Mantra Yoga: Many religions and schools advocate the use of a *mantra,* or a series of words, to create a vibrational effect, in order to purify the mind and to bring about mental focus and concentration. The result leads to *Samadhi*-like experiences when practiced often and wholeheartedly. Some schools advocate the combining of the breath with the *mantra* as well. One thing is certain: All types of transcendental experiences do occur with dedicated practice. Many students repeat the *mantra* throughout the day, as well as during a specific meditation time. In the

Catholic faith, the rosary or short prayers can be considered similar to *mantras*.

"The ability and power of mantras are unfathomable and unknown, and are therefore called the 'Secret School.' It's not the mantras themselves, but the power of the mantras that is secret. This is the meaning of Secret School."

— Master Hsuan Hua

Mantra Yoga is the repetition of a word or series of words to a particular deity or God with the purpose of gaining mental or material power. If we use this power to harm others, we will likely incur the wrath of the deity invoked. This practice results in the loss of our personal power and even can bring additional devastation. We can, however, use these *mantras* to help others, but the result is the loss of some vital energy.

In India, the *mantras* often represent a certain vibration that create, by the science of sound, a specific means of winning over a deity or obtaining a certain power to manipulate or control nature. When the mind is concentrated intensely upon the subtle five elements, for example, the resulting power causes the materialization into the physical reality, called *panchikarana* in Sanskrit. The success of using a *mantra* depends on our own inner purity and exemplary character and conduct, as well as the degree of concentration. This ability is called miraculous in the West; however, in the East, it is considered merely the result of mastery over the mind.

Some of the most common *mantras* in India use the actual names of Gods, such as Rama or Krishna. Other *mantras* are from the non-dual tradition. They emphasize the relation of the individual with formless, impersonal Total.

Aham Brahman Asmi (I am Brahman)
Ayam Atma Brahman (I am Thou)
Om Tat Sat (Om is the truth of Reality)

As mentioned before, each *mantra* has specific requirements of lifestyle and also ritualistic practices, depending on its nature. Ideally, when the Guru gives a *mantra,* he or she actually transfers his or her actual seed power lying hidden in the core of the *mantra.* All of creation is made up of energy and is vibrating at different frequencies. The higher more powerful frequencies are spiritual vibrations. Being subtler, these vibrations pervade the grosser material and influence or change these lower levels. This special gift of grace is given to the disciples to assist them in beginning their individual spiritual journey with protection and an elevated vibration.

Patanjali Yoga: The Patanjali Yoga System is an all-encompassing system that includes practices for every level of the human being, from physical to divine. The Indian philosopher, Patanjali is believed to have compiled his commentary on *Yoga* around the 3rd or 4th century BC, although there is archeological evidence that suggests that *yoga* was practiced in ancient India much earlier than 5000 BC. *Yoga* practices are a means of purification to attain at-one-ment with Brahman on the mental level. The serious minded student uses these practices as a stepping stone to the Truth.

The problem is that many teachers have compartmentalized the process into separate practices. Specializing in one aspect or another of the system, each teacher sees their specialty as an end in itself, instead of a means to the next step toward enlightenment. The teacher and student should know when the time has come to move to higher practices and go beyond the physical goals of *Hatha Yoga*. It is for the teacher to say, "I cannot help you to move on to the next level of spiritual practice. You must find another teacher."

Therefore, spirituality is a process of a slow ascension up the rungs of an intricate and involved ladder in the Patanjali *Yoga* System. This discipline requires hours of personal time and effort; therefore, spiritual progress using this system remains a closed door for the majority of us who are householders with limited time and energy.

"The goal of Yoga *is Self-realization by a regular process of self-analysis and withdrawal, so as to enable one to rise above body consciousness into higher cosmic and super-cosmic consciousness." Only a few men of exceptional physical endurance, long life and extraordinary capacity for not forgetting the distant goal can, in our time, pursue Patanjali's* Ashtang Yoga *to its logical conclusion: its highest purpose of at-one-ment with Brahman..."*

— Kirpal Singh

Hatha Yoga has developed as a means to control the body and physical activities in order to quiet the mind. Its practice involves different postures and cleaning procedures which render the body pure, strong and immune to diseases, also increasing chances of longevity. Usually the highest level achieved by the *Hatha yogi* is *Trikuti,* or the Third Eye *Chakra*. [See Table 12. Map of Inner Regions.]

Some of the benefits of *Hatha Yoga* are physical strength and well-being, inner joy, steady mind, quick understanding, enhanced concentration, detachment regarding the pairs of opposites, and stamina for spiritual practices. Although the practitioner may achieve peace of mind, the *Samadhi* experienced from *Hatha Yoga* usually only constitutes a lower experience called *Jar Samadhi*, which is the closing down of conscious awareness, as if in a sleep state. Only the higher *Samadhis*, based on knowledge, can change the very nature of the mind. Since it is temporary, *Jar Samadhi* means the monkey mind will return to play its pranks as usual, acting out of restlessness, comparable to a mind returning to wakefulness from deep sleep.

Pranayama Yoga or Breath Control is always practiced under the guidance of a *Guru*. Control of the breath is practiced by students who also practice moral codes, such as truthfulness, temperance, moderation in diet, humility, patience, chastity and freedom from addictions.

"For mind and life-breath (prana) *expressed in thought and action, diverge and branch out, but they spring from a single root. When the mind is fixed on a single point, and gets absorbed by breath-restraint, the mind will die."*

— Ramana Maharshi

The purpose of *Pranayama* is to awaken the coiled serpentine energy of the *Kundalini*. As the serpent energy rises, the various subtle centers or *nadis* become illuminated until the *Kundalini* reaches *Sahasrar,* the Fountain of Light at the top of the head. At this time, the veil covering the "Radiance of Eternity" is destroyed, so that the mind is quickly absorbed in the light of this radiance. Mental concentration follows of itself and is no longer an effort. So the benefit of *Pranayama* is mental concentration and control, as well as attaining certain powers over objects of the creation. Further, the Zen school clearly states that by merely watching the breath, the breath becomes united with the mind and *Samadhi* occurs naturally.

In an advanced form of purification by air, some *yogis* perform the "nine-step bottled-wind" practice. They have defined certain milestones in the purification process. The end result is some masters are able to transform their bodies into realms of light at the time of their death. This entire practice is said to take thirteen years of intense dedication to a precise series of disciplines.

This practice begins with the transforming of the seminal fluid into *jing* (or *ojas* in Sanskrit), then into subtle energy, or *chi*, during the first 100 days. This energy helps in the subsequent spiritual practices and is essential for spiritual progress in general. Hence, we have the practice of chastity in most of the world religions.

After ten months of this practice, the *chi* or energy transforms into *shen* or spirit, a subtle energy form. During the next three years, the subtle energy form is transformed into what is called "emptiness." After this stage, one devotes nine years to the "no-thought" phase, or what is referred to as the higher stages of emptiness.

In the Tao school, the various phases of cultivating *jing* into *chi* and *shen* correspond to "attaining the fruit of *Hinayana*" cultivation. Yet, it is said that one must go beyond this point to achieve higher enlightenment, or Buddhahood (in the Buddhist schools). These advanced practices are mentioned in order to bring an understanding of certain gross and subtle changes in the mind and body complex that actually occur as the mind becomes quieter and the Soul becomes stronger.

"Remember: if you can cease all restless activity, your integral nature will appear."

— Lao Tsu

Kundalini Yoga practice is used for the purpose of opening of the *Sushuma* central channel located in the spinal column to give off light and heat. This opening occurs as a result of focusing the attention on the Third Eye *Chakra,* behind the space between the two eyebrows in order to open the *chi* or *prana* channels, called *ida* and *pingala* in Sanskrit.

In the same way the Patanjali's *yoga* uses certain postures, breath work and concentration exercises, this practice requires the guidance of an adept teacher. When the attention becomes focused, all the *prana* force moves up to the Third Eye *Chakra.* The process involves the air element, for the wind or *chi* or *prana* element gives rise to the fire or *kundalini* element, which in turn gives rise to the water element, which forms in the pituitary gland. The force activates the pituitary gland to emit subtle drops that bring on a type of physical bliss. This bliss helps the spiritual practice for it enhances concentration, thereby, causing *Samadhi*-like experiences.

Other systems of *yoga* encourage concentration on the feet, navel or top of the head. If the attention is focused in a certain area, then the *chi* or *prana* force follows. The *Sant Mat* tradition prescribes focusing on the space between the eyebrows or slightly above, while at the same time repeating a given *mantra,* called *Simran.* In the same manner, the Tao school maintains that when the *chi* goes to the Third Eye *Chakra,* the *chi* transforms into light, or *shen.*

Several schools of Buddhism, including the Tsong Khapa School of Tibet, Shakyamuni, and Zen, as well speak of the benefits of seeing the light by using this same method. Some schools focus on other *chakras* to bring the *chi* force into the central channel. By bringing on a state of mental calmness, the *Kundalini* rises.

Depending on the point of view of different schools, four distinct blissful states, already mentioned, are said to occur. The blissful states are a means of clearing the subtle channels and aiding in concentration and detachment to the world, but they are not the final goal. It should be cautioned that if *Kundalini* practices are done improperly, or performed without a virtuous and chaste lifestyle, they can cause both mental and physical problems. Also, we must be aware of the danger of becoming an "experiential junkie." Again, *Kundalini* practice is a valid *means* in reaching the goal, but an extremely difficult one in today's hectic times.

"Life has grown too complex to allow any man the leisure time to pursue all of the branches of yoga. ... The mistake is to consider this or that branch as the ultimate and fritter away time in pursuit of physical prowess or magical powers."

— Kirpal Singh

Chapter Forty-four

Other Spiritual Practices

Prayer: Many Saints in the Catholic Church, as well as other world religions were able to transform prayer into a form of *Samadhi,* or god-like experience. The object of prayer is to eliminate all the random unrelated thoughts that clutter and distract the mind, so that the devotee can focus on God or the object of devotion. When the seeker gives up all thoughts of self-concern, which are usually aspects of the "lower mind," God's greatness comes through in the form of unfathomable bliss and knowledge.

Since prayer is a method of surrendering, prayer generally begins with an invocation of established words, which can be either vocal or mental. Essentially, the spiritual student asks for purification and inner peace. Again, the prayer requests God's help in stepping out of the lower mind of wants and needs, and in focusing on the higher mind of the Greatness of God. Christians call the result "grace," or "union with God," or "Pure Prayer." The Hindus and *yogis* call it *Dhyana.*

In Buddhism the act of surrendering oneself is called the "cloud of unknowing," or a state of emptiness and purity. Yet, the Buddhist prayer practice is said to take a person only to the "lower heaven" regions of heavenly beings, and acknowledges the need for more advanced practices to be able to go to higher states of consciousness.

"And see that nothing in thy working mind remain, but a naked intent stretching unto God — not clothed in any special thought of God in himself, or any of His works, but only that He is as He is."

— The Cloud of Unknowing

Visualization: Visualization is often practiced along with prayer, especially in the Buddhist, Tao and Hindu schools. The result of visualization can bring concentration and a single-minded *Samadhi*, or a stage called "stopping" of thoughts that would interfere with subtle bliss states of knowing.

In the Buddhist school, the *chi* and *mai* elements of the body are transformed into a deeper state of mental calm — or subtle mental elements called *shen* (subtle energy).

Two techniques of visualization can produce the *Samadhi* state of emptiness. In the first method, the contemplator focuses on an object until it becomes clear, then switches the attention to emptiness. Or one can focus on an object until it reduces to nothing.

The idea in both cases is to stop the "mad rush of thoughts" and go into the resulting emptiness with fully alert concentration. Through this practice, the mind attains a quietude that contains no dullness. It moves into a super awareness or consciousness — quite the opposite of dullness. The drawback of this method is that the "no thought" state is still a subtle thought and is not a higher form found in the *Samadhi* of Infinite Consciousness. It is recommended, therefore, that this practice be used as a means of quieting the mind. Further, Sawan Singh discouraged the practice of visualization because it involves the intellect, and the objective is to go beyond the intellect.

Detached Observation: There are several techniques to aid in having the attitude of a disinterested, uninvolved observer of different aspects of the creation. Probably the easiest practice is watching the breath. The mind dissolves into the breath as sugar dissolves into a liquid. When Buddha first went to China from India, he preached the practice of watching the breath. When we watch the breath, eventually both mind and breathe cease.

However, the experience of "no-thought" means nothing unless we can contemplate the emptiness of mind and, thereby, see the illusion in mental thought and physical things. All kinds of beneficial powers can come from this practice, such as longevity and good health.

The practitioner watches the silent gap between thoughts, until he or she realizes that the thoughts appear to come out of nothing and go back into nothing. They are comprehended as unreal. Gradually, the gap between thoughts becomes longer and, eventually, cessation of thought occurs. This method is a valid means of purifying the mind and increasing concentration.

Certain practitioners of *Vedanta* and *Abhidarma* of Buddhism are able to include the practice of "non-involved" observing in their day to day life. They remain rooted in an understanding that the observer is separate from the observed.

Further, by avoiding becoming involved in the reactions of the programmed mind and quietly observing it as it jumps around, we become more detached and peaceful. As a result, our meditations and connections with higher levels of reality become more and more profound.

"The greatest discovery of my generation is that a human being can alter his life by altering his attitudes of mind."

— William James

Table 17. Synthesis of Spiritual Practices

Religion or Discipline	Scripture	Rituals	Object of Devotion	Code of Ethics	Meditation or Practice
Sant Mat	*Anurag Sagar* Personal reports of Saints	None	Living Saint, *Sat Purush*, Supreme Lord	Non-injury Vegetarian Diet Perform one's duties	Visualization of Light Five Holy Names Sound Current
Hinduism 3,000 BCE	Vedas, Upanishads *Bhagavad Gita* Brahma Sutras	Performed by Brahman priests in temples Prostrations	Brahma, Vishnu, Shiva, divine Mother	Perform one's duties or *dharma* with detachment Good conduct Non-injury	Patanjali Yoga Raja Yoga Study of Scriptures Rituals
Judaism 2000 BCE. Kabalists	Bible: Old Testament Torah	Prostration	One God Angels Prophets	Talmud Commandments Loving Kindness	Prayer Chanting Five Secret Names
Greek/Roman	Writings of Pythagoras, Plato and Aristotle	Gods Goddesses	Gods Goddesses		Discourses for higher mind

Buddhism 600 BCE	Diamond Sutra Lotus Sutra	Performed in monasteries by monks for the well-being of all.	Gods Goddesses Boddhisattvas	Conscience	Chanting prayers Mindful meditation Visualization *Koan* practices
Christianity Catholicism Gnostics	Bible: Old and New Testaments Writings of Saints	Mass Prostrations	Trinity Jesus Mary Saints Angels	Ten Commandments Beatitudes Canon Laws Loving Kindness Conscience	Gregorian chants Meditation Pure Prayer Five Sacred Names
Islam 600 CE	Koran	Prostrations to Allah	Allah	100 virtues and vices Self-control	Prayer Fasting Chanting
Sufism	Mystically inspired	God	God	Monastic/ Ascetic	Meditation
Sikhism 1469 CE	Guru Granth Sahib	None	God and Guru	Right living	Prayer Meditation

Chapter Forty-five

Yoga of Jesus

Whether Jesus is understood as a prophet by the Jews and Muslims or as a Godman by the Christians, Jesus was born into this world, like all the rest of us, and made vulnerable to its suffering. At which point Jesus became fully enlightened into his Oneness with God, we do not know for sure. Even so, we do know that, as a twelve-year-old with no formal education, he was able to teach the rabbis and scholars of the temple, based upon a profound and personal experience.

Jesus had a system. He called it "love." If you consider "love," you see that it is a single-pointed, single-minded practice, founded upon a discovery in the mansion of the Heart *Chakra*. From the Heart Center, the Soul goes up to the Third Eye *Chakra* and beyond. Jesus didn't settle for the standard theoretical knowledge offered by the Rabbis, but he spoke from the levels of direct experience within.

Some scholars claim that Jesus went to India to learn from the Masters there, and others say he just went into the desert and meditated. All we know for sure is that the end result was love — absolute love. "God is Love" are the words Jesus used to describe His knowledge of God.

What about the rest of us Christians? How do we reach this goal? In Catholicism, we have a rich history of practitioners of the *Yoga of Love*. Some of their lives are remarkable in their demonstrations of mystical experiences reached by loving and experiencing God. What did these Saints do? They led unique lives in different times and suffered, as all humans do, under distinct circumstances. However, their personal experiences fall under the category of mysticism, or simply stated, a mystery. Catholicism recognizes a different Saint for every day of the year. What techniques did they use? They all had altars for rituals, rosaries for prayer, prophets for inspiration, and, finally, they had their devotion.

"Fasts and vigils, the study of Scripture, renouncing possessions and everything worldly are not in themselves perfection, as we have said; they are its tools. For perfection is not to be found in them; it is acquired through them. It is useless, therefore, to boast of our fasting, vigils, poverty, and reading of Scripture when we have not achieved the love of God and our fellow men. Whoever has achieved love has God within himself and his intellect is always with God."

— St John Cassian

The Yoga of Love is the *Yoga of Devotion* in church or temple or mosque. Devotion begins with the withdrawing of the senses from the world into the magical realm of beautiful stained glass windows, incense, music, chanting and flowers. Compared to our dreary, boring world of ticky-tacky boxes and cubicles, this enchanting setting has a way of drawing our attention toward association with God. When the withdrawal of attention from the outside world happens, the place of worship and the object of worship start to look appealing. For those who live an austere life with few outward temptations, withdrawal from the senses is easier and faster.

The next step is contemplation on God or Jesus, or Mary, as some prefer. The chanting, prayers and rosary begin to take effect and out of an innocent belief in God, even a child can begin to feel moved. The busy mind is given a job to do — prayer and chanting and singing — until it begins to withdraw. In the Heart *Chakra,* an acknowledgement of the love of God becomes an experience of one's Soul. As the mind becomes quieter and the practice becomes subtler, a relationship develops between the practitioner and object of worship. The devotee begins seeing glimpses of the clear space between thoughts. The space becomes longer and brighter, more and more profound. In this quiet space, one begins to hear what Christians call "the voice of God."

"Accustom yourself continually to make many acts of love, for they enkindle and melt the soul."
— Saint Teresa of Avila

Next we bring in the grace factor, which includes all the angelic forces that Catholicism and many other world religions recognize. When the practitioner perceives grace, a true relationship with God begins.

As the efforts to reach God increase, the imagination begins to create a relationship with God, which deepens and intensifies. St. Ignatius Loyola, the Patron Saint of Retreats, founded the Jesuit Order based upon the technique of withdrawing from the world and turning inward with practices of devotion using imagination and prayer. Through these practices, contact with God was established.

The rosary is one of the most popular forms of prayer. The use of beads along with reciting of prayers can be traced to India where people today still use beads, or a *mala,* for worship. From India, the use of prayer beads spread to Buddhism and

Christianity, as well as to the Islam religion. The beads help keep the mind focused. The chanting and repetition of prayer quiet the mind and prepare us for contemplation. The use of the rosary focuses on the various themes of Jesus' life: his birth, crucifixion and resurrection. Or the theme may be Mary's service to the life of Jesus as Mother of God.

Prayer with beads was practiced in the seclusion of the monasteries. Since the senses were not active with living and surviving in the world, withdrawal to mystical heights was possible. One would then go to a deep place within — where God was experienced intuitively. Some Catholics refer to this experience as *Pure Prayer.*

Three of the most famous mystics of the Catholic Church had transcendental experiences that they later described. St. Catherine had numerous visions and ecstasies. St. Teresa of Avila experienced a "let go and let God" principle by letting the Higher Power "override the mind." St. John of the Cross was a mystic who wrote about the longing of the Soul, or dark night of the Soul, and the inner journey of healing through meditation.

"This dark night is an inflowing of God into the Soul, which purges it from its ignorances and imperfections habitual, natural and spiritual and which is called by contemplatives as infused contemplation, or mystical theology. Herein God secretly teaches the Soul and instructs it in perfection of love...

— St. John of the Cross

Today many Catholics meet with others from all over the world in retreats to practice various types of contemplation and meditation. In a common technique, the seeker focuses attention on a single point, for example, the breath, which eventually stills the mind. Another technique is called "mindful meditation," in which the mind observes the flow of thoughts, feelings and sensations that are passing through awareness (similar to the Eastern detached observation practice). Also, *mantra* meditation or repetitive prayer, using a contemplative phrase or God's name, is often practiced, as in the East.

As the physical body experiences deeper states of relaxation than ever before, the awareness, intelligence and creativity of the mind increases. Virtually, all psychological systems become positively influenced by meditation. As a result, meditation is being taught in hospitals all over the country. One Benedictine Monastery in France reported a marked improvement in the well-being and health of its monks after the Gregorian Chant was reintroduced into the monastery's services. The chanting is said to unify body, mind and spirit. This "unification" is what the sages in India referred to as the goal in spirituality called "yoking" or *yoga*.

This moment is when the "whole eye becomes single." There is no further debate between the needs of the body, desires of the mind, or the questions of the intellect. All this opposing and divergent business gets resolved into one powerfully captivating focus of tremendous peace and joy in which all else is forgotten and made to seem trivial. These singular spiritual experiences of the one Spirit override all other concerns of the lesser bodies because these experiences are so profound — being so profound, they are much more Real.

"The name of Jesus should be repeated over and over in the heart as flashes of lightning are repeated over and over in the sky before rain..."

— Saint Hesychios

Chapter Forty-six

Culmination of Practices

The process of becoming a true *yogi* is a long and arduous series of practices in which the awareness moves up through the *chakras* into higher centers. A simpler approach is possible with the aid of a competent Master, who, with the technique of opening the awareness to the subtle Sound Current, can help the practitioner begin the withdrawal process at the Third Eye *Chakra*. This method is far easier then than the *yoga* techniques that require a long elaborate withdrawal from the physical body with arduous techniques designed and used in earlier times when life expectancy was much longer with fewer demands in life. The practice of the Sound Current given by the Master and the repetition of the charged Five Names, called *Simran*, provide a super-charged method of easily withdrawing to the Third Eye *Chakra*.

Most *yoga* practices eventually take us to the Third Eye *Chakra* — *Trikuti*, or the Second Region. They are extremely difficult to accomplish in the short amount of time that we have to spend each day while earning an honest living and performing our duties to family and society. Yet our expectations as aspirants are high.

Ultimately, the body can only serve itself in the perfection in *Hatha Yoga*. The mind can only serve itself by practices of devotion that bring great peace and happiness. Similarly, the intellect can only have its answers through the intellect. How do we, with these various vehicles, come to know and serve the Soul? The three *yogas* of action, devotion and knowledge can only take us as far as the instruments of practice, but not beyond. How can one know Soul? How can the Soul come to know God?

This process requires the assistance of a human being who knows God and, therefore, can give the aspirant back to God. The God-realized Saint uses certain techniques to wake up the adept. He is like an awake person looking down at a dreamer. He knows the waking state, so he can use a method of sound or splashing water or a shove to cause the dream to fall away from the dreamer. What remains is the state of waking up, so an awakened one emerges. From the Saint's reality, he uses a technique that awakens the slumbering Soul. These techniques purify and assist the Soul in its journey to greater realms of higher and higher vibration until that Soul meets and merges into its source. At that time, the dreamlike state of body, mind and intellect with its mundane preoccupations is left behind ... the Soul goes back to God.

Samadhi is the highest form of *yoga*, connecting with the Divine. Even so, in a few rare cases, some individuals may reach a level of *Samadhi* in childhood. It occurs spontaneously, seeming effortlessly, without any difficult rigors of a specific discipline. These cases are due to past lifetimes in which they would have labored long and hard at spiritual practices.

Bhava Samadhi: While dancing, jogging, singing or listening to music, we may temporarily become absorbed and lose awareness of the physical body. However, this experience does not give at-one-ment with the Divine.

Jar Samadhi: This level produces a state of sleep in which there is no super-sensory experience. We are able to completely shut down the physical processes and still remain alive for some days.

Kumbhak Samadhi: This lower *samadhi* state is achieved by stopping the breath; thereby, one is able to lock out sensory connections with the body.

Savikalpa Samadhi: There is an experience of phenomenal bliss, but a duality is present, for there is an individual who knows, "I am blissful." At this stage, we still do not completely lose ourselves and become one with all.

Nirvikalpa Samadhi: This experience removes all past *karmas*. When the aspirants come back into the world, they are centered on the Divine.

Chaitanya Samadhi (also called *Kaivalaya Samadhi):* This experience is a super-conscious state beyond the three *gunas,* or modes of energy, where the consciousness is absorbed in its own Divine Essence.

At the time of *Samadhi,* we are able to feel the inherent bliss of the Soul. At this time, the mind comes to reside and be absorbed in the Third Eye Center. This level corresponds to the *Trikuti,* in the Second Region. The veil of mind is removed, so that we rise above the higher intellect, which is self-conscious. The experience is pure Soul. Ceasing to be interested in the paltry pleasures of the world, we seek absorption into Absolute Bliss. The higher *Samadhis* are as though seeing through the Soul's eyes directly, instead of through the indirect vision of the mind and intellect. When this opening manifests, the Self shines in its own luminosity.

At this juncture, we may note that the *Samadhi* of the *yogi* is considered to be the highest form of enlightenment. According to the *Upanishads*, it is considered to be "the Truth knowing which the mind and words turn back," that is, the mind is dissolved into Brahman. This experience occurs only when the mind sheath gets removed from the Soul. Of this *Samadhi*, Santji explained that beyond all *Samadhis* of the *yogis* is the *Samadhi* of the *Naam* within — the "God-in-Expression Power, the Light and Sound, tasting the Nectar of which renders all tastes insipid." Further, the Masters declare, "You cannot experience this *Samadhi* by arrogance, force or command, but only through initiation and devotion to the Master."

"By deep and silent meditation, one must merge his very being in the sweet contemplation of the Beloved within and lose himself in the Great Soul of the Universe. This is the highest contemplation and it leads to the most coveted goal of Samadhi.

"This state goes beyond intuition and is a direct experience of the Soul. The mind becomes completely absorbed in divine radiance. The Soul realizes, 'I am Thou.' This is the state of awareness of Consciousness or perfect Bliss. It is achieved by either one-pointed attention upward toward subtle abstract regions, or through 'faith, energy and memory.' As the yogi progresses, the type of Samadhi *experienced will be subtler and more encompassing. The ultimate goal of the true spiritual practitioner is* Chaitanya Samadhi *where the consciousness is likened to a super-conscious state in unison with the super-consciousness."*

— Kirpal Singh

In explaining the lower *Samadhi* states, Santji told the story about a *yogi* who, by practicing *Kumbhak Samadhi,* a form of focusing attention, would be able to shut down his awareness of his body sensations to such an extent that he could lie on the ground and allow a steamroller to stand on his chest. He could even give an interesting discourse while in this position. He would also wind a rope around his neck and allow fifty people to pull from either side, but they could not make him move an inch. In another feat, he would be buried underground for six days and nights, but he remained unaffected by the lack of oxygen. One day, Santji asked him to describe the condition of his mind. The *yogi* replied, "It's okay. As long as I remain in *Kumbhak,* it's all right, but when I come out of that state, my mind goes back to its usual disturbed condition again."

As phenomenal as this state of mind seems, it is not the *Samadhi* that the Masters refer to, but a *Samadhi* of the lower regions. All *Samadhis* only take the aspirant through the Third Region to the Void Region, the threshold of Fourth Region. In order to cross the Void Region, one must have a true Master Saint, whose light can bring the disciple through this dreaded zone. Otherwise, the void is virtually impenetrable.

Without this grace, Souls may remain stuck, thinking that they have reached the highest form of bliss or joy, not understanding that the Soul has a further journey to be able to reach eternal peace. The mendicant or spiritual practitioner typically only reaches *Daswan Dwar,* the Third Region, where the mind dissolves into Brahman.

Each religion has its prophets who helped to teach others the way, and, like Catholicism, they have a group of mystics and set of mystical practices. These practices are always more advanced than the theories and dogmas handed down in the traditional teaching.

Islam: The Sufi is a mystical sect whose members practiced mediating on different names of God. While sitting together in a circle, they would bring on experiences of an ecstatic state using their *dhikr*, rosary, with the meditation. This sect grew out of the Mogul Empire during 1,500 to 1,700.

Judaism: The mysticism of the *Kabbalah* is a secret teaching and practice, transferred by the Master to the student who is emotionally and spiritually mature. There are individuals such as Rabbi Simeon bar Yochai, who lived in a cave for thirteen years. From this experience, he was later able to express the mysteries of communion with God and the Angels. Secret names of God, comparable to the *Simran* of *Sant Mat* tradition, were given to him. He was told these names had "great power." Included in the secret teachings, the theory of reincarnation was given and adherence to a vegetarian diet was stressed.

Sikhism: In India there is a spiritual group called the Sikhs, which was a sect born out of the synthesis of the Hindu and Muslim traditions. This new religion taught that people can experience mystical union with God by practicing inner devotion. Some of the *Sant Mat* Saints were also Sikh Gurus.

"By singing the Guru's hymns, I, the minstrel spread the Lord's glory. Nanak, by praising the True Name I have obtained the perfect Lord."

— Guru Nanak

Buddhism: Gautama Buddha's teaching and practices extended throughout India, China, Japan and Tibet. Not only does the practice begin with the cultivation of love for all beings as Christ taught, but the teaching contains some very advanced practices for the attainment of mystical states. These practices include devotion to deities who reside over different aspects of creation and the Zen practices of meditation on the non-dual, complete, immediate, selfless aspect of Self.

Jainism: A mystical religious group in India formed in India by Mahavir, a contemporary of Buddha. The monks are believed to be the world's earliest aesthetics. They practiced meditation for years while enforcing rigorous self-denial routines, including never staying in one place overnight, eating only begged food, and traveling "sky-clad" throughout their travels.

Egyptian Gnostics: This sect were said to have meditated on five sacred names, similar to the *Sant Mat* tradition of five charged names, called *Simran*. The Gnostics also understood the principle of the Negative Power — or lower force — with its ability to distract and prevent the liberation of the Soul from the physical realm.

Whatever the mystic sect in whatever the time, the common elements are based upon certain sacred practices designed to help the Soul purify and withdraw into its God mansion. It is not uncommon to hear the expression that "religion without practice is superstition," for mysticism is a direct result of practice, not just a system of dogmas for dealing with the world. True practices take the seeker to Soul and beyond — there all mystics are in agreement.

"Just like the luminous and pure sun is obscured by clouds, the afflictions are cloud, which if removed, allow the sun of the essential Nature to shine brightly."

— Buddha

"The physical universe is not complex, it is simple. The laws of energy can be mastered. When the highest laws of spirituality are understood, all smaller or lesser laws are understandable. By connecting with the subtle, spiritual energy, the greatest secrets of the physical and mental worlds can be comprehended because it is the same energy. ..."

"Humankind is about to enter into a great period where faith becomes knowledge, belief is a twin to science and true religion means 'I bind (yoke) together'!"

— Phylos, the Tibetan

Chapter Forty-seven

Inner Journey on Sant Mat Path

Sat Purush gave a method to awaken Souls to Kabir and other Masters who passed the knowledge down to the lineages on earth — a gift to those Souls who cry out to be free. This gift comes not from this world, but from other realms. It consists of two parts, the Sound Current and *Simran,* the charged *mantra.* This system of *Yoga* requires no particular age, religion, belief system or culture, so it is open to all. The only requirement is a commitment to the discipline. Therefore, for those who are ready to give up the lures of the world and are willing to turn inward a few hours a day, this system is a viable path.

"The very source from where the Unmanifest comes into manifestation, the Formless assumes form, the Nameless Name. It was this completeness of the inner journey made possible by the Yoga of Sound."

— Kirpal Singh

The Sound Current is the energy vibration that supports the entire creation; the current emanates from the source. The Sound Current flows down through the regions of subtle vibration to the gross earth. When the Soul is introduced to the current through the *Sat Guru,* the Soul follows the current beyond the Third Eye *Chakra,* then through all of the worlds of astral and causal nature and to the spiritual regions. Each of these regions has a different vibration of purer and subtler nature, accordingly the sound also changes. In the same way the sound of water changes when it hits different objects, the inner sound takes on distinct forms when it passes through the different regions.

The Soul follows this sound naturally, dropping its coverings of grosser nature from the physical sheath, to the etheric sheath, to the lower mind sheath, and intellect sheath. The Sound Current helps carry the Soul upward from region to region, in spite of any hardships that are encountered, such as blinding light or pitch darkness. Finally, the Soul sheds its causal body and merges in the greater realm of Brahman to continue its journey back to *Sat Lok,* where the Soul meets the Creator — *Sat Purush.*

Table 18. Practices of the *Sant Mat* Path

- Repetition of *Mantra* while focusing on Third Eye area, called *Simran,* which are the five names of the Lords of the five spiritual regions.

- Listening to the Sound Current, called *Bhajan,* which is the connection to the inner regions.

- Practice of a pure (vegetarian) diet.

- Practice of righteous living: moral conduct, including non-injury to others in thought, word and deed.

- Devotion and remembrance of the Masters and God.

Since the Third Eye Center is the source out of which the currents travel down into the body's *chakra* system, the serious student only need start with the Sound Current at the Third Eye and move forward by closing down the activity of the five senses. So, this journey with the Sound Current begins in the Third Eye Region, the region we experience in the waking state. This region radiates with one thousand rays of lights, called *Sahasrar.*

Concentration is improved through the practice of using a special *mantra,* called *Simran,* given by the Saint. *Simran* consists of the five charged names of the five inner rulers of the five upper regions. These regions are likened to the realms of the *chakra* system of the body. In fact, they can be considered as higher *chakras* of the spiritual bodies. Imbued with power of the Saint who has given the *mantra, Simran* helps the Soul withdraw from its body and reside in the Third Eye Region. Here the Master Saint opens the door to the astral region and accompanies the Soul back to its original home. The vibration of *Simran* protects the Soul from sabotage by the celestial beings on its return journey, similar to the Soul's passport. The light and sound emanating out of *Sat Lok* become the ticket.

The Master who accompanies the Soul is the Captain. He is able to help the Soul to land only when appropriate, to avoid all pitfalls of being stuck when the destination is not known, and to show the final goal beyond all expectation. Otherwise, how would a Soul know where to go? Not knowing any better, we could have settled for any intermediate stage.

The guideline is simple: The lighter the thoughts, the higher the vibration; that is, the more selfless and pure the thoughts, the better the afterlife. A person who lives a spiritual life and does not mix themselves up with astral forces is virtually free of an astral body connection at death. Therefore, their point of exit is not the Solar Plexus Center, but a higher energy center. Similarly, an individual's mental body can be shattered and eliminated as he or she becomes connected to the Soul. The Soul's light or energy is said to be instrumental in shattering, not only the astral body, but also the mental body in time. This process is accelerated with the Words of Power given by a Master. Their use expands the mental body until it finally dissipates into subtle particles.

The Words of Power that the devotee receives at initiation have a specific vibration. The vibration represents a color, tone, or form, which is of a certain energy quality. Just as in a chemistry laboratory, when the chemist adds one chemical to another, the original chemical is altered; by consciously adding spiritual practices or higher energy into our lives, we can completely alter our destiny in life, as well as the afterlife.

As a result of the very subtle nature of the inner light and sound, plus the inner guidance and protection of the Master, we are able to make the great journey through the five inner regions to our eternal home. These practices are of such an incredible vibration that we finally arrive in the subtle abode of the All Pervasive Lord.

The Master, Kabir, often referred to meditation as a battlefield because Kal, the Negative Power, resides in the Third Eye *Chakra*. This is the region that *"ahamkara,"* the ego, has its foothold, so it is the site where the Soul must take command in order for higher experiences to take place. When the Soul is free of the enemies, ego being last to go, it can naturally return to its source, no longer held by the illusion of the pull of the mind. So the mind finds its happiness in the Third Eye *Chakra*, while the Soul gets to return to its source: the higher spiritual region.

"It is in the kingdom of truth, contentment and purity,
That this battle is raging; and the sword
That rings forth loudest is the sword of His Name.
When a brave knight takes the field,
A host of cowards is put to flight.
It is a hard fight and a weary one,
This fight of the Truth-seeker. ...
The Truth-seeker's battle goes on day and night,
As long as life lasts it never ceases."

— Kabir

At initiation the Master connects the disciple to the spectrum of Light coming down from *Sat Lok*. This Light must be distinguished from the early perceptions of light that the beginner experiences as one progresses through the *chakras*. The light seen when one withdraws the attention up to the Third Eye *Chakra* is the light of the Peace of the Void, the abode of Kal. The light of Kal, which leads the Soul no higher than the Third Eye *Chakra*, is similar to the light that many people see at the time of death. They often mention that they were told that they have more work to do on earth, a reminder that Kal is the perpetuator and maintainer of the creation.

Unless one has the initiation practice given by the Master, one progresses only as far as the Void Region and cannot go beyond the light of the Third Eye *Chakra*. When the Master gives the initiation of Light and Sound Current, the initiate receives two vehicles for the Soul to follow out of the lower regions of the body into the higher realms of existence and experience of the Free Spirit, for both Light and Sound Current originate in *Sat Lok*.

As one's Soul vehicle becomes purer and subtler in vibration by exposing itself to the subtle spiritual practices, it is actually refining its vibration to a subtler and purer mode in the same way ice changes to water. Thereby, the Soul is able to perceive the subtler regions. Ice can remain frozen solid on the mountaintops indefinitely. Still, when it is exposed to the bright warm radiance of the sun, it is able to cascade into a myriad of forms as it travels across varied terrains, finally to spill into a great ocean. With greater exposure to the sun, the same water is able to evaporate into the sky to experience a subtler arena of existence.

In order to become a free spirit, the Soul must cross an inner ocean, the *Gagan,* which separates the region of *karmic* bondage and the realm of Free Spirit. This ocean is of such incredible heated temperatures that grosser forms cannot enter it. Through the vibrational change in association with the Inner Radiant Form of the Master and the spiritual practices, the Soul merges into the radiant form and is able to cross this great divide with grace and ease. Of this terrible journey for the Soul, the Master Saint is often referred to as the boat that safely carries the Soul across the "Ocean of Samsara" or the cycle of rebirth.

"His Soul shall wing homeward, born on the stream of Shabd *[holy word], towards its point of origin, the heaven of bliss and peace ... its Radiant Friend is always beside it to lead it past, and protect it from, its pitfalls."*

— Sawan Singh

A Master has spent many years in profound meditation and does not need to use others to boost his image, or to provide money for his upkeep, or to exploit anyone for personal motives. Established in the God Power, the Saint takes directions from the Higher Power. Having dissolved their ego in Universal Oneness, they call themselves Servants of God. Knowing God is their source of power, yet they never refer to themselves as Masters or Godmen. They always quote their personal *Gurus* or Scripture as authority. Knowing their Universal Oneness, they are the embodiment of compassion. Being stainless, they reflect the love of God. They no longer take dictation from an individual Soul that has weathered thousands of incarnations, but reflect the will of God and God Power.

The Master Saint is sent by the Supreme Lord, not to start a religion or philosophy, which will only enable us to make a temporary trip to the higher realms, but to rescue the Soul completely from the realms of birth and death. The Master Saint takes the Soul back to its real and original home. Not all God-immersed beings have the special mission to take souls back to _Sat Lok_. To find one is extremely rare and a great blessing.

Chapter Forty-eight

Gifts of the Spirit

It is a new era, a time of the dawning of True Being, an era of the opportunity of lifetimes for many Souls. It is a time for awakening and an occasion for hope. It is an era for our Souls to end the bondage of human form and step out of the box of the physical body. The time has come to feel expansive and no longer contracted. We are learning to drop the points of distinction that separate us, as humans, from one another. As we purify and simplify our lives, we emerge a strong and central figure of our own God-realization. We are given the opportunity of vibrating at a higher, more refined modality, while removing the unhappiness of being stuck.

Spiritual practices that serve to align us with our Spiritual Nature transform us. With the progress on the inner journey, we will reap the rewards of identifying with the Whole, and not its parts. *This integration was the way we, the Souls, were before we fell into earthly forms.* In the beginning, we knew our identity with the Whole, then we lost it by experimenting as separate vehicles of experience.

All the practices mentioned in this book are a means of getting unstuck from the barbed-wire minds of ourselves and of others. In the isolating experience of humanness, we began to build forts around ourselves, creating forgetfulness, isolationism and loneliness in our lives. From these conditions, so unnatural for the Soul, the mind seeks its own remedies, thereby robbing the Soul of its energy and power and taking it on a downward spiral through grosser and lower vibrational experiences—in its efforts to escape the dilemma of being finite, the Soul has gone into greater forgetfulness.

This heritage is a poor fate for the Soul, cut off from the source of Life. Conversely, when the Soul is fed from the God-Source, it becomes so empowered that the mind, its servant, can perform any task in the Soul's service, so that the Soul can experience the kingdom on earth. "May my journey help you in your journey; may you come to know and have all by the blessings of our eternal Lord.

God Speed you in your noble spiritual pursuits.

Soul speaks to Soul
Mind to Mind
When the Soul of the Saint touches the Souls of others
When the Soul gets its energy
It feeds it to the mind
The mind can create and manifest easily
Whatever the Soul requires –
When the Soul does not get
Its God energy and sustenance,
But is left to the devices of the mind
It falls to the addictions
Of the lower charkas and its spirit
Becomes dull and deadened
Then it is lost for a long time to
Its source of subtle energy and uplift –
To true happiness and love –
A requirement of the Soul.
Finally with the help of the Saint
The soul can reverse its course
Of lifetimes of hardships
To return to its
Home of God and light and love

Afterword

Saints are humble servants who do not announce themselves, nor do they come to form organizations. They do not attach themselves to others, but are free and independent of the world. While in conversation with Phil, Santji mentioned a few words about the next person who would offer initiation and take responsibility for the souls. Based upon those conversations and other information, Phil and I have gone to India to look for the new source of grace and happiness so that our children and others would benefit. This trip was one of the most exhilarating experiences of my life. There was so much grace and bliss pouring down on us that we felt rewarded for making the effort. Although it was revealed to us that the time was not yet right for the physical meeting with the Saint, we were able to establish the groundwork for a future meeting with him. We are optimistic that the Saint will be available to serve humankind soon, by the grace of God. Contacting the publisher will help you if you wish to know more about him.

www.TenthGatePublishing.com
email address: MaryAnne@TenthGatePublishing.com

Glossary

Agam Lok: *Seventh inner spiritual region, described as inconceivable.*

Alakh Lok: *Sixth inner spiritual region, called indescribable.*

Ahamkara: *Egoism or self-conceit; the sense of "I."*

Amrit: *Heavenly nectar, food for the Soul, which strengthens and purifies so that the Soul may continue its upward journey to its source.*

Anami: *Eighth and final spiritual region, "one without a name." In this region, the Soul remains forever peaceful and content in a nameless formless state.*

Ananda-maya kosha: *Soul body or covering, made of the subtle cause forms, or etheric material.*

Anna-maya Kosha: *Physical covering of human being, which is made of food, or the earth element.*

Astral Body: *Emotional, or desire body of subtle matter. The sheath covers a living being's life essence, consciousness, and Soul.*

Astral Region: *First region containing heavens and purgatories. The first region a Soul passes through on its inner journey back to the Source.*

Atma: *True identity of individual as Self, pure limitless beingness, also means Soul or Spirit.*

Bank Naal: *Soul has reached the Shore of the Inner Master and begins to hear the sound of a conch and OM. This point is the beginning of the Second, or Causal, Region — Trikuti.*

Bhakti Yoga: *Practices to develop devotion and openness of the heart, or love.*

Bhajan: *The act of listening to the inner Sound Current to purify the Soul and lead it to its Source.*

Bhanwar Guph: *Fourth Region, containing 88,000 continents, where the Soul becomes intoxicated with the rarefied atmosphere. The Soul practices surat and nirat in this region*

Bindu Drops: *Subtle drops from the pituitary gland that flow into the Third Eye, Heart Chakra, and the Solar Plexus, thereby forming the four Samadhis.*

Brahma Lok: *Causal Region, or Trikuti. This region is supposed to be the region from where the ancient Vedas of India originated. Immersing one's Soul in Brahman is going to the place where the mind and words turn back. Many prophets descend from this region.*

Brahman: *The impersonal God, devoid of all qualities. It pertains to the first three regions.*

Causal Body: *Also referred to as the Soul Sheath, which corresponds to Trikuti, the Second Region of experience.*

Causal Region: *Second spiritual region, called Trikuti or Brahma Lok.*

Chakra: *Vortex of energy that forms at the intersection of various nadis, responsible for psychological and physiological functions.*

Chi: *Life force, the body's wind element.*

Darshan: *The transference of spiritual power or energy from the Soul of a Master Saint to the Soul of the receptive devotee through either the physical eyes or inner form of the Master.*

Daswan Dwar: *Third Region, considered first home of the free spirit. From this center, the whole world emanates.*

Etheric Body: *Vital body, manages the autonomic nervous system and other sub-conscious functions of the physical body.*

Gagan: *Inner ocean of incredible heated temperatures that separates the region of karmic bondage and the realm of the free spirit.*

Hansa: *Literally, "swan," but the title indicates enlightenment, which corresponds to the third region, Daswan Dwar.*

Hatha Yoga: *Beginning practice for controlling the body, breath and mind, which helps to improve one's concentration or focusing power.*

Jing: *Seminal essence which transforms into chi or life force with meditation, helping one to progress in spiritual practices.*

Ida: *Nerve current flowing through the left nostril, then down the spinal column, or the left side of the Sushuma Channel.*

Jnana Yoga: *Intellectual understanding through the study of Vedanta.*

Kal Niranjan or Kal: *The son of Sat Purush, who performed such intense spiritual practices that he was given the authority to reign over the three regions: Physical, Astral and Causal.*

Karma: *Force that empowers the law of cause and effect, which binds the individual Soul to the wheel of birth and death.*

Karma Yoga: *Emphasizes right attitude and actions.*

Kosha: *A sheath or covering or the essential being. A human has five coverings: physical, etheric, astral, mental and Soul.*

Kundalini: *Subtle energy (fire element) that is the primordial cosmic energy that lies coiled like a serpent in the base or Muladhara Chakra.*

Maha Sunn: *This means the great void. This region is located between the third and fourth regions. The darkness here is so intense that only a disciple accompanied by a Saint can pass through.*

Mahatma: *"Great Soul" or realized sage.*

Mai or Nadi: *Tiny energy channels in the body.*

Mano-maya Kosha: *Mental covering, which is made of emotions and feelings, or the fire element.*

Mantra: *Sacred words or phrases invoking a god.*

Meditation: *Concentrated focus, subtler and freer than thought itself. It is a way of synchronizing all the energies in order to perceive inner vistas of the Soul.*

Naam: *Holy name (of God). It is of two varieties: that which can be expressed or uttered and later that which can only be heard within. The latter has a power that emanates from the Supreme Being and draws the Soul back to it.*

Nadi: *Tiny energy channels in the body.*

Nine Gateways: *The nine gateways, holes, in which impressions from the external world can enter the body or flow out of the body in the form of attention. They are two eyes, two ears, two nostrils, mouth, and two lower apertures.*

Nirat: *Faculty of inner seeing.*

Nirvikalpa Samadhi: *an ecstatic state of integration with no modifications of the mind in which oneness with God is experienced.*

Nishta: *Rooted in the God state.*

Ojas: *Seminal essence which transforms into chi or life force with meditation, helping one to progress in spiritual practices.*

Panchikarana: *In Sanskrit (literally "caused by combination of five"). A process in which the five kinds of elementary constituents of the universe combine with one another to form the gross material that makes up the physical world.*

Pingala: *Nadi, or nerve channel, on the right side of Sushuma, the central current in the subtle body.*

Pituitary Gland: *Master endocrine gland, secretes hormones that stimulate and control the functioning of almost all the other endocrine glands in the body. Pituitary hormones also promote growth and control the water balance of the body.*

Pineal Gland: *Manufactures and releases the melatonin that has many effects principal among which is regulation and coordination of circadian (wake-sleep) and other biological rhythms (hibernation, menstruation).*

Plexus: *Points where the nerves, arteries and veins interlace each other. In the etheric body, and on subtler levels (such as the astral), the nadis come together to form the subtle plexus or chakras.*

Prana: *Life force, vital energy, the body's wind element.*

Prana-maya Kosha: *Covering composed of five senses of human being, which is made of voluntary and involuntary functions of the body, or the water element.*

Pranayama: *mastery over the vital airs and the life force.*

Rajas: *quality of activity, movement and anger that is spurred on by desire and intention.*

Samadhi: *a heightened state of concentration in which normal thoughts cease. Proficiency in Samadhi leads to enlightenment. Also see Nirvakalpa Samadhi*

Sat Lok: *Fifth Region, also referred to as Sach Kand. Region where the Soul sees the Supreme Lord, Sat Purush. From this point, Sat Purush takes over the duty of guiding the Soul to the higher regions.*

Sattwa: *The quality of brightness, love, knowledge, understanding, wisdom, serenity and joy.*

Shakti: *Power, strength, the dynamic aspect of Divine Being.*

Simran: *Special mantra given by the Master Saint. Simran consists of the five charged names of the five inner rulers of the five higher regions. It also means repetition and remembrance of the five holy names.*

Shabd: *Word, sound or Sound Current. As the Soul manifest in the body as consciousness, the word of God manifests itself as Inner Spiritual Sound. There are five forms of the Shabd within every human being. The secret of which can only be imparted by a True Master or Saint.*

Shen: *Chinese term for spirit or illumination. Also means light (tejas in Sanskrit) that results from transformation of chi.*

Shiva: *The god of destruction of creation, one of trinity of Hindu gods.*

Sound Current: *The Sound Current is the energy vibration that supports the entire creation. It flows down through the regions of subtle vibration to the gross earth.*

Surat: *Faculty of inner hearing for the Soul.*

Sushuma: *Central energy channel that runs up spinal column through which the subtle energy (fire element), also called Kundalini, rises with spiritual practices.*

Tamas: *Quality of darkness, dullness, ignorance.*

Tanmatra: Rudimentary element in an undifferentiated state of the Causal Region before the process of panchikarana, or materialization.

Tenth Gate: The inner doorway through which the Soul leaves the physical realms and enters into the spiritual regions. The lower nine gates are two eyes, two ears, two nostrils, mouth and two lower apertures.

Third-Eye Chakra: Seat or headquarters Soul as well as the mind, referred to as the Tenth Gate. If the Soul wins out it's the Causal, if the mind wins, it is not.

Trikuti: The Second Region. Trikuti is a huge ocean which every initiate encounters inside themselves; it is impossible to cross without the "boat" of Grace of a Master. The headquarters of Brahman, it is considered the highest heaven in many systems of yoga.

Upanishads: Philosophical section of each of the four Vedas that reveals the essential oneness between God and man. These treatises are believed to have been compiled from 800 to 500 B.C. from an oral tradition, dating back from 2,500 to 5,000 years ago.

Vedanta: System of non-dualistic philosophy based on the Upanishads, Bhagavad Gita and Brahma Sutras. Vedanta proves the oneness of the individual Self (Atma) and the Supreme Self (Brahman).

Vedas: Major collection of Hindu scriptures; four principal books of knowledge of the Hindu religion.

Vigyana-maya Kosha: Intellectual covering, made of thoughts and logic, or the air element.

Vishnu: The god of maintenance of creation, one of the trinity of Hindu gods.

Void Region: The Void Region is an extremely dark, dense vacuum that separates the Third Region (of the three worlds) from the Fourth Region. The region where Kal Niranjan, the Negative Power, is said to reside. It is located in the Third Eye, or sixth, Chakra of the body and is considered to be the arena where the Soul asserts its dominance over the mind in meditation, so that it can finally be free of the influence of the mind, its first and last enemy.

About the Author

Mary Anne Ayer began asking more about spirituality and metaphysics than her Catholic upbringing and parochial school provided. She graduated from the University of Washington with a B.A. in cultural anthropology and became interested in meditation and Christian mysticism. In search of more answers, she attended an intense two and a half year course of study in India in Vedanta in the Sanskrit medium. This was a twelve-year course condensed into two and a half years, designed to create monks and nuns who would teach the ancient scriptures embodied in "the path of knowledge" to students around the world. Mary Anne was a teacher of Vedanta, meditation and Eastern philosophy and religion for over ten years in Seattle, Vancouver Canada and Boston.

With a profound longing for greater insights and spiritual experiences, Mary Anne expanded her understanding with the study of other systems of Yoga such as Hatha, Kriya and Raja Yoga. In her search she traveled throughout India meeting many yogis and sages. She broadened her search to the study and practices of Tibetan and Zen Buddhism in monasteries and retreat centers as well.

Receiving a Masters Degree at Tufts University to teach foreign languages, as well as the study of foreign language at Harvard University and The Sorbonne in Paris, she was able to study the writings of Spanish and French speaking saints and mystics of Catholicism in their native tongue.

Her studies and her spiritual practice culminated in the meeting of a Living Saint and with the meditation practices of the Sant Mat (Path of the Masters) tradition, where she has been a student and practitioner for the past 20 years. She felt compelled to write about her experiences not only to benefit her children but for others who may share her interest in spirituality.

She now lives in Naples, Florida with her husband and two children.